Interconnectivity, Subversion, and Healing in World Christianity

Also Available from Bloomsbury:

The African Christian Diaspora, Afe Adogame
Charismatic Healers in Contemporary Africa, Edited by Sandra Fancello and
Alessandro Gusman
Indigeneity in African Religions, Afe Adogame

Interconnectivity, Subversion, and Healing in World Christianity

Essays in honor of Joel Carpenter

Edited by
Afe Adogame and Aminta Arrington

BLOOMSBURY ACADEMIC
LONDON • NEW YORK • OXFORD • NEW DELHI • SYDNEY

BLOOMSBURY ACADEMIC
Bloomsbury Publishing Plc
50 Bedford Square, London, WC1B 3DP, UK
1385 Broadway, New York, NY 10018, USA
29 Earlsfort Terrace, Dublin 2, Ireland

BLOOMSBURY, BLOOMSBURY ACADEMIC and the Diana logo are trademarks of Bloomsbury Publishing Plc

First published in Great Britain 2023
This paperback edition published 2025

Copyright © Afe Adogame, Aminta Arrington and Contributors, 2023

Afe Adogame and Aminta Arrington have asserted their rights under the Copyright, Designs and Patents Act, 1988, to be identified as Editors of this work.

Cover image: *Mustard Tree Birds* by Keng Sen Chong, pen and ink on paper, 10 × 11 inches. This image is used with the gracious permission of the Overseas Ministries Study Center at Princeton Theology Seminary (OMSC@PTS).

All rights reserved. No part of this publication may be reproduced or transmitted in any form or by any means, electronic or mechanical, including photocopying, recording, or any information storage or retrieval system, without prior permission in writing from the publishers.

Bloomsbury Publishing Plc does not have any control over, or responsibility for, any third-party websites referred to or in this book. All internet addresses given in this book were correct at the time of going to press. The author and publisher regret any inconvenience caused if addresses have changed or sites have ceased to exist, but can accept no responsibility for any such changes.

A catalogue record for this book is available from the British Library.

Library of Congress Control Number: 2023931563

ISBN: HB: 978-1-3503-3339-0
PB: 978-1-3503-3343-7
ePDF: 978-1-3503-3340-6
eBook: 978-1-3503-3341-3

Typeset by Newgen KnowledgeWorks Pvt. Ltd., Chennai, India

To find out more about our authors and books visit www.bloomsbury.com and sign up for our newsletters

Contents

Foreword   vii
    Retief Müller

Introduction   1
    Aminta Arrington and Afe Adogame

1   The Contribution of Joel A. Carpenter to World Christianity   7
    Tite Tiénou

2   Revive Us Again: A Deeper Understanding of Fundamentalism's Continuing Role in American Life   19
    Alexandre Brasil Fonseca

3   Academic Border Crossing and an Anthropologist's Excursions into Research on Theology and African Christianity   31
    Mwenda Ntarangwi

4   Translatability and Identity: A Korean Diasporic Exegesis on Jacob's Name Change   43
    Won W. Lee

5   Contextualization, Social Science Insights, and the Interpretive Task   55
    Melba Padilla Maggay

6   Crucial Lessons to Construct Democracy: From the Protestant Reformation to the Mexican Revolutions   69
    Mariano Ávila Arteaga

7   Pathways for a Protestant Social Ethics in Latin America   81
    Raimundo C. Barreto

8   Christianity among the Nankani in Ghana   97
    Rose Mary Amenga-Etego

9   Pyongyang and Protestantism: Imaged as Sodom, Jerusalem, and Babylon, 1866–1945   109
    Sung Deuk Oak

10 Rediscovering Women Leaders in the History of Chinese Protestantism   123
    Li Ma

11 A Dream Deferred? The Lingering Effects of White Supremacy on
    Christian Young Adults in South Africa Today   137
    Nadine Bowers Du Toit

12 African Traditional Pediatric Hospitals in Northern Nigeria:
    Shapeshifting Identities and the Future of World Christianity   149
    Matthew Michael

13 Ante-Sacred-Space and the Interreligious Sphere in a Covid-19 ICU Room   161
    Izak Y. M. Lattu

14 Ubuntuism and Africa: Actualized, Misappropriated, Endangered, and
    Reappraised   173
    Francis B. Nyamnjoh

15 The Significance of Ancestors in Shaping and Understanding Christian
    Theology: A Samoan Perspective   185
    Featunai Liuaana

16 Primal Religious Spirituality and Charismatic Revivalism: The Mizo
    Christian Experience   197
    Lalsangkima Pachuau

List of Contributors   209
Index   213

Foreword

Retief Müller

Some of the greatest contributors to the study of World Christianity entered the field more or less unpredictably. Or, perhaps, to say they entered it by providence would be a more appropriate turn of phrase. Among the people who made World Christianity a vibrant field in academic scholarship, several names could potentially be mentioned, which I am not going to do in this brief foreword. However, the great Andrew Walls, whose recent passing is still fresh in memory, comes to mind as someone who, in the words of Brian Stanley, could justifiably be described as the "inspirer and architect" of the field of World Christianity.[1] As Stanley further points out, Walls never did any of the standard things that might be expected of an undisputed leader in an academic field, such as writing a doctoral dissertation or publishing an academic monograph. Instead, Walls' reputation was built over a long career of dedicated scholarship in smaller yet incrementally accumulating segments and through the mentoring of students.

Although there are numerous obvious differences between Walls and Joel Carpenter and their respective careers, I find at least one interesting connecting point between the two in the fact that Carpenter, like Walls, entered a leadership position in the field via a somewhat unconventional route. Unlike Walls, Carpenter did indeed attain a doctoral degree and published an academic monograph. In fact, Carpenter had the highest of academic credentials as I will elaborate on below. However, he did not train as someone who might be expected to become a World Christianity expert, let alone a leader. His field of expertise is American religious history. Or, rather, this *was* his field, because over the past couple of decades, he has become without a doubt one of the preeminent voices worldwide promoting the study of World Christianity.

What made Carpenter's contribution to this field both significant and highly successful has perhaps something to do with the way in which he understood his own role within the process. Always a keen observer of scholarly discourses, Carpenter—under the inspiration of the works of Walls, Lamin Sanneh, Kwame Bediako, and others who since the late twentieth century were proposing a dramatic reorientation regarding how the global church should think of itself, its history, and trajectory—became convinced of the need for high-level academic attention to movements and trends among the churches and Christian populations within the majority world. Yet, with his background as a historian of American Christianity, Carpenter understood that he could serve the field of World Christianity best by being an enabler and facilitator of research done by local scholars and experts in the various contexts of Asia, Africa, and Latin America, which had all become growth areas in the increasingly majority world dominated by the World Christian movement. The demographic realities of World Christianity, with its center of gravity situated in the Global South, seemed to demand new ways of doing theology. No longer would it be adequate for scholars in Africa, Asia, and Latin America to subsist on a diet of prepackaged theology produced by individuals and institutions of learning in Europe and North America. No, the indigenous context where the most vibrant forms of Christianity were increasingly situated had to speak and moreover write, and theology had to be localized. At the same time, the world remained interconnected, and in fact toward the close of the previous century when the field of World Christianity really got its bearings, with the iron curtain apparently lifted in Europe, and repressive ideologies like apartheid in South Africa passing away into history, it seemed that globalization would characterize the future state of human affairs like never before. Hence, there remained a role for well-heeled academic institutions in the North. Carpenter, among several of his peers, understood that this would be an important role in relation to the new World Christianity, but also that it would have to be a very different approach from the ways in which the West and its Christian institutions have traditionally interacted with the rest.

The Nagel Institute, founded in 2006, was the brainchild of Joel Carpenter, who was also its founding director. In important ways, the Nagel Institute was created as a direct answer to the question alluded to above: what role can Western Christian academia play in assisting and strengthening the burgeoning growth in majority World Christianity? From its inception, the Nagel Institute, with Carpenter at the helm, set for itself an expansive overarching goal, which was to promote the study of World Christianity in the contexts where it was growing most vociferously, to partner with people and institutions who were equally involved in this general aim, and to provoke a renewed understanding of and commitment to World Christianity among churches and Christians in the North Atlantic regions. As such, the Nagel Institute would act as a kind of nexus that would facilitate the scholarly conversations and partnerships that could attain diverse aspects of this broad goal. In practical terms, this meant that the Nagel Institute would often act as a kind of broker between the interests of philanthropic foundations in the Global North and Christian scholarly communities in the South and East. As Nagel's director, Carpenter initiated and oversaw several larger and smaller ventures in Asia, Africa, and Latin America that served to bring scholars together in their research on diverse aspects of World Christianity. Among other things, he also initiated a visiting scholars' program for the benefit of this developing network at Nagel's home base, Calvin College (today University), in Grand Rapids, Michigan, USA. As a result of these and other initiatives, the Nagel Institute has become a pivotal name among institutions dedicated to the study of World Christianity. The very existence of this institute and its ongoing commitment to theological, historical, and social scientific research into Christian realities within the majority world is perhaps Carpenter's greatest legacy to this field of study.

To broaden the picture regarding how this all came to be, it might be helpful to mention a few things about Carpenter's academic biography up until he became the founding director of the Nagel Institute. I made brief reference to Carpenter's scholarly acumen earlier. To say a bit more about that, he received his PhD in history from Johns

Hopkins University in 1984, and he is the author of the award-winning book *Revive Us Again: The Reawakening of American Fundamentalism* (Oxford University Press, 1997). In his pre-Nagel years, Carpenter occupied various academic roles. A noticeable trend in his professional trajectory, which started to develop early on, is his strong administrative and, moreover, fundraising ability, which he managed to combine with regular academic work.

From 1983 to 1989 he served as Director of the Institute for the Study of American Evangelicals at Wheaton College. Among various administrative duties, he was responsible for writing grant proposals and subsequent financial and narrative reports as well as for teaching in the history department. During this period, he raised over $1 million in grant funding.

An even more formative period, particularly in light of his later work at the Nagel Institute, followed when he joined the Pew Charitable Trusts from 1989 to 1996 as Religion Director. In this capacity, Carpenter served as a grant maker, and it is notable that a number of the projects he supported were what might be inherently classified as World Christianity projects. This included, among others, the African Theological Initiative, based in Abidjan, Côte d'Ivoire; the Research Enablement Program for the Overseas Ministries Study Center, New Haven, CT, which gave international awards for research on missions and non-Western Christianity; and Hispanic Theological Initiative at Emory University, which was a national scholarship, mentoring, and networking program for Hispanic graduate students in ministry, theology, and religion. And, if possible, even more auspiciously, he channeled funding for Currents in World Christianity at Cambridge University, which provided international research awards and operated as a publishing program for studies of Christian movements and traditions in Africa, Asia, Latin America, and the Pacific.

In 1996 Carpenter returned to his alma mater, Calvin College, where he had completed his undergraduate degree many years before, to take up the role of provost in which he remained until 2006. In this capacity, he made productive work of exhibiting his World Christian commitments as illustrated by several initiatives he pioneered in this direction at Calvin. To give just a few examples, five new off-campus semester programs were established, which included Ghana and Honduras; the enrolment of international students and underrepresented US minorities doubled during this period; and a new comprehensive plan and policy for advancing Calvin's work in race relations, cross-cultural engagement, and multicultural partnerships was established.

This brings us toward the end of Carpenter's tenure as provost and the founding of the Nagel Institute, which counts among several other educational and research centers/institutes founded at Calvin during this period. On more than one occasion, I heard Carpenter describe the events leading up to the founding of Nagel in what could only be called religious language. To say that he experienced a profound sense of calling might be putting things too mildly. More definitely, it seems that he experienced a sense of being gripped by the Spirit of God, an experience that made him realize not that the path he had been walking on was wrong, of course, but nonetheless that God was showing a new path that he should walk from there on further. I heard Carpenter tell the story of how he approached Gaylen Byker, then president at Calvin, with the idea of an institute devoted to the study of World Christianity. Carpenter was also able to convince Byker to allow him to step down from his role of provost to become the founding director of this new institute, which the college was able to establish with the generous support of Doug and Lois Nagel, the founding donors of the Nagel Institute and after whom it is named.

Joel Carpenter remains a senior research fellow with the Nagel Institute. In this capacity, he continues to serve as editor of the impressive "Studies in World Christianity" book series of Baylor University Press. He is also currently engaged in the writing of a highly anticipated biography of the late Ghanaian theologian Kwame Bediako.

Through the networks he established, the research projects and programs he fostered, and the publications he has generated and continues to generate, Joel Carpenter will be known as among the foremost leaders in the establishment of World Christianity as an academic field and scholarly enterprise.

Note

1. Brian Stanley, "Andrew Finlay Walls (1928–2021)," *International Bulletin of Mission Research* 45, no. 4 (2021): 319.

Bibliography

Stanley, Brian. "Andrew Finlay Walls (1928–2021)." *International Bulletin of Mission Research* 45, no. 4 (2021): 319–29.

The cover art for this book is titled "Mustard Tree Birds," by artist Keng Sen Chong (pen and ink on paper, 10 × 11 inches). This work is inspired by the Parable of the Mustard Seed, which is included in all three synoptic gospels. In this image, the gathered birds express the vibrant new life and community that can emerge from an underestimated and subversive mustard seed. The image is used with the gracious permission of the Overseas Ministries Study Center at Princeton Theological Seminary (OMSC@PTS) in sincere gratitude to Joel Carpenter for his leadership stewarding OMSC's Research Enablement Program and service on OMSC's Board of Trustees from 2016–2020.

Introduction

Aminta Arrington and Afe Adogame

The field of World Christianity is maturing. As an interdisciplinary field, World Christianity does not simply describe Christian belief and practice outside of North America and Europe; it also examines Christianity within and between these contexts that host Christian diasporas coming from the Global South. Further, as this book's title makes clear, the field of World Christianity exhibits various thematic elements, among them interconnectivity, subversion, and healing; that is, the field of World Christianity recognizes not just the existence of Christian communities on six continents but also the absolute necessity of such communities for the Christian project globally.

Much of the advancement in the field of World Christianity is due to Joel A. Carpenter. This book, intended to recognize his many accomplishments in the field, is a festschrift in his honor. All contributors to this volume have encountered Joel one way or another, through project leadership and collaboration, mentorship, networking, institutional exchanges, study trips, and so on. By founding the Nagel Institute for the Study of World Christianity at Calvin College (now Calvin University), Joel played a foundational role in shaping the emerging field considerably. Furthermore, for over a decade, Joel has been successful in receiving large grants that have increased the academic amplitude and enabled the work of younger, early career scholars in the Global South.

For someone whose work is so closely associated with the growth of the interdisciplinary field of World Christianity, as Retief Müller attests in the foreword, Joel Carpenter's pivot toward World Christianity was an unexpected turn of events since he began his academic career as a scholar of American religion, more specifically American Christian fundamentalism.

Tite Tiénou fills in the outline of Carpenter's academic journey, demonstrating that this "pivot" was a result of Joel Carpenter's own disposition toward respecting the religious proclivities of ordinary people, as well as several fortuitous encounters with international students, particularly from Africa (Chapter 1). Joel Carpenter's significant and long-lasting contribution to the field of World Christianity, as both Müller and Tiénou acknowledge, came less through focusing on his own research and writing and more through amplifying the voices of others globally. In so doing,

Carpenter helped lay the foundation and build the scaffolding for a structure that would allow scholars and theologians from around the world to be heard and for the field of World Christianity to grow and mature.

The essays in this volume reflect this maturity. The book is organized around the three themes of interconnectivity, subversion, and healing. Interconnectivity posits that connection, and the benefit that comes with it, goes both ways. The global cosmos continues to be interconnected in ways that have implications for religion, culture, politics, and economics. No longer is communication a one-way street, as in much of the mission era; rather, each stream of Christianity in the world has much to offer and learn from the others, making connection critical. Further, interconnectivity implies that this connection is dynamic, continuous, and ongoing.

As Christianity has become a global phenomenon, connection among denominations, among churches, and even among individual Christians has increased enormously. Migration and diaspora, digital technologies and globalization, transnational ties and movements, all have served to foster sustained connection. While Cabrita and Maxwell have argued that the term World Christianity "privileges attention to the local, the particular and the regional, and thus simultaneously obscures larger-scale connection and networks as well as cross-cultural continuities," the chapters in this volume demonstrate that interconnectivity, with its implication that we need one another, is a fundamental piece of World Christianity.[1] World Christianity seeks to understand how Christian communities embody historical and cultural experiences locally and globally; thus, it fosters the study and practice of both local and trans-local ways of knowing and doing. "Christianity, past and present, has shaped all geographical, religious, and cultural contexts in which it has found itself, but all these various contexts, cultures and religious traditions have in turn also had an impact on Christianity in manifold ways. An exploration of this reciprocal interaction is important for our global age."[2] As contributions in this book vividly demonstrate, interconnectedness and mutuality of influences need further contextual understanding and analysis. And as Isaac M. T. Mwase has written, "mutual reliance … has to win the day."[3]

This interconnectivity, as pointed out by Alexandre Brasil Fonseca, is noticeable in that both the United States and Brazil, along with many other Latin American countries, continue to grapple with religious fundamentalism. Brasil Fonseca examines the lasting impact of Joel Carpenter's writing on American fundamentalism in the 1930s and 1940s and its continuing impact on the historiography of evangelicalism (Chapter 2). For Mwenda Ntarangwi, in his reflexive chapter on "Academic Border Crossing" (Chapter 3), interconnectivity might involve academics moving to new disciplines and new subjects, taking their "old" knowledge along with them. Joel Carpenter exemplifies this interconnectivity, trained in American religion but making perhaps his greatest contributions in African Christianity; Ntarangwi himself was trained as an anthropologist and then encouraged by Carpenter to apply his ethnographic skills to African Christianity. Likewise, Won Lee examines how his hybrid identity as a Korean American scholar connects him to the Bible, showing the reciprocal relationship between the authoritative biblical text and his own reality as a reader of said text coming from a Korean diasporic context (Chapter 4). Melba Padilla

Maggay discusses the interconnectivity between the deep structures of a culture and the core themes of the biblical text, resulting in a "contextualization from within" method of biblical interpretation (Chapter 5). Mariano Ávila Arteaga connects the political theology of John Calvin to the Latin American democracy project (Chapter 6). Still within the Reformed tradition, Raimundo Barreto shows the efforts of Richard Shaull to draw on Latin American liberation to unsettle his own North American Reformation theology and how each can contribute to the development of Protestant social ethics (Chapter 7).

Yet while interconnectivity implies equality, inequalities have abounded in Christian practice. Dominant narratives have obscured lesser-known but not less important ones. Hegemonic discourses have elevated theological interpretation from some parts of the world over others. Colonialism has meant that power imbalances were present in many new Christian communities from their very start. Thus, an element at the core of World Christianity is subversion. As Andrew F. Walls has stated, a World Christian consciousness has yet to fully inform our structures, our teaching, and our theology. In the face of such, "Deliberate subversion may be the only way forward."[4]

There is much to subvert. The Western missionary movement of the last few centuries was transformative, but we would be remiss not to note the hierarchies and inequalities it left in its wake. Sadly, the "equality of believers" was often not practiced.[5] Colonial hegemonism and the European Enlightenment frame, both of which have cast their long, defining shadows over Western thinking and practice for centuries, require subversion as well.

Reading and writing are themselves subversive activities. Likewise, giving full weight to local expressions of Christianity is subversive. Rose Mary Amenga-Etego disrupts the historiographical narrative of Christianity in Ghana, showing that the conveniently forgotten history of the northern mission complicates the dominant *tabula rasa* narrative (Chapter 8). Likewise, Sung Deuk Oak challenges the monolithic historiographical image of Pyongyang as the "Jerusalem of Korea," revealing that, in fact, Pyongyang had many contested images prior to 1945 in its complex history (Chapter 9). Li Ma examines the historiography of Christianity in China, showing that while women have long been the majority of Protestant Christians in the country, the histories focus on the actions of well-known male leaders (Chapter 10). Subverting the long history of white supremacy in South Africa, Nadine Bowers du Toit brings to light its lingering effects on Christian youth in South Africa today (Chapter 11).

Subversion, though often necessary, is not a righteous end unto itself. Subversion recognizes that harm has occurred, but ultimately, in World Christianity both interconnectivity and subversion aspire to something greater—healing.

Physical healing plays a prominent theme in several of our essays. Matthew Michael sees a nexus of Christianity with African spirituality at traditional pediatric clinics in Nigeria—sites of healing of the physical bodies of children as well as the symbolic bodies of children as the source of communal and family continuity and hope (Chapter 12). Izak Lattu, in an autoethnography of his own hospitalization with Covid-19, examines interreligious prayer as a source of physical, spiritual, and interfaith healing in multireligious Indonesia (Chapter 13).

Healing can also be a recovery of what has been lost, a return to wholeness and shalom. Francis Nyamnjoh presents Ubuntuism, which sees wholeness in relational connection and reciprocal obligation, as a feasible framework for emancipatory social change that is both participatory and inclusive (Chapter 14). For Samoan Christians, remembering is a form of wholeness. Feauna'i Liuaana shows how remembering the ancestors, which was a key part of primal Samoan religion, has shaped Samoan Christianity and theology. Reclaiming ancestor remembrance and veneration from the missionary narratives, which classified it negatively and, unfortunately, as ancestor *worship*, has been healing for Samoan Christians (Chapter 15). And Kima Pachuau demonstrates that the healing power of revivals for Mizo Christians in Northeast India draws from the primal religious spirituality of the Mizo people (Chapter 16).

These three—interconnectivity, subversion, and healing—demonstrate that World Christianity is in fact a field with an agenda. Not content with detailed histories or elucidative ethnographies, World Christianity carries a normative load.[6] Interconnectivity, subversion, and healing are moral activities that place the development of Christianity around the world in contradistinction to the more insular, nativist, and nostalgic strains of religious fundamentalism. World Christianity as a field remains a postcolonial project in which the main actors, centers, institutes, conferences, and funding remain centered in the Global North. Joel Carpenter, through his initiatives, has contributed to the decentering of the field, a process that gained considerable momentum thanks to his successful initiatives that have empowered scholars from the Global South. Understanding that global voices were critical and seeing the potential of World Christianity to change the discourse, Joel Carpenter helped lay a path forward through enabling theologians, historians, social scientists, and other scholars to have their work speak not just into their local contexts but also into the global conversation. This volume is dedicated to Joel Carpenter, his vision, and his work. We are immensely grateful to Afia Sun Kim, Ruth Amwe, and Katrina Reimer for their editorial assistance through several stages of this project.

Notes

1. Joel Cabrita and David Maxwell, "Introduction: Relocating World Christianity," in Joel Cabrita, David Maxwell, and Emma Wild-Wood, eds., *Relocating World Christianity: Interdisciplinary Studies in Universal and Local Expressions of the Christian Faith* (Leiden: Brill, 2017), 4.
2. Afe Adogame, Raimundo Barreto, and Richard Young, Editorial, "World Christianity and Reciprocal Exchange," *Studies in World Christianity* 28, no. 2 (2022): 151.
3. Isaac M. T. Mwase, "Shall They Till with Their Own Hoes? Baptists in Zimbabwe and New Patterns of Interdependence, 1950–2000," in Lamin Sanneh and Joel A. Carpenter, eds., *The Changing Face of Christianity: Africa, the West, and the World* (Oxford: Oxford University Press, 2005), 63.
4. Andrew F. Walls, "Overseas Ministries and the Subversion of Theological Education," *International Bulletin of Mission Research* 45, no. 1 (2021): 11.

5. See, for example, Richard Elphick, *The Equality of Believers: Protestant Missionaries and the Racial Politics of South Africa* (Charlottesville: University of Virginia Press, 2012).
6. Cabrita and Maxwell, "Introduction," 4.

Bibliography

Adogame, Afe, Raimundo Barreto, and Richard Young. Editorial. "World Christianity and Reciprocal Exchange." *Studies in World Christianity* 28, no. 2 (2022): 151–5.

Cabrita, Joel, and David Maxwell. "Introduction: Relocating World Christianity." In *Relocating World Christianity: Interdisciplinary Studies in Universal and Local Expressions of the Christian Faith*, edited by Joel Cabrita, David Maxwell, and Emma Wild-Wood. Leiden: Brill, 2017, pp. 1–46.

Elphick, Richard. *The Equality of Believers: Protestant Missionaries and the Racial Politics of South Africa*. Charlottesville: University of Virginia Press, 2012.

Mwase, Isaac M. T. "Shall They Till with Their Own Hoes? Baptists in Zimbabwe and New Patterns of Interdependence, 1950–2000." In *The Changing Face of Christianity: Africa, the West, and the World*, edited by Lamin Sanneh and Joel A. Carpenter. Oxford: Oxford University Press, 2005, pp. 63–80.

Walls, Andrew F. "Overseas Ministries and the Subversion of Theological Education." *International Bulletin of Mission Research* 45, no. 1 (2021): 7–14.

1

The Contribution of Joel A. Carpenter to World Christianity

Tite Tiénou

Introduction

World Christianity exists. World Christianity is real. In light of the astonishing number and variety of publications dealing with "World" or "Global" Christianity, these opening statements may seem like truisms to many people, especially readers of the essays in the present volume. The abundant literature, the numerous academic programs, as well as the existence of numerous centers and institutes on World or Global Christianity provide further evidence of the reality of the global nature of the Christian faith. It is one thing to acknowledge the fact of World Christianity, to study it, and to understand its nature and its diversity. It is another thing to assess the connections between "World Christianity" and Christianity in one's "local" setting. For example, what significance, if any, does the worldwide development of the Christian faith have for Christians in the United States? Consider the following two viewpoints: the first expressed by theologian Carl F. H. Henry in the last quarter of the twentieth century, and the second by historian Joel A. Carpenter in the first decade of the twenty-first century.

In comments made to the Faculty of Asbury College (now Asbury University, Wilmore, Kentucky) on January 28, 1987, Carl F. H. Henry stated:

> The Christian Church—or some significant remnant of it—may indeed experience renewal, and it may even achieve spectacular gains on Mainland China and in certain African and Asian Third World countries. But that is another story, one marginal to the moral destiny of the West and to the fate of American evangelicalism.[1]

Contrast Henry's observation with the remark made by Joel A. Carpenter in the preface to *The Changing Face of Christianity: Africa, the West, and the World*: "Africa is fast becoming a heartland for World Christianity, and anyone who would understand the dawning of this new dispensation in world religious history would do well to study its African dimensions."[2] Additionally, in "The Evangelical Complexion," a contribution to *The Immanent Frame*, a blog published by the Social Science Research Council on August 7, 2008, Carpenter advances the idea of the presence of explicit links between the reality of evangelicalism in the United States and evangelicalism in other regions of the world. In this piece, he notes that "as American evangelical Christianity is increasingly made of people and movements from every part of the world, some things may change in evangelical outlook ... Evangelicals ... are coming from all over the world, and they are expressing revivalist Christianity in more ways than ever before."[3]

The views expressed by Henry and Carpenter show that awareness of World Christianity can mean different things to different people. An examination of factors related to the variety of perceptions pertaining to the implications of World Christianity can be rewarding and instructive. That, however, is beyond the scope and concerns of this essay. Attention has been drawn to the perspectives offered by Henry and Carpenter in order to situate the contribution of Carpenter to World Christianity in the broader context of his understanding of its place and significance. Carpenter's assessment of, in his words, "this new dispensation in world religious history," the present essay argues, should guide anyone interested in his contribution to World Christianity. In light of this, here I explore how Carpenter contributed to World Christianity by considering, first, his disposition and, secondly, his enablement of others by securing resources for their work and by a resolute commitment to collaboration and networking. We now turn to the qualities of mind and character, that is, the disposition sustaining Carpenter's work in World Christianity.

Disposition

The consideration of disposition matters for our purposes here because human achievements, scholarship included, are usually rooted in biography. Persons choose and pursue their work in light of certain interests, passions, or a particular disposition. In the case of intellectual endeavors, these interests and passions may be referred to what Aristotle identifies as "habits or trained faculties"[4] or what Loïc Wacquant describes as "the implicit cognitive, conative and emotional constructs through which persons navigate social space and animate their lived world."[5] How, then, does Carpenter's biography relate to his work in World Christianity? Through what "habits" does he "navigate" the world of globalized Christianity?

The words Carpenter chose to articulate and characterize what he learned from Professor Timothy L. Smith, his dissertation supervisor, reveal an important aspect of his own habits and disposition. In a paragraph expressing gratitude to Smith, Carpenter notes: "Tim's great respect for the religious creativity and integrity of ordinary people was a lesson I shall never forget."[6] The "lesson" learned from Smith depicts a habit, a quality, I have observed and appreciated in Carpenter over the years. One can see this quality of mind in his study of Christian fundamentalism in the United States, in his interactions with participants at academic conferences and various venues, and in his perspective on grassroots religious movements. Given his "respect for the religious creativity and integrity of ordinary people," Carpenter's interest and active role in promoting World Christianity, "a remarkable case of 'globalization from below,'"[7] should not surprise anyone. Carpenter's "respect for ordinary people" manifests itself in the attitude of a learner, another facet of Carpenter's biography and habit. I know of no better evidence for this character trait than the autobiographical statement Carpenter provided in the inaugural lecture of the Paul G. Hiebert Center for World Christianity and Global Theology at Trinity Evangelical Divinity School (TEDS) (Deerfield, Illinois) on March 22, 2017. In the opening comments of this lecture, Carpenter informed the audience that he "taught history for five years at Trinity College" and spoke of "having warm memories" of those years. Carpenter specified that "among the most memorable encounters I had while at Trinity were with African students coming to TEDS. Far beyond what I understood at the time, it was the beginning of a major change in my own calling as a scholar and as a promoter for Christian scholarship."[8] Here is an American professor indicating learning from "foreign" students and acknowledging their influence on the course of his scholarship! That Carpenter recounts this many years after the "encounters" is even more remarkable. The reader should take good note of the self-disclosure of disposition Carpenter makes here. Scholars rarely reveal that much about their own intellectual habit and character.

The intellectual habit of a learner is further displayed in Carpenter's interest and participation in interdisciplinary scholarship. Evidence of interdisciplinary scholarship is discernible in the following books with Carpenter as one of the editors: *Earthen Vessels: American Evangelicals and Foreign Missions, 1880–1980* (1990), *The Changing Face of Christianity: Africa, the West, and the World* (2005), and *Christian Higher Education: A Global Reconnaissance* (2014). These books are outcomes of his interactions with a wide range of scholars such as historians (his discipline), theologians, anthropologists, missiologists, educators, and philosophers. In a comment on the study of Christianity in Africa, Carpenter writes: "Just as the charts of Western modernity are inadequate for exploring African Christianity, so are the modern divisions in scholarship. This book [the 2005 publication mentioned above] offers a thoroughly interdisciplinary approach."[9] Note that this clearly expressed commitment to interdisciplinary scholarship relates to one of the "tribes"[10] of the family called World Christianity. But, does Carpenter limit this approach to what some may consider "exotic" forms of Christianity? A brief examination of his work on fundamentalism may provide an answer to this question.

In 1984 Carpenter's interest in and study of Christian fundamentalism in the United States culminated in a PhD degree from Johns Hopkins University. He was guided by Smith in the research and writing of his dissertation titled "The Renewal of American Fundamentalism, 1930–1945." The revised and matured version of this work was published in the 1997 book, mentioned earlier, *Revive Us Again: The Reawakening of American Fundamentalism*. Scholars recognized the significance and quality of the work with laudatory expressions. I offer Grant Wacker's commendation as one example. He writes that Carpenter "weaves theological, cultural, and social strands into a mosaic that is as sweeping in its breadth as it is beautiful in its telling."[11] Some readers may find Carpenter's analysis to be narrowly focused on the "cultural and social trends" of white fundamentalism. One can expect such criticism, especially given the passing of time. This kind of quibble, warranted or not, must take historical context into account. Were Carpenter writing in 2021, he would have certainly been in conversation with current scholarship, such as Timothy Gloege's *Guaranteed Pure: The Moody Bible Institute,*

Business, and the Making of Modern Evangelicalism (2015), Mary Beth Swetnam Mathews' *Doctrine and Race: African American Evangelicals and Fundamentalism between the Wars* (2017), and Daniel R. Bare's *Black Fundamentalists: Conservative Christianity and Racial Identity in the Segregation Era* (2021); and he would have broadened his scope to include, for example, Black fundamentalism. One should therefore situate Carpenter's analysis of fundamentalism in the time the work was conducted and assess it on its merits.

A major strength of Carpenter's investigation resides in the way he brings the dimensions of theology, society, and culture into his analysis of fundamentalism in the United States as a "grassroots religious movement," often with lay persons as leaders.[12] This approach is akin to the one taken by Smith in his 1978 article "Religion and Ethnicity in America." In this study, Smith stressed the role of lay leaders in the life of immigrant religious organizations in the United States and propounded that the exploration "of the relationship between religion and ethnicity demonstrates that we have now come to the point where anthropological, sociological, psychological, and historical perspectives on ethnicity can coalesce."[13] One can reasonably conclude that the clear articulation of the value of interdisciplinary scholarship, discernible in this statement, is part of what Carpenter retained from Smith. As we will see next, Carpenter's disposition hallmarks his contribution to World Christianity through enabling the work of a considerable number of scholars with expertise in a wide range of disciplines.

Enablement

Why and how can an aspect of Carpenter's contribution to World Christianity be identified as *enablement*? I suggest that an elucidation of the use of this word is found in the grant-making chapter of his professional life. From 1989 to 1996, Carpenter was the director of the Religion Program at Pew Charitable Trusts, Philadelphia, Pennsylvania. He was, in fact, the first religion officer of the trusts. Immediately prior to his work at Pew, Carpenter had been at Wheaton College (Illinois) where he taught courses in history, directed operations and planning, and engaged in fund-raising for the college's Institute for the Study of American Evangelicals.[14] One can detect his interest in World Christianity in the Institute's June 1986 conference on the theme "A Century of World Evangelization: North American Evangelical Missions, 1886–1986." He organized this conference by securing support and funding for it. He mobilized the participation of an international lineup of scholars for this academic forum.[15] The 1990 book, *Earthen Vessels: American Evangelicals and Foreign Missions, 1880–1980*, edited by Joel A. Carpenter and Wilbert R. Shenk, resulted from papers, panels, and discussions that occurred at Wheaton College in 1986.

At Pew, Carpenter had responsibility for all aspects of the work of the foundation pertaining to the domain of religion in the United States and beyond. With this position locating him on the other side of support and funding for projects, Carpenter applied his planning and administrative skills to resourcing work in religion through grant-making.[16] One grant-making scheme, the Research Enablement Program, awarded funding "for the advancement of scholarship in studies of the world Christian movement." Bearing this in mind, I submit that the word *enablement* represents a significant characteristic of the contribution of Carpenter to World Christianity. Let us now take a closer look at the Research Enablement Program.

The rubric "Noteworthy" of the April 1993 issue of the *International Bulletin of Missionary Research*[17] announced a number of initiatives in World Christianity funded by the Pew Charitable Trusts. First on this list of announcements is the Research Enablement Program. For the sake of history and perspective, I offer here the beginning two paragraphs pertaining to this program:

> The Research Enablement Program, administered by the Overseas Ministries Study Center in New Haven, Connecticut, has awarded twenty grants totaling $247,000 to scholars from eleven countries. The program is devoted to the advancement of scholarship in studies of Christian Mission and World Christianity.
>
> The grants, funded by the Pew Charitable Trusts, support both younger scholars engaged in dissertation-related field research and established scholars engaged in major writing and research projects dealing with mission and Third World Christianity.[18]

After this introductory description, the announcement provides an enumeration of the grant recipients, with their project titles, under specific categories. Here are the categories, with the number of grantees for each one: dissertation field research (six), postdoctoral book research and writing (five), missiological consultations (two), English translations (two), oral history projects (two), planning grants for major interdisciplinary projects (three). The results of the work produced by this international group of twenty grantees have advanced the scholarship on World Christianity.

In April 1993, readers of the *International Bulletin of Missionary Research* who paid attention to the announcement about the grant recipients of the Research Enablement Program would not have anticipated seeing similar announcements in the next five April issues of the journal. Here are the numbers of grant recipients reported by the Overseas Ministries Study Center for these years: 1994 (twenty-one grantees), 1995 (eighteen awardees), 1996 (eighteen grant recipients), 1997 (sixteen grantees), 1998 (nineteen awardees).[19] So, over the course of six years, the Pew Charitable Trusts provided funding to support the research and writing in World Christianity by 112 scholars. Carpenter had a strategic role in the birth of the Research Enablement Program. The work produced by scholars as a result of the funding by Pew can and should legitimately stand as evidence of Carpenter's contribution to World Christianity.

Carpenter's work at Pew also provided a catalyst for three other foundation-funded initiatives announced in the April 1993 issue of the *International Bulletin of Missionary Research*. The first two, described as "major projects of collaborative missiological research," focused on "African Proverbs" in one case and on "Christianity in Modern China: From Western Missions to a Chinese Identity" in the second case. Significantly, in contrast to the other grants announced, and as if to highlight the aspect of collaboration, the members of the Review and Selection Committee for these two initiatives are specified: Joel A. Carpenter, Lamin Sanneh, Wilbert Shenk, and A. Christopher Little. The third initiative, labeled "a program to foster the building of a community of Christian scholars, researchers, and trainers in sub-Saharan Africa," was simply titled the African Theological Initiative.[20] Some of its features, such as its explicit Africa-centered nature and the configuration of its administrative structure, set it apart from the other programs reviewed thus far. For these reasons, and for others that will become clear later, the last grant-making scheme warrants further comment.

It is proper and fitting to start with noting my personal involvement in this initiative because this information is publicly available, for example, in the 1993 announcement of the grant. While such an indication could provide minimal expression of a statement of disclosure, for the sake of integrity, I think a clear and unambiguous declaration is necessary. Therefore, I hereby declare my participation in the planning and initial implementation of the African Theological Initiative.[21] No elaboration is necessary beyond the brief remark made here. Persons interested in more of my reflections can examine them in my article "Church and Theological Education: Legacies of the African Theological Initiative" (text of the Tenth Kwame Bediako Memorial Lecture).[22]

In addition to the previous observation, one must acknowledge Carpenter for the crucial role he had in the entire process of formulating and focusing the African Theological Initiative. Indeed, the chronicles of the initiative would be inaccurate and incomplete without a reference to the efforts and influence Carpenter expended in order to secure the commitment of the Pew Charitable Trusts to supporting an "offshore" program, especially one based in Africa. It is not an exaggeration to assert that the African Theological Initiative owes its existence to Carpenter's passion and considerable diplomatic skills. What other explanation could one offer for the commitment of an American foundation to finance what the proposal for funding described as "a bold and comprehensive multi-year program designed to address the needs of African theological education"[23] by promoting Christian scholarship and strengthening the formation of a community of researchers and practitioners on the African continent in the 1990s?

In the first decade of the 1990s, at the time of the beginning of the post-1945 bipolar world, making the case for the African Theological Initiative was no easy task. Advocates of the program had to provide evidence for its worthiness, a condition required of all requests for funding. Additionally, they faced issues such as the focus on Africa, the institutional location for administering the grant, and the question of fiscal responsibility and reporting. A brief review of these three issues reveals the magnitude of the task and helps pinpoint the significance of Carpenter's contribution.

The geopolitical environment of the world in the early 1990s represented a challenge for anyone seeking financial support for Africa-specific projects. This was a climate where gloomy portrayals of the African continent and its people, with depictions of a bleak future, spread like a virus. Sometimes referred to as "afro-pessimism," these characterizations, long-standing traits of the discourse on Africa and Africans, are evident, for example, in the words chosen by Lance Morrow in 1992 to set the continent apart from the rest of the world, "the basket case of the planet, the 'Third World of the Third World,' a vast continent in free fall,"[24] or in the oft-cited 1994 article "The Coming Anarchy" by Robert D. Kaplan. Evaluations of the state of scholarship in the continent also painted a picture similar to the sense of hopelessness expressed in publications purporting to assess the entire situation of Africa. Abiola Irele's article,

"The African Scholar," represents a case in point. After observing that "black Africa" may "ha[ve] entered upon the Dark Ages of scholarship," Irele asserted: "Despite individual achievements and reputations, African scholarship is at best marginal, and at worst nonexistent in the total economy of intellectual and scientific endeavor in the world today."[25] How stunning that the Pew Charitable Trusts should make a multi-year grant of nearly 2 million dollars to fund a program in Africa in this context of extensive and devastating pessimism about the continent. Carpenter deserves appreciation and credit for his role in guiding the process that made the commitment of the Philadelphia-based foundation possible.

Moreover, he provided wise counsel essential for addressing concerns related to the operation of an Africa-based grant-making initiative. His guidance facilitated the crafting of a creative administrative structure of awarding the grant to a US fiscal agent, in this case a well-known philanthropic organization, with other aspects of the implementation of the program located in an academic institution in Africa. This creative structure ensured compliance with the regulatory requirements of the US government pertaining to fiscal oversight; it also empowered African agency in the execution of the initiative. Looking back, any of the three issues reviewed (the Africa focus, the institutional location, or governmental regulations) represented a significant challenge; together they constituted what seemed an insurmountable obstacle. The obstacle was overcome because Carpenter made key contributions to the formulation of an acceptable solution to problems that could have hindered the approval of the grant application.

The approval of the proposal empowered the implementation of the "bold" African Theological Initiative. Over the course of its existence, the initiative fostered faculty development through the provision of scholarships for doctoral studies, contributed to the enhancement and development of infrastructure for academic life, and facilitated continuing education and church-related leadership development. These outcomes of the African Theological Initiative, indicators of *enablement*, represent specific and notable examples of how Carpenter has strengthened World Christianity by resourcing and stimulating the work of individuals and institutions.

The resourcing of people and institutions is not limited to the Research Enablement Program, the African Theological Initiative, or Carpenter's tenure at Pew Charitable Trusts. This characteristic applies to Carpenter's lifetime contribution to World Christianity. Observable prior to and subsequent to the time he directed the religion program at Pew, facilitating and amplifying the voices of others globally became more visible during the years he led the Nagel Institute for the Study of World Christianity at Calvin University. On April 11, 2018, the online newsletter of the Christian Reformed Church in North America announced Carpenter's retirement from the directorship of the Nagel Institute. In this newsletter, Nicholas Wolterstorff articulated his appreciation for what Nagel achieved during the twelve years of Carpenter's directorship in the following statement:

> What most impresses me about the work of the Institute under Carpenter's leadership, … is the extent to which it has gone … to assist Christians in other countries in finding their own voices in scholarship, education, and the arts

and to bring American scholars, educators, and artists into dialogue with their counterparts in other countries, especially Africa and Asia.[26]

These words express the essence of the contribution Carpenter made to World Christianity. They point to the great many individual scholars whose work he furthered either by facilitating the procurement of funding for their projects or by engaging them in collaboration and networking. Over the years, these scholars and Carpenter produced a massive oeuvre on various aspects of World Christianity. Taken together, the completed research projects, the seminal academic conferences, the articles and books published establish solid documentary evidence of Carpenter's stature. This considerable body of work, made possible by Carpenter's choice to invest in *people*, stands as an abiding tribute to him for his multifaceted contribution to World Christianity. By investing in people worldwide, Carpenter amplified their voices, thus making their participation in what he described as a "new dispensation in world religious history." Investment in people constitutes Carpenter's lasting legacy.

Conclusion

World Christianity represents a complex and living reality that requires sustained collaborative inquiry. The contribution of Carpenter to the scholarship on World Christianity, as presented in this essay, exemplifies the fact that "nothing we do, however virtuous, can be accomplished alone."[27] As Carpenter has honored numerous scholars by inviting them to join him in accomplishing the work of World Christianity, it is right and proper for us, his colleagues, to express gratitude and honor to him.

Notes

1. Carl F. H. Henry, *Twilight of a Great Civilization: The Drift toward Neo-Paganism* (Westchester, IL: Crossway Books, 1988), 23–4.
2. Joel Carpenter, "Preface," in Lamin Sanneh and Joel A. Carpenter, eds., *The Changing Face of Christianity: Africa, the West, and the World* (Oxford: Oxford University Press, 2005), viii.
3. Joel Carpenter, "The Evangelical Complexion," *Immanent Frame* (blog), Social Science Research Council, August 7, 2008. https://tif.ssrc.org/2008/08/07/the-evangelical-complexion.
4. Aristotle, *The Nicomachean Ethics* (trans. F. H. Peters), 10th ed. (London: Kegan Paul and Trench Trübner, 1906), 43, book II, Chapter 5, paragraph 6.
5. Loïc Wacquant, "A Concise Genealogy and Anatomy of Habitus," *Sociological Review* 64 (2016): 64–72. doi.10.1111/1467-954X.12356.
6. Joel A. Carpenter, *Revive Us Again: The Reawakening of American Fundamentalism* (New York: Oxford University Press, 1997), ix.
7. Carpenter, "Preface," vii.
8. Joel A. Carpenter, "A Center for Global Theology: Fresh Opportunities for Christian Thinking in America: Remarks at the Opening of the Paul Hiebert Center for

Global Theology," Trinity Evangelical Divinity School, Deerfield, IL, March 22, 2017. Unpublished Manuscript.
9. Carpenter, "Preface," viii.
10. Andrew F. Walls observes: "In its essence, western Christianity is tribal religion, and tribal religion is fundamentally more about acknowledged symbols, and custom and recognized practice, than faith": "The Missionary Movement: A Lay Fiefdom," in Deryck W. Lovegrov, ed., *The Rise of the Laity in Evangelical Protestantism* (London: Routledge, 2002), 170-1. Following Walls, I use "tribe" in reference to the configuration of Christianity present in Africa.
11. Grant Wacker, "Advance Praise for *Revive Us Again*," back cover.
12. See Carpenter, *Revive Us Again*, "Chapter 1" (pp. 13-32) and "Conclusion" (pp. 233-46). It is worth noting that in the 1980s, Carpenter's work on fundamentalism included publications such as *Making Higher Education Christian*, coedited with Kenneth W. Shipps (Christian University Press and Eerdmans, 1987 and reissued in 2019 by Wipf and Stock), and *Reformers of Fundamentalism: John Ockenga and Carl F. H. Henry* (New York: Garland Press, 1988), being issue no. 45 in the series "Fundamentalism in American Religion, 1880-1950," edited by Joel A. Carpenter. A review of these publications is beyond the scope of the present essay.
13. Timothy L. Smith, "Religion and Ethnicity in America," *American Historical Review* 83, no. 5 (December 1978): 1185. In an article published in 1993, Leslie Woodcock Tentler states: "Lay initiative is an important theme in Smith's seminal 'Religion and Ethnicity in America' ... which still stands as a model for the social analysis of religion": "On the Margins: The State of American Catholic History," *American Quarterly* 45, no. 1 (March 1993): 124, n. 15.
14. Established by Wheaton College in 1982, the Institute for the Study of American Evangelicals ceased to exist on January 1, 2015. See "The Institute for the Study of American Evangelicals Closes," *Wheaton Record*, November 7, 2014. https://thewheatonrecord.com/2014/11/07/the-institute-for-the-study-of-america-evangelicals-closed.
15. The collaboration with missiologist Wilbert Shenk is worth noting. So is the dedication to J. Herbert Kane, referred to as "missionary, teacher, scholar, world Christian." See *Earthen Vessels: American Evangelicals and Foreign Missions, 1880-1980* (Grand Rapids, MI: William B. Eerdmans, 1990), v.
16. In the 1990s the Pew Charitable Trusts made grants to support religion projects in the United States, such as the "Pew Evangelical Scholars Program" and the "Pew Younger Scholars Program." See Michael S. Hamilton, "Philanthropic Funding, the ISAE, and Evangelical Scholarship," *Evangelical Studies Bulletin*. www.faithandhistory.org/wp-content/uploads/2014/11/Hamilton-on-ISAE.pdf.
17. *International Bulletin of Missionary Research* at the time, now *International Bulletin of Mission Research*. In 1993 the Overseas Ministries Study Center was located in New Haven, Connecticut. In 2020 it relocated its operations and programs to Princeton Theological Seminary, Princeton, New Jersey.
18. "Noteworthy," *International Bulletin of Missionary Research* 17, no. 2 (April 1993): 74. I retain the expression "Third World" for the sake of historical integrity.
19. For the 1994-8 announcements, see the following issues of the *International Bulletin of Missionary Research*: 18, no. 2 (April 1994): 74-5; 19, no. 2 (April 1995): 66-7; 20, no. 2 (April 1996): 72-3; 21, no. 2 (April 1997): 74; and 22, no. 2 (April 1998): 58-9.
20. "Noteworthy," *International Bulletin of Missionary Research* 17, no. 2 (April 1993): 75.
21. I served as the first director of the African Theological Initiative from 1993 to 1997.

22. Tite Tiénou, "Church and Theological Education: Legacies of the African Theological Initiative. Tenth Kwame Bediako Memorial Lecture, 13 June 2018," *Journal of African Christian Thought* 21, no. 2 (December 2018): 7–13.
23. See "African Theological Initiative: Proposal Presented to Pew Charitable Trusts" by MAP International, July 1992, p. 2.
24. Lance Morrow, "Africa: The Scramble for Existence," *Time*, September 7, 1992, 42. Kaplan's piece, "The Coming Anarchy," published as an article in the February 1994 issue of the *Atlantic Monthly*, 44–76, was expanded into the 2001 book *The Coming Anarchy: Shattering the Dreams of the Post-Cold War*. An abundant literature exists on "afro-pessimism." I suggest a few articles in English: Aimable Mugarura Gahutu, "Afro-Pessimism and Globalization: The Stakes of Symbolic Death of Africa," *Rwanda Journal of Arts and Humanities* 2, no. 2 (2017): 5–17. https://dx.doi.org/104 314/rj.v2i2.2A; Abubakar Momoh, "Does Pan-Africanism Have a Future in Africa? In Search of the Ideational Basis of Afro-Pessimism," *African Journal of Political Science* 8, no. 1 (2003): 31–57; Toussaint Nothias, "Definition and Scope of Afro-Pessimism: Mapping the Concept and Its Usefulness for Analysing Media Cover Age of Africa," *Leeds African Studies Bulletin*, no. 74 (December 2012): 54–62; and Handel Kashope Wright, "Is This an African I See before Me?" https://ccie1-edu.sites.olt.ubc.ca/files/2018/04/DIME_Wright_African1.pdf.
25. Abiola Irele, "The Africa Scholar," *Transition*, no. 51 (1991): 63.
26. Nicholas Wolterstorff quoted in "Nagel Institute's Joel Carpenter to Retire." www.crcna.org/news-and-events/news/nagel-instiutes-joel-carpenter-retire.
27. Reinhold Niebuhr, *The Irony of American History* (New York: Charles Scribner's Sons), 63.

Bibliography

Aristotle. *The Nicomachean Ethics* (trans. F. H. Peters), 10th ed., bk. II. London: Kegan Paul and Trench Trübner, 1906.

Carpenter, Joel. *Revive Us Again: The Reawakening of American Fundamentalism.* New York: Oxford University Press, 1997.

Carpenter, Joel. "Preface." In *The Changing Face of Christianity: Africa, the West, and the World*, edited by Lamin Sanneh and Joel A. Carpenter. Oxford: Oxford University Press, 2005, pp. vii–ix.

Carpenter, Joel. "The Evangelical Complexion." *The Immanent Frame* (blog), Social Science Research Council, August 7, 2008. https://tif.ssrc.org/2008/08/07/the-evangelical-complexion.

Carpenter, Joel. "A Center for Global Theology: Fresh Opportunities for Christian Thinking in America: Remarks at the Opening of the Paul Hiebert Center for Global Theology." Trinity Evangelical Divinity School, Deerfield, IL, March 22, 2017. Unpublished Manuscript.

Carpenter, Joel, and Wilbert Shenk. *Earthen Vessels: American Evangelicals and Foreign Missions, 1880–1980.* Grand Rapids, MI: William B. Eerdmans, 1990.

Gahutu, Aimable Mugarura. "Afro-Pessimism and Globalization: The Stakes of Symbolic Death of Africa." Rwanda *Journal of Arts and Humanities* 2, no. 2 (2017): 5–17.

Hamilton, Michael S. "Philanthropic Funding, the ISAE, and Evangelical Scholarship." *Evangelical Studies Bulletin*. www.faithandhistory.org/wp-content/uploads/2014/11/Hamilton-on-ISAE.pdf.

Henry, Carl F. H. *Twilight of a Great Civilization: The Drift toward Neo-Paganism.* Westchester, IL: Crossway Books, 1988.
Irele, Abiola. "The African Scholar." *Transition*, no. 51 (1991): 56–69.
Momoh, Abubakar. "Does Pan-Africanism Have a Future in Africa? In Search of the Ideational Basis of Afro-Pessimism." *African Journal of Political Science* 8, no. 1 (2003): 31–57.
Morrow, Lance. "Africa: The Scramble for Existence." *Time*, September 7, 1992.
Niebuhr, Reinhold. *The Irony of American History.* New York: Charles Scribner's Sons.
Nothias, Toussaint. "Definition and Scope of Afro-Pessimism: Mapping the Concept and Its Usefulness for Analysing Media Cover Age of Africa." *Leeds African Studies Bulletin*, no. 74 (December 2012): 54–62.
Smith, Timothy L. "Religion and Ethnicity in America." *American Historical Review* 83, no. 5 (December 1978): 1185.
Tiénou, Tite. "Church and Theological Education: Legacies of the African Theological Initiative. Tenth Kwame Bediako Memorial Lecture, 13 June 2018." *Journal of African Christian Thought* 21, no. 2 (December 2018): 7–13.
Wacker, Grant. "Advance Praise for Joel A. Carpenter, *Revive Us Again*." Back Cover. New York: Oxford University Press, 1997.
Wacquant, Loïc. "A Concise Genealogy and Anatomy of Habitus." *Sociological Review* 64 (2016): 64–72. doi.10.1111/1467-954X.12356.
Walls, Andrew F. "The Missionary Movement: A Lay Fiefdom." In *The Rise of the Laity in Evangelical Protestantism*, edited by Deryck W. Lovegrove. London: Routledge, 2002, pp. 167–86.
Wright, Handel Kashope. "Is This an African I See before Me?" https://ccie1-edu.sites.olt.ubc.ca/files/2018/04/DIME_Wright_African1.pdf.

2

Revive Us Again: A Deeper Understanding of Fundamentalism's Continuing Role in American Life

Alexandre Brasil Fonseca

The opening scene of the 1960 film *Inherit the Wind* frames the façade of the Hillsboro Courthouse, where a clock is set at 7:59 a.m. The soundtrack suggests some suspense. The film credits are shown, and time passes by. It is now 8 a.m. The camera starts to pan away, and the suspenceful music gives way to a woman chanting the traditional spiritual "Old Time Religion" in its distinctly southern form, "Gimme Dat," which appears in the play in the middle of Act 1.[1] The camera, after focusing for a few seconds on the façade of the building, begins to slide, engrossed by a musical crescendo. The city's mayor walks to the town square, where other prominent figures are gathered: the prosecutor, bailiff, pastor, journalist, and photographer. These men march through the streets toward a building on which is written, at the top, "Hillsboro Consolidated School." They are there to arrest, in front of his students, a science teacher who teaches about human evolution.

In the stage version, there is a remark at the beginning of the script: "Time: Summer. Not too long ago. Place: A small town." Hillsboro does not refer to a specific city, although there are more than a dozen cities with that name in the United States. In fact, the play is a reference to what happened in the small and sweltering town of Dayton, Tennessee, in Rhea County, the name of the courthouse where the famous "Monkey Trial" took place in July 1925.

The dispute between God and Darwin, between evolutionism and creationism, was the context chosen by the playwrights to indicate that something from the American past seemed to be reviving. A reality associated with darkness, with total lack of reasonableness, and with denialism regarding the knowledge produced by humanity. The "Monkey Trial," an episode that had national repercussions, was a game-changer in relation to the public perception of an important sector of society, leading to the repudiation, at some level and in certain aspects, of the worldview and perspective known as fundamentalism.

If the 1920s represented the crisis and the loss of power of the fundamentalists, Joel A. Carpenter's proposal in 1997 when he published *Revive Us Again* was to look at the next two decades. For him, the 1930s and 1940s were a classic era for fundamentalism, when it not only survived but prospered, achieving outstanding success in the free market of American popular religiosity, and began to influence other evangelical movements and traditions in the United States and around the world. Fundamentalists took the lead in new "evangelical" coalitions and stood out as influential in the postwar global evangelical resurgence.

In this chapter, I will start by highlighting some central points in Carpenter's book. Then I will identify how more recent historiographical books dialogue with Carpenter's work. The choice of these books was pragmatic. In July 2020, I coordinated a course at the Djanira Institute (www.djanira.com.br) in Rio de Janeiro. Our participants were scholars dedicated to the historiography of religion in the United States, and our focus was on the relationship between evangelicals in the United States and corporations. In organizing the course, we gathered a vast historiographic bibliography, to which I now return.

It was a rich exercise to consider the questions Carpenter addressed and how they contributed to the reflection of other authors. This became even more evident when considering other academic literature, particularly in the social sciences, where one notices a scarcity of references to Carpenter's work, which then leads to ignoring important aspects of fundamentalism Carpenter addresses.

As Carpenter says, fundamentalism presents itself as a kaleidoscope. He looks precisely at the period when its visibility had decreased and points out, "The recovery of American fundamentalism is an amazing story."[2] Hence, understanding this recovery, its nuances, its characters, and processes was his challenge and ended up being the important contribution he made to the historiography of religion in the United States.

Fundamentalism: Revisiting Some Aspects

Glancing at the first edition of *The Fundamentals*, published in the 1910s, is an interesting experience. The Bible verse chosen for the book's epigraph is particularly significant in relation to much of the vision and posture that would characterize fundamentalism: "To the Law and to the Testimony" (Isa. 8:20).

The focus on law, order, and norms came under the leadership of—words from the book's preface—"two intelligent and consecrated Christian laymen" Lyman and Milton Stewart, owners of the Union Oil Company of California. The beginning of the twentieth century was probably the time when secularization was at its most evident. The emphasis of fundamentalism was on the defense of the Law (capitalized because it is from God), the defense of "right doctrine," and the choice of the cognitive and ideological battleground, thus characterizing it, according to Marsden (1980), as hailing from a Calvinist lineage.

The formation of a dispute in the cultural field was another important aspect that characterized fundamentalism. The fundamentalists made culture a battlefield and sought to act firmly to recover the influence and cultural power they felt they had in the past. This came back recently in a very significant way when we saw proposals to "make America great again." It was around fundamentalism, at the beginning of the twentieth century, that many came together and congregated as the "true American patriots." Fundamentalism "portrayed itself as standing for the eternal verities in the face of destructive modern innovation, billing itself as the 'old-time religion' of America's better days gone by."[3]

In the challenge of unraveling the characteristics of this movement and how it continues to influence American religiosity and beyond, Carpenter's book joins works such as those of Sandeen (1970) and Marsden (1980). I consider these three works as critical for a better understanding of what evangelical fundamentalism is and how it built a reaction to its time involving a wide range of interdenominational leaders. These leaders built a network of schools, magazines, publishing houses, mission centers, and agencies: "The postwar evangelical movement reached into the older denominations, the offices of Capitol Hill, the studios of Hollywood, and up the Hit Parade charts as well."[4] Its message and practice used both mass media and mass marketing.

Fundamentalism, as a popular religious movement, represents an important characteristic of American culture, and understanding its continuing role in American life is a challenge that was posed in a significant way at the beginning of the twenty-first century, particularly in the face of the events surrounding Donald Trump's victory in 2016 and how religion has recently occupied such an important place in American politics. A similar scenario has occurred in Brazil amid the rise of Jair Bolsonaro and other indicators of agendas that are characteristic of fundamentalism in several Latin American countries as well as the United States (Cunha 2020). In the face of these more recent events, returning to Carpenter's work is extremely useful for a more qualified and nuanced interpretation. The point Carpenter stresses is that the time that should have seen the downfall of fundamentalism was much more than that; it was a time of restructuring that allowed fundamentalism to be reinvented and to meaningfully remain in society.

This reinvention had to be nuanced, especially with the negativity the term "fundamentalism" had begun to carry in the wake of the "Monkey Trial" and the split between a so-called rural or less-educated America, represented by this vision, and a so-called modern and liberal America. Thus, new names, with nuances as well, started to be triggered. The central point here is that everyone agrees that there is a reference to this fundamentalist reality that was so prevalent in American popular religiosity at the beginning of the twentieth century. There is a continuum. What Carpenter concentrates on is precisely the understanding and origin of those features that managed to survive, observing a time neglected by many authors, but that was, nonetheless, central to the way American evangelical Christianity is constituted today.

An important point other authors may have lost sight of is the fact that the period observed by Carpenter is the interwar years, in which the premillennial discourse of the fundamentalists seemed correct to a generation that had experienced the first great war and, a few years later, would see itself embroiled in a second one. Thus, the preaching of those evangelicals who affirmed human damnation and total depravity seemed to be corroborated by the evident historical facts that frightened everyone, most of all the working and lower middle classes, the locus in which fundamentalism gained strength, being constituted by people and groups that desired to prosper and experience social mobility, but who felt most significantly the impact of the war and the dismal prospects.

Thus, in the postwar period, the resources and prosperity that were achieved seem to have been associated with this religious discourse by some parts of American society, for they experienced a correct diagnosis and a proper response through access to social and income support networks via precisely the religious groups that, in the south of the United States, were protagonists in the diverse processes of economic prosperity.

Another important aspect is the adoption of a position defined today as prolife and profamily, assuming, for example, firm opposition to the legalization of abortion, a posture "that represent[s] deep and long-standing cultural conflict in modern America."[5] In general, its practice can be characterized by an antimodernist militancy, and Carpenter also emphasized the fact that this position goes beyond a generalized antiliberal and antimodern mentality. There is a project, a strategy, a movement, on the one hand; on the other hand, it also highlights a certain inconsistency when discovering that "self-righteous militancy and self-mortifying piety could coexist, and often did to a perplexing degree, in the same individuals."[6]

In this context, Carpenter refers to a poem by T. S. Eliot ("Burnt Norton") to suggest that fundamentalism could be, for many, the desired "still point" of the turning world, a safe and comforting space amid so many changes, violence, and crises. A certainty, a refuge, and, at the same time, a refreshment for myriads of people, perhaps the "golden chalice of hope." Carpenter considers it important to emphasize that fundamentalism is not synonymous with intolerance, fanaticism, or anti-intellectualism, even pointing out that it represents "the most dynamic and widely influential American evangelical impulse."[7] Even so, it has often been used popularly as an inaccurate term that serves more to write off others or disparage opponents.

It is this "still point" that experiences an amazing story in its recovery, in the 1930s and 1940s, of this "distinctly fundamentalist remnant" in the United States. This is the history that Carpenter presents to us, when he says that "one of [the] most important purposes of this book is to explain how it happened": "Fundamentalists became the chief organizers of a new evangelical coalition and were some of the most influential agents in the postwar evangelical resurgence."[8]

Contributions of "Revive Us Again" in Recent American Historiography

In this section, I attempt to identify how and when the book *Revive Us Again* is mentioned in nine recent books that have looked at various aspects of the evangelical presence in American society. As stated in the introduction, the selection of these texts took place in the context of a course in which many authors cited here participated, presenting some aspects of their books and debating with a qualified group of Brazilian social scientists, historians, and theologians on the theme of corporations and evangelicals. Knowing a little more about the shape and presence of evangelicals in American society has become even more relevant in view of the similarities and proximities between the strategies adopted in politics by former US president Trump and those used by former Brazilian president Jair Bolsonaro.

An important aspect to think about in the Brazilian context is the role of evangelicals closest to the dominant profile in the United States and the various bridges and interactions between these groups today. At the beginning of 2019, for example, in several cities of Brazil there were huge meetings of The Send, an initiative created in the south of the United States and which arrived in Brazil with its name spelled in English, with American preachers, with support by missions with logos and names also from the United States, and with the involvement of some national leaders, including President Jair Bolsonaro himself, who participated in one event.

I understand initiatives like this, as well as their dissemination to other locations in the world, as a strong example of what Carpenter underlined in the introduction to *Revive Us Again*: the importance of considering fundamentalism's "continuing role in American life." If understanding and exploring this was important in 1997, I would say that in the 2020s this has become mandatory for anyone who wants to understand the role and presence of evangelical religion in the United States and other countries.

The nine books selected here were published between 2009 and 2020. What led me to bring these works together was the relationship between religion and corporations; it is Philips-Fein (2009) who highlighted the existence of a symbiotic process between businessmen and postwar initiatives in the evangelical field. These processes give the impression, according to the author, that in fact the goal of many evangelicals seemed to be not the salvation of souls but the salvation of American capitalism. This interpretation can be found in other authors such as Kruse (2015), who argues that it was corporate America that created Christian America, and not the other way around.

Thus, Philips-Fein starts to explore aspects in which several symbioses between evangelicals and companies were experienced, emblematic cases such as the emergence of the Christian Business Men's Committee (CBMC) created in 1930, and the overall concern "to demonstrate that capitalist principles did not in fact contradict Christian ethics."[9] Some anti–New Deal preachers are also named, such as Abraham Vereide of Seattle, and James Fifield of Los Angeles.

James Fifield, known as the Apostle of the Millionaires (Kruse 2015), adapted his preaching in defense of "freedom under God" and the free market. Fifield argued that the sermon should be simple and accessible to all. Complex or uncomfortable issues that could possibly exist in one's preaching should be removed; it should only offer content that is easy to consume, easy to swallow. In Los Angeles, he was accused of being a racist and acted to remove from the city's schools some material from UNESCO that he considered contrary to the Christian faith.

He also opposed the Universal Declaration of Human Rights, and the movement he led, called Spiritual Mobilization, had as one of its goals to mobilize evangelical leaders against "pagan statism." This fight would take place based on the following philosophy: "I am only what is mine; I am the sum of the material things I possess and control."[10] This position was pointed out to be closer to dialectical materialism than to Christianity and was one of the reasons that led Ralph Roy, in his 1953 work *Apostles of Discord*, to refer to "the well-financed groups dedicated to the promotion of libertarianism [who] in place of the social ideals of Christianity would substitute the narrow dogma of extreme laissez-faireism."[11] At the beginning of the chapter "God and the 'Libertarians,'" Roy is straightforward in indicating that some of these promarket groups go beyond a conservative stance, assuming a reactionary character.[12]

The author indicates that in the fundamentalist milieu it is also possible to identify anti-Communist preachers such as Carl McIntire and Billy James Hargis. These conjugated the defense of economic freedom with the task of confronting theological liberalism, preaching the gospel while fighting the New Deal. On this anti–New Deal stance, Philips-Fein quotes a speech by J. Howard Pew, an executive of Sun Oil: "My attack on the New Deal has not been prompted by materialistic considerations, but rather by a desire to preserve in America an opportunity for coming generations." It is Dochuck (2012) who retrieved a 1949 report from the National Association of Evangelicals in which the approval of legislation related to the New Deal was defined as a situation in which "the police-state is near at hand if these bills pass," revealing "that legislative trends were pointing to collectivism."[13]

It is in this imbricated relationship to enlist religion explicitly in the defense of laissez-faire economics that Philips-Fein refers to Carpenter's work, commenting on attempts to integrate Christianity and anticommunist politics, the desire of the business conservatives to find ways to show that market principles are compatible with divine truths. It is about the relationship between the CBMC and other entrepreneurs with Youth for Christ that the reference deals; Philips-Fein states that in 1945 about a third of the youth organization's bases were financed by the CBMC.

Carpenter (1997) adds an important and relevant aspect to this issue. Initially, he recognizes the generous investment of financial resources made by entrepreneurs for organizations such as Youth for Christ, but with the caveat that their relationship with these organizations did not take place on a fascist basis, as might be expected by many, highlighting that there was no attempt by these entrepreneurs to shape the movement's ideology. There was a convergence between part of their visions and desires with those of these movements, given that their contribution to these movements represented a "fresh injection of the pragmatic, optimistic, enterprising, and nonsectarian spirit that had characterized evangelical revivalism in the past."[14]

In this fruitful relationship between economic sectors and evangelical groups, an important factor can be identified in the postwar period, a time awash with societal demands and a period of recovery for the nation. On this issue, Schäfer's book (2012) dialogues with Carpenter's work (1997) in addressing both the evangelical rediscovery and its reengagement with the state. He opts to approach what he identifies as neo-evangelicals, a term coined by Harold J. Ockenga, who along with Carl Henry was concerned with positioning himself as belonging to a movement other than fundamentalism. Neo-evangelicals presented themselves as a third way, located beyond fundamentalist separatism and liberal theology. Carpenter's book uses this term a few times, most often when proposing a differentiation of this group that began to take shape in the late 1940s, which he calls "progressive fundamentalist." Another expression also used in historiography is post-fundamentalism, adopted by Donald Dayton.

Du Mez (2020) dialogues with these questions by indicating that the use of "evangelical" represents a rebranding effort. It was precisely these conservative evangelical groups that benefited from the economic prosperity that occurred in the postwar period and which participated in the developments that led to the new formation of the American religious landscape, as proposed by the Center for Religion and Civic Culture at the University of Southern California in the 2018 report "The Varieties of American Evangelicalism." In it are included groups that enthusiastically supported Donald Trump's administration, called "neo-fundamentalists," which are conservative groups that deny a militant and active devotion to Trump but supported most of his decisions and actions, since these largely aligned with their desires and agendas. The proposed classification also indicated the existence of a new evangelical group they called "Trump-vangelicals," which brings together militant and staunch supporters of the former president.

Examining Carpenter's (1997) work shows this is not a new phenomenon. He identified that a "remarkable convergence was taking place":[15] financial investment, a new vision of society, and the desires of evangelical groups originating from fundamentalism that were restructured in the 1930s and 1940s and were able to assume a prominent position in the second half of the twentieth century and an important role at the beginning of the twenty-first century. In addition to the aspects related to economic recovery, there was ample access to surplus materials and equipment from the war that were made available at affordable prices to fuel the international expansion of mission agencies. This in a context in which "military planners increasingly regarded missionary enterprises as useful for the promotion of US national interests,"[16] in which "evangelicals reasserted previously marginalized theological concepts such as Armageddon, the Antichrist, and the Apocalypse by linking them to America's new global role as 'defender of the Free World.'"[17] All the tension experienced during the Second World War and the concrete possibility of imminent destruction fit like a glove for the spread of revivalist preaching.

Regarding the nuances between evangelicals and fundamentalists, Du Mez (2020) identifies in the figure of Billy Graham, defined as an "All-American Male," an important and beautiful face decanted by the evangelical logic so in vogue today that gives strong support to what Trump stands for. In it she identifies important points of this ideal of white male evangelical power. In this process, Du Mez mentions excerpts from *Revive Us Again* to situate the reader in relation to Graham's ministry. For the author, the values and rationale introduced by fundamentalism in American culture remain.

At this point it is important to remember once again the "continuing role" affirmed by Carpenter in relation to fundamentalism and its importance in contributing to the formation of an American evangelical culture that spread across the country and abroad throughout the twentieth century. It is here that Du Mez's contribution is particularly interesting in identifying some aspects of this current culture that originated from fundamentalism, and which argued that "a strong nation was a virtuous one; sexual morality was an issue of national significance."[18]

This permanence is one of the points that Fea (2016) refers to in Carpenter's work (1997), demonstrating the establishment of a kind of evangelical subculture involving an intricate network of organizations, companies, and agencies; articulating the missionary yearning for business management; and becoming so deeply involved in

American culture, configuring important and relevant aspects related to the values and rationale that are so important in decision-making processes. If, on the one hand, we have this question so well portrayed by Carpenter (1997), on the other hand, there is a negation of the fundamentalist label, as pointed out by Fea: "former fundamentalists, now choosing to describe themselves again with the less combative label 'evangelicals.'"[19]

In this role of establishing an evangelical subculture and involving wide borders and taking on the contestation of cultural policy as an important task, we can highlight the Moody Bible Institute (MBI). As Gloege states, "It is difficult to think of an interwar fundamentalist that did not have or attempt to establish some connection to MBI ..., it served as a primary hub of an informal religious network that spread across America and the world."[20] It was initiatives and rationales like these, portrayed by Carpenter in his book, that gave the basis and the structure for subsequent broad action.

The question of good management and entrepreneurial spirit is very evident in the case chosen by Moreton (2009) for his study. He looks at the formation of Walmart, the company with the highest market value in the world at the beginning of the twenty-first century and that appears in the cradle of American white evangelical Christianity, in the Ozark region portrayed in the play *Inherit the Wind* as "the buckle on the Bible belt." Moreton's dialogue with Carpenter's work takes place at various times, highlighting aspects such as the contribution of fundamentalism to American culture, church–business relations, and the growth of this relationship in the postwar period.

The idea held by many that "self-realization placed salvation back into the center of American public life"[21] seemed totally wrong in view of the impact on public life the New Christian Right had from the 1980s. It was only at that moment that it began to realize that the aspirations about life of some were not shared by everyone. Instead, it was realized that "a powerful counterculture of conservative Christianity had been building strength."[22] To this end, Moreton starts to name the organizations and initiatives mentioned by Carpenter (1997) and then concludes: "Rather than ending in secularism, self-realization placed salvation back into the center of American public life."[23]

In this context, business–church–state relations during the immediate postwar period are an aspect that was also explored by Schäfer (2012), and which Carpenter had also addressed. In Moreton we have a specific and richly documented example in which we see in a localized way a successful case, looking at Fellowship Bible Church of Northwest Arkansas, the church of many of Walmart's executives. Moreton says: "Fellowship was at once an explicit companion to Walmart, an inheritor of a specific regional religious history, and an active innovator of novel trends in postwar Christianity."[24] When looking at this specific case, Moreton's work sheds light on several of the perspectives addressed in the historiography of religion in the United States. The issue of access to financial resources and the comfort achieved in the postwar era were materialized in this specific case that involved the structuring of Walmart in the Ozarks, a situation defined as a "fertile cross-pollination between the Cold War American military and evangelical power centers."[25] The combative language and the support of technical staff—such as pilots and radio operators, for instance—who served in the war set the tone and greatly contributed to the advancement and conquest of new lands, now through the preaching of the gospel.

Also focusing on the business side of things, Grem's book (2016) accesses Carpenter's work to affirm that he demonstrated that fundamentalism "was never apolitical or confined to an uncomplicated and easily demarcated" spiritual realm "set apart from public life or politics."[26] An important point for the author is the understanding that the search for revival was a cultural policy "to reinstate America's lost evangelical character." This is in a context where the "revival was not about the past but the future. It was about crafting a new faith, a new means of religious belief and experience directed on businessmen's terms."[27] An important part of this war strategy was the partnership established with businessmen, with a participation that went well beyond resources and that included a whole ethos and rationale, in Grem's words, based "upon the principle of infiltration."[28] Here he takes up a point well underlined by Carpenter, the idea that the leaders of evangelical missionary organizations could and should come from the business world, in a contribution that went beyond financial resources and was also given in the logic of "taking over the business": "'Every evangelical,' businessmen included, 'should find his place in the implementation of the modern evangelical resurgence in Christianity.'"[29]

Dochuk (2011), on the other hand, in telling the story of the transposition of the evangelicals from the Bible Belt to the Sunbelt, is interested in dialoguing with Carpenter in a better characterization of this evangelical movement that would spread throughout North America. Initially, he recalls the socioeconomic profile of the group, the prevalence of the working class among the faithful, and how it is presented in the book *Revive Us Again*.

When approaching the National Association of Evangelicals (NAE), Dochuk accesses Carpenter's work as a source for the constitutive "ecumenical character" of the NAE involving, on the one hand, a wide range of sectors and groups and highlighting, on the other hand, the centrality of premillennialism among fundamentalists. This understanding of the "end of time" served "to focus their attention on missions and evangelism, and any endeavor that gave priority to spiritual revival and personal salvation," leading to significant activism and an extension of the range of its message and worldview in a form of preaching that—in a quote from Carpenter introduced by Dochuk—presents "a genteel version of Christianity that would reinforce their cosmopolitan, optimistic outlook and elite perspective."[30]

The last book I will address is the work of Worthen (2013) in her search for an American evangelical mentality. For the author, the modus operandi adopted by the fundamentalist movement, and which was portrayed by Carpenter, was also used by the Church Growth Movement: "The movement's network of academic centers, seminar programs, publications, and traveling speakers was, in some ways, merely an updated version of the classic fundamentalist media-driven subculture that historian Carpenter has described."[31] Also quoting *Revive Us Again*, she comments on the experiences of the MBI and the Bible Institute of Los Angeles (Biola). Corroborating Carpenter's analysis of fundamentalism in the 1930s and 1940s, Harvard's Pluralism Project identifies that the loss of space and prestige of the group did not throw it into a mobilizing ostracism, but rather laid the foundation for its reorganization "to form an extensive subculture which served as an incubator for a range of fundamentalist and neo-evangelical forms of Christianity" (fundamentalism, evangelicalism, and Pentecostalism[32]) in the years to come.

In general, what all these authors did was to recognize and dialogue with the important contribution the book *Revive Us Again* represents for understanding the shaping of American fundamentalism. In the introduction to his book, Carpenter states that one day it will be "possible to begin a book like this without pausing first to define fundamentalism and locate it within the American religious and social landscape."[33] That day has not yet arrived. Given the current reality, it is necessary to celebrate the important and central contribution of Joel A. Carpenter's work and reflections in the understanding of this important social phenomenon.

In a 2008 article, Carpenter pointed out important clues that can help in understanding and looking at the evangelical universe in the United States today. The focus of his text is the need to consider the changes and new perspectives that are imposed in the face of "recent patterns of immigration." Fundamentalism, its history, and its culture have remained within the white evangelical church for a long time. A good question to think about is what metamorphoses will happen through the meeting of the new agendas and perspectives that Asian Americans, Arab Americans, African Americans, and Latin Americans, increasingly numerous, bring to this evangelical culture. Much of the presence and of the current evangelical growth in the United States is a result of what is happening in the congregations of immigrants and ethnic minorities. Changes are in sight that require us to think about the configuration of this religious field about the historical contribution of fundamentalism vis-à-vis the challenge arising from growing evangelical ethnic diversity. What are the possible syntheses and developments of these two realities? This is an important question for researchers and scholars interested in understanding and discussing religion in contemporary society, both in the United States and in other countries, a task that will certainly be better developed by considering the reflections and contributions of Joel A. Carpenter.

Notes

Translated by Raphael Freston.
1. J. Lawrence and R. E. Lee, "Inherit the Wind," in A. Woods, ed., *Selected Plays of Jerome Lawrence and Robert E. Lee* (Columbus: Ohio State University Press, 1995), 21.
2. Joel A. Carpenter, *Revive Us Again: The Reawakening of American Fundamentalism* (New York: Oxford University Press, 1997), 4.
3. Ibid., 246.
4. Ibid., 233.
5. Ibid., 4.
6. Ibid., 246.
7. Ibid., 237.
8. Ibid., 4.
9. K. Philips-Fein, *Invisible Hands: The Businessmen's Crusade against the New Deal* (New York: W. W. Norton, 2009), 70.
10. M. A. Hennessey, "Saving Los Angeles from the UN," *The Reporter*, November 11, 1952, 31. www.unz.com/print/Reporter-1952nov11-00028.
11. J. Rorty, "Commentary," in Ralph Lord Roy, *Apostles of Discord*, November. www.commentarymagazine.com/articles/apostles-of-discord-by-ralph-lord-roy.

12. R. L. Roy, *Apostles of Discord: A Study of Organized Bigotry and Disruption on the Fringes of Protestantism* (Boston: Beacon Press, 1953), 285.
13. D. Dochuck, *From Bible Belt to Sunbelt: Plain-Folk Religion, Grassroots Politics, and the Rise of Evangelical Conservatism* (New York: W. W. Norton, 2012), 118 and 119.
14. Carpenter, *Revive Us Again*, 172.
15. Ibid., 171.
16. A. R. Schäfer, *Piety and Public Funding: Evangelicals and the State in Modern America* (Philadelphia: University of Pennsylvania Press, 2012), 106.
17. Ibid., 87.
18. K. K. Du Mez, *Jesus and John Wayne: How the White Evangelicals Corrupted a Faith and Fractured a Nation* (New York: Liveright, 2020), 23.
19. J. Fea, *Was America Founded as a Christian Nation? A Historical Introduction* (Louisville, KY: Westminster John Knox Press, 2016), 43.
20. T. Gloege, *Guaranteed Pure: The Moody Bible Institute, Business, and the Making of Modern Evangelicalism* (Chapel Hill: University of North Carolina Press, 2015), 227.
21. B. Moreton, *To Serve God and Wal-Mart: The Making of Christian Free Enterprise* (Cambridge, MA: Harvard University Press, 2009), 88.
22. Ibid., 87.
23. Ibid., 88.
24. Ibid., 96.
25. Ibid., 238.
26. D. E. Grem, *The Blessings of Business: How Corporations Shaped Conservative Christianity* (New York: Oxford University Press, 2016), 46.
27. Ibid., 42 and 43.
28. Ibid., 53.
29. Ibid.
30. Carpenter, *Revive Us Again*, 10.
31. M. Worthen, *Apostles of Reason: The Crisis of Authority in American Evangelicalism* (New York: Oxford University Press, 2013), 134.
32. https://hwpi.harvard.edu/files/pluralism/files/fundamentalism_evangelicalism_and_pentecostalism.pdf.
33. Carpenter, *Revive Us Again*, 4.

Bibliography

Carpenter, J. A. "The Evangelical Complexion." Brooklyn: Social Science Research Council, 2008. https://tif.ssrc.org/2008/08/07/the-evangelical-complexion.

Carpenter, J. A. *Revive Us Again: The Reawakening of American Fundamentalism.* New York: Oxford University Press, 1997.

Cunha, M. N. "Fundamentalisms, the Crisis of Democracy and the Threat to Human Rights in South America: Trends and Challenges for Action." Salvador: Koinonia, 2020. https://kn.org.br/wp-content/uploads/2020/10/FundamentalismsIN.pdf.

Dochuck, D. *From Bible Belt to Sunbelt: Plain-Folk Religion, Grassroots Politics, and the Rise of Evangelical Conservatism.* New York: W. W. Norton, 2011.

Du Mez, K. K. *Jesus and John Wayne: How the White Evangelicals Corrupted a Faith and Fractured a Nation.* New York: Liveright, 2020.

Fea, J. *Was America Founded as a Christian Nation? A Historical Introduction*, rev. ed. Louisville, KY: Westminster John Knox Press, 2016.

Gloege, T. *Guaranteed Pure: The Moody Bible Institute, Business, and the Making of Modern Evangelicalism*. Chapel Hill: University of North Carolina Press, 2015.

Grem, D. E. *The Blessings of Business: How Corporations Shaped Conservative Christianity*. New York: Oxford University Press, 2016.

Hennessey, M. A. "Saving Los Angeles from the UN." *The Reporter*, November 11, 1952. www.unz.com/print/Reporter-1952nov11-00028.

Kruse, K. *One Nation under God: How Corporate America Invented Christian America*. New York: Basic Books, 2015.

Lawrence, J., and R. E. Lee. "Inherit the Wind." In *Selected Plays of Jerome Lawrence and Robert E. Lee*, edited by A. Woods. Columbus: Ohio State University Press, 1995, pp. 9–69.

Marsden, G. M. *Fundamentalism and American Culture: The Shaping of Twentieth Century Evangelicalism: 1870–1925*. New York: Oxford University Press, 1980.

Moreton, B. *To Serve God and Wal-Mart: The Making of Christian Free Enterprise*. Cambridge, MA: Harvard University Press, 2009.

Philips-Fein, K. *Invisible Hands: The Businessmen's Crusade against the New Deal*. New York: W. W. Norton, 2009.

Rorty, J. "Commentary." In Ralph Lord Roy, *Apostles of Discord*, November 1953. www.commentarymagazine.com/articles/apostles-of-discord-by-ralph-lord-roy.

Roy, R. L. *Apostles of Discord: A Study of Organized Bigotry and Disruption on the Fringes of Protestantism*. Boston: Beacon Press, 1953.

Sandeen, E. *The Roots of Fundamentalism: British and American Millenarianism, 1800–1930*. Chicago: University of Chicago Press, 1970.

Schäfer, A. R. *Piety and Public Funding: Evangelicals and the State in Modern America*. Philadelphia: University of Pennsylvania Press, 2012.

USC Center for Religion and Civic Culture. "The Varieties of American Evangelicalism," 2018. https://crcc.usc.edu/report/the-varieties-of-american-evangelicalism.

Worthen, M. *Apostles of Reason: The Crisis of Authority in American Evangelicalism*. New York: Oxford University Press, 2013.

3

Academic Border Crossing and an Anthropologist's Excursions into Research on Theology and African Christianity

Mwenda Ntarangwi

Introduction

Dr. Joel A. Carpenter was trained as a historian and, in his doctoral work, focused on American religious history. After a series of high-level administrative positions, his training in history started to expand as he encountered scholars and practitioners of the Christian faith from the Majority World, mostly Africa, Asia, and Latin America. These scholars helped Joel find connections between his own interests in American religious history and the history and practices of (especially) Christianity in Africa, Asia, and Latin America. He particularly grew a keen interest in Africa and forged strong networks with scholars and lifelong friendships. I first met Joel Carpenter in Grand Rapids, Michigan, in the fall of 2006 when I was visiting Calvin College (now Calvin University) to give a presentation and explore the possibility of relocating to Grand Rapids from Illinois where I was teaching at the time. Carpenter's name had come up several times as someone I should meet with while in Grand Rapids. At the time he had just set up a research institute focused on the study of World Christianity named after Doug and Lois Nagel, who gave the initial funding to set up the institute. As I came to learn later, Carpenter had a deep interest in Africa and was involved in a number of initiatives to support theological thinking and research on African Christianity. As a scholar, I had not yet traversed into the field of African Christianity. It was later, while working at Calvin University and through close contact and collaboration with Carpenter and other colleagues, that I started researching and writing on Christianity in Africa.

This chapter captures the spirit of the personal and professional relationship that grew out of my initial meeting with Joel in 2006, focusing on what I have learned from him about bringing together different disciplines and scholars to think, work, and produce scholarly work to benefit multiple players. The key outcome of this relationship is a focus on African Christianity, both as a scholarly endeavor and as a practice. I am a trained anthropologist by profession and a follower of Christ by choice. I was a Christian before I became an anthropologist, but it was my professional work at Calvin University that helped clarify and blend the two identities. For me the intersection between my professional training in anthropology and my faith founded in African Christianity had started emerging from my life and research in Kenya and further augmented by being part of a vibrant campus culture at Calvin, especially the Nagel Institute where Carpenter was serving as director.

Over time I attended numerous presentations by visiting scholars and practitioners and learned a great deal from events involving scholars from different disciplines gathering to focus on Christianity and art, all hosted by the Nagel Institute. Out of these interactions, I found myself seeking to curve out a research agenda for my newfound interest in anthropology and Christianity. The issues the scholars were raising in their talks were familiar to me from my own experiences in Kenya and other parts of the world where I had visited and conducted research. I was inspired to see how my own training had equipped me to explore different topics, so I decided to start a new research project on Christianity. I first consulted with colleagues, especially with Carpenter (who helped me pick out relevant books), and immediately realized I needed to get some further grounding in the topic. I convened a faculty book reading group on African Christianity as a way of introducing me to some of the current thinking about Christianity in Africa as I sought to develop my research topic further. With funding from both the Calvin Center for Christian Scholarship and the Nagel Institute for the Study of World Christianity, I brought together a team of eleven colleagues for the reading group. We met for five months (2008–9) on a regular basis and read selected texts by different authors, including Ogbu Kalu, Kwame Bediako, Mercy Oduyoye, J. Kwabena Asamoah-Gyadu, and Emmanuel Katongole, among others. Out of this gathering came a volume I edited titled *Jesus and Ubuntu*, published in 2011, in which we explored the social significance of the growing Christian presence in Africa. In 2012 I was invited to serve on the board of directors for the Nagel Institute and, at the same time, to lead an international organization that brought Christian universities together. With all these networks and knowledge, I was convinced I needed an opportunity to explore how ethnography can bring useful insights to contemporary Christian practices in Africa. I chose to focus on ethnographic research study of Christianity and popular music in Kenya, which culminated in a publication titled *Hip Hop and Christianity in Kenya*. I had to straddle more than two disciplinary paths and come up with a product that would represent both approaches. Luckily I had Carpenter to look up to as an example. All along he insisted that there is a need to bring in scholars from different disciplinary traditions and positions to interact with each other on similar topics, mostly Christianity.

Ethnography is a tested methodology that mostly seeks to see cultural phenomena through the perspective of the practitioner. Anthropologists call this the view from below or the native point of view. My own studies have undertaken this as the best approach to understanding African Christianity and faith realities. By ethnography I adopt John Brewer's definition:

> Ethnography is the study of people in naturally occurring settings or "fields" by methods of data collection which capture their social meanings and ordinary

activities, involving the researcher participating directly in the setting, if not also the activities, in order to collect data in a systematic manner but without meaning being imposed on them externally.[1]

Brewer further explains the assumption behind ethnography as field research within the social sciences:

> Ethnography is premised on the view that the central aim of the social sciences is to understand people's actions and their experiences of the world, and the ways in which their motivated actions arise from and reflect back on these experiences ... knowledge of the social world is acquired from intimate familiarity with it, and ethnography is central as a method because it involves this intimate familiarity with day-to-day practice and the meanings of social action.[2]

Straddling between anthropology and Christianity through ethnography seemed like a strategic approach for me in my research. But it was not as easy as it may sound.

Anthropology and Christianity: Strange Bedfellows?

My journey into this border-crossing between anthropology and Christianity has been complicated due to some inherent challenges I have had to embrace. As Brian Howell has noted, anthropologists and theologians "working at the intersection of anthropology and religion have argued for a recognition, if not embrace, of the incommensurability or incompatibility of anthropology and theology."[3] For me there was this unspoken view among my fellow Christians that anthropology was antithetical to Christianity, and among fellow anthropologists that Christians are irrational and guided by emotions rather than scientific facts. It did not help that anthropology as a discipline upholds a methodological approach to culture based on relativism, in which a culture's values and practices are gauged according to the culture's own internal logic, not that of another culture. Anthropology also views human life as having emerged through an evolutionary path linked to primates as compared to the Christian view of creation. Some ground has, however, been covered on this front with some Christian scholars seeing no contradiction between creation and evolution.[4] I became a more committed Christian following my training in anthropology because it provided me analytical tools and a perspective that enhanced my understanding of scripture culturally while also introducing a reflective stance for my own faith journey and practices. Instead of shaking my faith, anthropology led to a stronger ownership of my faith.

A quick look at the history of anthropology shows that Christianity is good for anthropology just as anthropology is good for Christianity. In the book *The Slain God*, Timothy Larsen notes that even though pioneer anthropologist Edward Tylor rejected Christianity and even belittled religion altogether in much of his writing, it was the basic tenets of his Quaker faith and its sympathies for the marginalized that led Tylor to the discipline of anthropology. In contrast E. E. Evans-Pritchard, Edith and Victor Turner, and Mary Douglas, all of whom kept their Catholic identity, were also steered toward their theoretical and methodological contributions to anthropology by their Christian faith. Their willingness to see rationality in the cultural practices and explanations of the African cultures they studied was in no small way shaped by the Christian principle of Imago Dei. The humanity of the people they studied was affirmed in their faith, and this led to their willingness to see those people, even though very different from the anthropologists themselves, as both rational and their explanations of social phenomena probable. These anthropologists understood that social phenomena need not always be observable to be real, even as they personally embraced the scientific method. Evans-Pritchard, for instance, did not personally believe in the efficacy of the Azande magic, but he saw it as representing the same rational behavior as that which he was accustomed to in his own British culture. Some of his conclusions were made following his understanding of the limitations of research methods as noted in his book *Theories of Primitive Religion* when he says:

> Statements about a people's religious beliefs must always be treated with the greatest caution, for we are then dealing with what neither European nor native can directly observe, with conceptions, images, words, which require for understanding a thorough knowledge of a people's language and also an awareness of the entire system of ideas of which any particular belief is part, for it may be meaningless when divorced from the set of beliefs and practices to which it belongs.[5]

This holistic approach to understanding a culture is the most valuable contribution anthropology has for our Christian witness.

Research in Christianity by anthropologists deals not only with what people say but also with what they do, and it is in the faith practitioners' activities and their performances that one will find meanings of their expressed faith. This is the approach that Carpenter encouraged me to highlight when I showed interest in studying African Christianity and reiterated later when we were brainstorming on a proposed research project for theologians in Africa that was later funded by the Templeton Trust. Theological studies that are anchored in ethnographic research, therefore, have the greatest potential to capture the vibrancy, authenticity, and diversity of Africa's faith realities today. But, I also understand it is difficult to fully study and comprehend matters of faith, matters that are very personal and often unarticulated in the same way we know and express reality. Therefore, ethnography becomes a key methodology to help in accessing those practices.

Building on interdisciplinarity and breaking established disciplinary boundaries, ethnography provides access to the experiences of people in different contexts and from various vantages, pointing to its efficacy even in humanities. It combines methods of data collection such as participant observation, interviewing, document analysis, mapping physical spaces, comparative analyses, and visual or audio-recording. These methods provide for rich data about a people, place, and period leading to opportunities for projections of experiences from one place to another. This is why it is possible, for instance, for Naomi Haynes to use her study of a congregation in a specific location in Zambia's Copperbelt to understand a national phenomenon. From her work of that small congregation, she was able to understand the role of a pastor and the expectations congregants have of him. That understanding is what she used to understand the responses Zambians had to Nevers Mumba's bid for the presidency, and especially why he was not able to garner much political support despite his standing as a prominent evangelical leader in a predominantly Christian country. When engaging ethnographic methods, anthropologists believe that repeated data collection through these methods allows for a deep understanding of sociocultural phenomena that enables one to describe a people and/or their culture.[6] That is the experience Carpenter has had in his work as a scholar and administrator especially with individuals, institutions, and communities in different African nations. It has helped him get a rich holistic picture of the issues and opportunities for local studies that he has championed.

Anthropologists apply the holistic approach to collect and analyze data, allowing them to see connectivity between otherwise different strands of observations and practices. In my own scholarly work on popular culture and Christianity in Kenya, I was drawn to connections between economic activities, social identities, and faith commitments. I was particularly interested in an economic analysis that was extended to development studies and then to Christian practice. A 1909 publication by Joseph Schumeter on the concept of methodological individualism (the sense that subjective individual motivation explains social phenomena) set in motion certain social analyses. The approach was used to explain many development projects and many techniques of microeconomics being framed through that approach. The connection between this approach and Christianity was not lost on me. Christianity emphasizes the individual in terms of personal salvation and individual prosperity, with converts primarily encouraged to think of themselves instrumentally as individuals because each will account for his/her individual deeds or sins on the judgment day. This has been amplified lately through the charismatic and neo-Pentecostal movements. One can therefore see the need to look at Christianity as part of a large ecosystem of being, a phenomenon that I argue is best approached through the ethnographic method. Through ethnographic methods, I was able to undertake comparative studies as well as a deeper understanding of Christianity. Here is an example.

The Advantages and Limits of Ethnography

There is an evangelical church that has a conservative theology with a liberal social style, meaning that members of the congregation may sometimes go dancing and have a drink here and there. The church is therefore not Pentecostal in the sense of being set apart from the world, but nonetheless is biblically based and takes the Bible to be literally or near literally true. The church assumes that the real authority in the world comes from the Bible and not from humans. The church meets in a gym or a school classroom as it is unlikely that the meeting will be in a church building; there is a contemporary music band; the target audience is the youth; it's the kind of church where people dress casually, and men primarily run everything. The congregation's point of faith is to have a relationship with Jesus; and to some extent, members are expected to share the Good News with other people because they believe that every single person in the congregation must have a vivid and supernatural experience of God. While this description may seem generic, it is a description of many churches I have had a chance to attend in my experiences both in Africa and the United States.

This description fits the church I attended between late 2017 and early 2020 in Nairobi called Mavuno Crossroads. It is a church that meets in a hall in a local primary school, and congregants dress casually and are committed to "winning souls." This particular description, however, is of Vineyard Christian Fellowship Church in Chicago where anthropologist Tanya Luhrmann spent two years carrying out ethnographic research on the growing movement of evangelical and charismatic Christianity in the United States. She wanted to answer these questions: How does God become and remain real for modern evangelicals? How are rational, sensible people of faith able to experience the presence of a powerful yet invisible being and sustain that belief in an environment of overwhelming skepticism? She was involved in a participant observation exercise that included attending morning Sunday services, being part of a house group, praying with people, and hanging out with them so she could truly understand how they interacted with and heard from God. She carried out a deep ethnographic study of the church. From this experience and the data she gathered, Luhrmann wrote a book titled *When God Talks Back: Understanding the American Evangelical Relationship with God.*

Luhrmann's study was purely a scientific undertaking that did not reflect her own faith commitment to Christianity or evangelicalism. Even when she prayed and participated in the various church activities, it was merely a way to understand the subject matter. I have argued above that there has been a conversation in anthropology regarding the "qualifications" of "insiders" during ethnographic studies. That is, can people embedded in the cultures they study truly provide insights that are credible? Can a Christian study Christianity? Or does such an activity require an outsider like Luhrmann? Luhrmann could describe specific practices and people's statements about their faith, but could not go all the way to explain how or if they heard from God because as an outsider, the anthropologist cannot answer such questions as those related to people's internal decisions or validity of what they believe. When asked to comment on whether she thought that people heard from God or not, she chose not to make such a conclusion. In an interview on US National Public Radio (NPR), for instance, she told *Fresh Air*'s Terry Gross:

> The way I think about it as an anthropologist, I don't have the authority to pronounce on whether God is real or whether God is not real. I don't feel like I have a horse in that race. I don't feel I have the authority to say whether God showed up to somebody or did not. I do think that if God speaks to someone, God speaks to the human mind. And I can say something about the social, cultural, and psychological features of what that person is experiencing.[7]

Luhrmann believes that the mind is the medium through which individuals communicate with God. She combined her training as an ethnographic researcher on how the mind responded to a series of questions known to psychologists regarding certain behavior. She found that people who scored highly in the absorption hypothesis had sharper images of hearing from God. Carrying out research on people's faith will raise questions about ethnography's ability to really present all the complexities of such a phenomenon.

Critiques of ethnography have often been around three major fronts—linguistic, feminist, and postmodern—which at times limit our full comprehension of cultural nuances. There are spaces and phenomena that ethnographers cannot access. Further, that the researcher can influence the outcome of the research in many ways through the questions asked, the analyses undertaken, and conclusions arrived at, all point to the unique role played by the researcher. As Christian Smith has noted when reviewing Timothy Larsen's book *The Slain God*:

> All sciences, as particular human practices, never finally transcend the humanity of the persons who engage in them. The very human personal characteristics of even the greatest scholars—including their religious or anti-religious proclivities—are often not irrelevant to the kind of scholarship they produce.[8]

So what does this tell us about anthropology and Christianity? Following Haynes' definition of theology as "a system or set of ideas about the divine; ... what people think about God and how they ought to relate to him,"[9] we can see Luhrmann's study as an attempt to describe and analyze an aspect of people's thinking about God by focusing on a specific congregation within a specific church in Chicago. But we have to question how someone not connected to the tradition can access the core of what another is experiencing. Luhrmann is a nominal Jew, which leads to one asking if there is a need to be a Christian to understand and explain beliefs and practices among Christians. As Haynes further asks, can we, as anthropologists studying Christianity, "write about divine action in a way that preserves the integrity of both our informants' experiences and that of anthropological frameworks"?[10] Can we capture the essence of what others are experiencing without compromising the integrity of our methods, especially ethnography? Can theology or anthropology truly capture the transcendent? Again, Haynes offers this answer:

> When theology is understood as a result of the critical work of people who are trying to understand God and, at least in the Pentecostal case, to make him act, we are able to write about God anthropologically because we can write about him ethnographically.[11]

Our focus then is on what people are trying to do as well as on our own proximity to their identity as Christians. Anthropology gives us the distance to observe, but Christianity gives us the proximity to understand. It is no wonder that in his 1965 book *Theories of Religion*, Evans-Pritchard cautions anthropologists on how to think about studying religion. People's traditional practices cannot be ignored when exploring their engagement with Christianity.

Scholars have, for instance, argued for the importance of taking African traditional religious and philosophical practices seriously when trying to understand contemporary African Christianity. It was Desmond Tutu who in the 1970s said:

It is reassuring to know that we have our own ways of communicating with deity, ways which mean that we are able to speak authentically as ourselves and as pale imitators of others. It means that we have a great store from which we can fashion new ways of speaking to and about God, and new styles of worship consistent with our new faith.[12]

Kwame Bediako's work also focuses a great deal on the question of identity and Christianity in Africa. Scholars working on Christianity in Africa often encounter certain beliefs and practices in their studies that show a close connection between Christianity and African traditional thought, especially in the realm of the supernatural. Such encounters often produce some tension between belief and practice, the logical and the illogical, and the expected and the manifested. Such tensions are not limited to African Christianity, though. Anthropologist Paul Hiebert wrote about his experiences in India in ways that are instructive to us today in Africa. In his essay titled "The Flaw of the Excluded Middle," Hiebert starts with the story in Luke 7:20 where John's disciples asked Christ, "Are you he who should come, or do we look for another?" Hiebert says, "Jesus answered not with logical proofs but by a demonstration of power in the curing of the sick and casting out of evil spirits."[13] Hiebert then shares how, in his own presentation of the Gospel, his Western identity led him to emphasize rational arguments instead of focusing on evidence of God's power in the lives of those with whom he was sharing Christ. Hiebert's experiences in India mirror my own observations in Kenya, where I could see that the narrative used by a street preacher was very similar to that used by a traditional healer. I have written of a preacher in a matatu in Nairobi using Isa. 65:23, which says, "they will not labor in vain, nor will they bear children doomed to misfortune," to promise the passengers that God will intervene in all their challenges in life, including prospering in business, getting a visa to go abroad, getting a US green card, and recovering from an illness.[14] I also talk of posters on streets and roads in Nairobi announcing traditional healers promising to deal with challenges similar to those enlisted by the matatu pastor. Clearly these are important topics for the people in the city, but there are two competing ideologies for responding to them. Are churches or prayers one of many market options available to Kenyan Christians seeking prosperity and spiritual assistance in everyday affairs? Hiebert confronted similar scenarios and says that when people converted to Christianity "they took problems they formerly took to traditional saints to the Christian minister or missionary. Christ replaced Krishna or Siva as the healer of their spiritual diseases."[15] The question then is how to make sense of these practices. I think this is where ethnography becomes critical. What is the value of ethnography to theology? Ethnography captures practices, and if we are to be involved in redemptive communities, then we need to have good ethnography that helps us to go beyond a mere academic exercise to an engagement involving an understanding of the intricacies of living a life of faith in the midst of the messiness of life.

Ethnography, therefore, is an important tool for capturing the realities of life expressed through the topics you are focused on because most of those topics are very much part of the lives of the people you are studying. To some extent, whether you talk about morals or historical injustices, faith in urban areas, or ethnic reconciliation, you are delving into the realm of life that the same people you are studying have their own understanding and even explanations of that phenomenon. Many of them have, for instance, ideas about why there is decline in morality or church attendance, the place of faith healing in today's world, or the best approaches for ethnic reconciliation. Many can tell what steps need to be taken to reconcile people from different ethnic backgrounds who have suffered historical injustices. But the danger with these individual explanations is that they are derived from personal knowledge, beliefs, or experiences that are partial even though often generalized. These generalized explanations hardly get critiqued or revised as things change because of the limited view individuals have of the entire spectrum held by the individual. At other times, because of being so close to the phenomenon itself, these individuals are unable to see these matters in distinct forms that help explain and understand them. They are taken as common sense. And because they are so common, they become part of habits that we rarely pause to explain. When we take ethnography to be both a method and a methodology, however, we can develop a sequence of steps that help eliminate individual biases because of extended and repeated observations of multiple sources of information.

The task of an ethnographer, therefore, is to make sure that research focuses on people's behavior in their everyday contexts rather than in unnatural or experimental circumstances the researcher has created. The researcher collects data through various techniques, but primarily by means of observations and in flexible and unstructured ways to avoid prefixed arrangements that impose categories on what people say and do. And the researcher's focus is on a single setting or a small-scale group with analysis of those data attributed to the meanings and actions the people one works with describe and explain.[16]

Conclusion

Increased complexity in the world today calls for a combined approach to scholarly work to get to as many facets of that complexity as possible. To do this I have suggested some academic border-crossing that allows the use of different scholarly approaches while remaining rooted in one's academic discipline. This approach is one that has been well practiced by Carpenter in his own work and in the work he has encouraged of others, including my own. I have found that combining my own training in anthropology with studies of Christianity as informed by theologians has allowed me to gain a good understanding of the practice of Christianity in contemporary Africa. This is because ethnographers have long understood that place and space are central to understanding the everyday lives and practices of the people they study. Place and space are not simply the backgrounds or settings to our stories, but rather important contributors to how we inhabit and interact as individuals and as communities. Place and space shape social relationships and create meanings that come out of social interactions and structures. To understand Christianity in such contexts, similarly complex approaches are required. Being grounded in one's discipline while flexible enough to cross borders by seeking out and applying other disciplinary approaches and practices, as Carpenter has done, is a sure way of unraveling the complexity of life.

Notes

1. John Brewer, *Ethnography* (Buckingham: Open University Press, 2000), 6.
2. Ibid., 11.
3. Brian Howell, "Anthropology and the Making of Billy Graham: Evangelicalism and Anthropology in the 20th Century United States," *American Anthropologist* 117, no. 1 (2015): 60.
4. There are many resources one can engage on this topic, including, but not limited to, John Walton's *The Lost World of Genesis One*; Kathryn Applegate and Jim Stump's *How I Changed My Mind about Evolution*; and Debra and Loren Haarsma's *Origins*. One may also find more resources at Biologos, a foundation that engages the intersection between science and faith, as well as the Colossian Forum that engages churches and Christians on divisive topics such as evolution.
5. E. E. Evans-Pritchard, *Theories of Primitive Religion* (Oxford: Oxford University Press, 1965), 7.
6. Naomi Hayes, *Moving by the Spirit: Pentecostal Social Life on the Zambian Copperbelt* (Oakland: University of California Press, 2017).
7. See "'When God Talks Back' to the Evangelical Community." www.npr.org/2012/11/16/165270844/when-god-talks-back-to-the-evangelical-community (accessed January 22, 2021).
8. Christian Smith, "God and the Anthropologists: A Review of the Slain God," *First Things*, 2015. www.firstthings.com/article/2015/03/god-and-the-anthropologists (accessed January 12, 2021).
9. See Naomi Haynes, "Grounded Theology," in J. Derrick Lemons, ed., *Theologically Engaged Anthropology* (Oxford University Press, 2018), 266.
10. Ibid.
11. Ibid., 279.
12. Desmond Tutu, "Whither African Theology?," in E. Fasholé-Luke, Richard Gray, Adrian Hastings, and Godwin Tasie, eds., *Christianity in Independent Africa* (London: Rex Collings, 1978), 366.
13. Paul Hiebert, "The Flaw of the Excluded Middle," *Missiology: An International Review* 10, no. 1 (1982): 35.
14. See Mwenda Ntarangwi, *The Street Is My Pulpit: Hip Hop and Christianity in Kenya* (Urbana: University of Illinois Press, 2016).
15. Hiebert, "The Flaw of the Excluded Middle," 39.
16. Paul Atkinson and Martyn Hammersley, "Ethnography and Participant Observation," in N. K. Denzin and Y. S. Lincoln, eds., *Strategies of Qualitative Inquiry* (London: Sage, 1998), 110.

Bibliography

Applegate, Kathryn, and Jim Stump. *How I Changed My Mind about Evolution: Evangelicals Debate Faith and Science*. Downers Grove, IL: IVP Academic, 2016.

Atkinson, Paul, and Martyn Hammersley. "Ethnography and Participant Observation." In *Strategies of Qualitative Inquiry*, edited by Norman K. Denzin and Yvonna S. Lincoln. London: Sage, 1998, pp. 110–36.

Brewer, John. *Ethnography*. Buckingham: Open University Press, 2000.

Evans-Pritchard, E. E. *Theories of Primitive Religion*. Oxford: Oxford University Press, 1965.

Haarsma, Debra, and Loren Haarsma. *Origins: Christian Perspectives on Creation, Evolution, and Intelligent Design*. Grand Rapids, MI: Faith Alive Christian Resources, 2011.

Haynes, Naomi. "Grounded Theology." In *Theologically Engaged Anthropology*, edited by J. Derrick Lemons. Oxford: Oxford University Press, 2018, pp. 200–79.

Haynes, Naomi. *Moving by the Spirit: Pentecostal Social Life on the Zambian Copperbelt*. Oakland: University of California Press, 2017.

Hiebert, Paul. "The Flaw of the Excluded Middle." *Missiology: An International Review* 10, no. 1 (1982): 35–47.

Howell, Brian. "Anthropology and the Making of Billy Graham: Evangelicalism and Anthropology in the 20th Century United States." *American Anthropologist* 117, no. 1 (2015): 59–70.

Ntarangwi, Mwenda. *The Street Is My Pulpit: Hip Hop and Christianity in Kenya*. Urbana: University of Illinois Press, 2016.

Smith, Christian. "God and the Anthropologists: A Review of the Slain God." *First Things*, 2015. www.firstthings.com/article/2015/03/god-and-the-anthropologists.

Tutu, Desmond. "Whither African Theology?" In *Christianity in Independent Africa*, edited by E. Fasholé-Luke, Richard Gray, Adrian Hastings, and Godwin Tasie. London: Rex Collings, 1978, pp. 364–9.

Walton, John. *The Lost World of Genesis One: Ancient Cosmology and the Origins Debate*. Downers Grove, IL: IVP Academic, 2009.

4

Translatability and Identity: A Korean Diasporic Exegesis on Jacob's Name Change

Won W. Lee

Church historian Lamin Sanneh argues that the translatability of Christianity is an essential theoretical framework for proclaiming its gospel, not just in the mission movement but also for a universal understanding of Christianity.[1] He contends that Christianity is not tied to a single language, people, or culture. It is translatable across borders from its original Hebrew-Aramaic texts and Judaic-Hellenistic roots to the destigmatized identity of Gentiles and eventually to the life of a new religion. In response, Christians across centuries and continents have both embraced *and* rejected the pluralistic nature of their religion when learning of new contextual expressions and translations of divine activity.

This chapter examines the dilemma that Sanneh's thesis poses for biblical studies. Drawing on my own experience as a Korean American biblical scholar, I find this challenge most significant. A Korean diasporic translation of scripture is epistemologically different from that of scholars born into, living in, and being received by their dominant culture. This difference is evident in the translation/interpretation of Jacob's wrestling match at Jabbok in Gen. 32:22–32. At the end of one very fitful night, Jacob emerges with a new name—Israel. Yet, his two names are used interchangeably in the subsequent narrative.[2] As such, Jacob/Israel is perceived as an inspiration for a hybrid identity. Therein lies the challenge of a culturally translatable and vital scripture.

Like Jacob who assumes a new name in a new context, Korean American biblical scholars are given a new identity, a new name, and new cultural standards of acceptance or rejection in everyday life. Like Jacob's struggle, and not dissimilar to the lives of other Asian Americans, the Korean diaspora lives 24/7 translatability. This frames our lives and scholarly work. Sometimes, we are praised for model minority aspirations. On other occasions, and particularly in the time of the pandemic, we have been scorned as part of a "yellow peril" threatening public health.[3] This is nothing new. There is no denying that the Chinese Exclusion Act, Japanese American internments, the American War in Vietnam, the colonization of the Philippines, the Hawaiian annexation, the Los Angeles Riots, and attacks on South Asians in the wake of 9/11 are all part of American history, and thus Korean American identity.

How, therefore, shall scholars of nondominant cultures render exegetical insight that is vital to Christianity, an essentially pluralistic religion? Will their works be regarded as mere additions to the cluster of traditional interpretations? Or can established academia be provoked into reinvigorating and reorienting itself because of their intentional engagements?

Translatability in Biblical Studies

Sanneh's conceptual missiological framework is that a translatable Christianity is contextual and pluralistic. Flexible translatability allows for a rich tapestry of religious encounters from recipient cultures, as translation allows space for scripture to be read, understood, and practiced anew. Thus, each translation should be understood as a legitimate expression of the divine activities in the world, and each takes a seat at the roundtable of interpretation. For Sanneh, this pluralism sets Christianity apart from the other Abrahamic religions. Judaism is predominantly the faith of a single ethnic group, and Islam is based upon the untranslatability of the Arabic Qur'an. As shown by his examination of missions in Africa, Islam penetrated every aspect of African life, insisted on unconditional submission to the revelation of the Arabic Qur'an, and co-identified Islamization with Arabization. By contrast, the driving force of Christian mission in Africa has been its openness to diverse linguistic and cultural translations.[4]

Sanneh's insight, especially for scriptural translatability into vernacular languages, provides a heuristic value for biblical studies. The Bible contains a plurality of texts, traditions, concepts, worldviews, and theologies that lie within its pages. Moreover, it resignifies received traditions, altering old traditions into new messages applicable to changing contexts. This multivalent nature of the Bible prompts ongoing debates as to whether there is a coherent message throughout the Bible. If it were to be identifiable, no one disputes that it should be reconstructed only through navigating, negotiating, and reevaluating contending accounts, retold stories, and expressions of faith by various authors and communities. The pluralistic and contextual features of the Bible imply that the Christian gospel may, at its core, be simple but never simplistic.

Translating the Bible is a hermeneutical dance of text and readers. Whereas the existence of a biblical canon closes the possibility of addition and subtraction to accepted scripture, all books within the canon are open for interpretation. Since biblical texts result from a long and complex transformation of once-proclaimed messages, their meaning is not fossilized. Rather, their meaning is potentially vital. Translators are not to excavate the texts, but they ought to let the texts speak for themselves. On the other hand, biblical translation makes the recipient people and culture the appropriate agents of and location for proclamation. Through translation, people receive revelation that either embraces or collides with what they already have and know. Their social and ideological situation is integral to translation.[5] The pluralistic and contextual character of the Bible engages the translator with living testimonies of faith, dialogue, comparison, contrast, disagreement, and reinterpretation.

Korean Diasporic Context

Given Sanneh's argument that the recipient people and culture are the true and final loci for Christian proclamation, how do I, a Korean American Christian, read the Bible? As a first-generation Korean American, I have been nurtured by and contributed to Korean Christianity, a Christian subculture renowned for its rapid growth, conservative theological orientation, missionary spirit, struggle against Japanese colonizers and Korean dictators, and its ample share of schism, materialism, and secularization. After immigrating to the United States, I endured physical, material, and spiritual separation. I struggled with internal strife and faced external hostility. I have had many names—permanent alien, hyphenated foreigner, model minority, outsider, and Asian American. These are all names that I did not have at birth. They were assigned to me in this new land.

So, at present, I belong neither to my motherland nor to this newly adopted home. I am perpetually marginalized. My scholarly training is in Western orthodoxy and the traditional historical-critical method of biblical interpretation. Still my vocation of teaching the Bible at a Christian university in the United States is a daily reminder of hybridity, living between two worlds, diasporic identity, marginalization, and day-in/day-out translatability. How, then, does my diaspora context affect reading the Bible?[6]

In the field of Korean and Korean diaspora scholarship, the dominant trend has been to take Korean diasporic identity, immigrant history, interreligious culture, and multiple social boundaries as the hermeneutical starting point in reading biblical texts. This "reader-in-context" approach is ultimately aligned with the idea that context dictates the production of meaning. Therefore, the Bible is a reference point, not the subject. It is one among many resources, albeit an important one. Accepting the legitimacy of this approach, I prefer another route, stressing the reciprocity between the text and the reader. Reciprocity takes seriously the authority of the scripture *and* the reality of diasporic context. Even if my Korean-ness serves as a point of reference, any biblical interpretation is still grounded in, verified by, and adjudicated by the biblical texts that it seeks to elucidate. This reciprocal approach considers the impact of the Bible in the diasporic context *and* the appropriation of the Bible by the diaspora interpreter. This captures the essence of hybridity—a state of being perpetually marginalized *and* simultaneously part of two worlds. This is living translatability. Diaspora interpreters are well practiced at navigating the shoals of pluralism and context when translating biblical texts.

A Korean Diasporic Exegesis of Gen. 32:22–32

Names matter for they constitute one's identity and individuality within the framework of family and community. For all diaspora, names are a window into how people perceive their identity in a foreign land. Among the Korean diaspora, a typical name consists of three units/syllables with Chinese characters denoting specific meanings. It begins with a family name (one syllable) and is followed by a given name (two syllables). The family name points to the origin of a common patrilineal ancestor and indicates the bearer's belonging to a particular family lineage. One syllable of the given name refers to one's place within the family genealogy and relates to the bearer's male siblings. And the other, having an individually distinct syllable, signifies a unique identity and is reflected in its Chinese character. For instance, my name is Lee, Won Woo. It reveals that I belong to a specific clan of the Lee family, which originated in the city of Gyeongju, the capital of the ancient kingdom of Silla (57 BCE–935 CE). I am placed in the seventy-third generation, indicated by "Woo." My distinct individual name (Won) means to be "the best."

But all this precisely articulated identity is lost in the United States. The English spelling of the name has no capacity to hold its embedded meaning. Should I add a familiar first name to avoid the tedium of repeating, spelling, or explaining my name? Should I change the given name entirely and invent a new identity? How should I call upon my name to connect to my siblings and extended families, which date back two millennia in Korean history? Struggling to hold onto my name in a new land epitomizes the identity crisis of living between two worlds. My name in English is a visible signifier of having a diasporic identity.

The struggle of being renamed leads me to focus on the renaming and identity of Jacob in Gen. 32:22–32. At a glance, there is an unusual amount of contextual ambiguity and obscurity in the text.[7] Did Jacob cross the ford of Jabbok? Why was he left alone? Why did the event take place at Jabbok? Why wrestle? Who is the opponent? Why are subject matters changed abruptly from a wrestling match to name inquiry, to the name change, and to a blessing? All these questions, directly or indirectly, deal with the issue of Jacob's name. For example, using the rare word "wrestle (אבק)" and specifying the place as "Jabbok (יבק)" creates an acoustical phenomenon with the name Jacob (יעקב). Note the consonantal similarity of these terms: יעקב - אבק - יבק. This similarity and the repetition of the name Jacob in the text (vv. 24, 25, 27, 28, 29, 30, 32) direct readers' attention to the name change. Jacob isolated himself far enough away from his entire family and possession, the sign of God's enormous blessings, and he alone wrestled with an unnamed man all night long. No rescue was readily available to him during that night.

Difficulties arise in understanding Jacob's wrestling match where his identity is challenged and transformed. Who is doing what to whom in vv. 25–27? The Hebrew text uses only personal pronouns for all subjects and objects, except for its mention of "Jacob's hip" in v. 25 and "Jacob" in v. 27:

> And he saw that he could not prevail against him, and he struck the hollow of his hip, and **Jacob's** hip socket was dislocated as he wrestled with him. And he said, "let me go, for the dawn is coming," and he said, "I will not let you go unless you bless me." And he said to him, "what is your name?" and he said, "**Jacob**."

Who could not prevail against whom? Who asked to be let go? Who demanded a blessing as the condition for the release?

By taking Jacob as the one who demanded a blessing in v. 26b, these verses have been translated as follows:

When **the man** saw that he could not prevail against **Jacob**, and he struck the hollow of his hip, and **Jacob's** hip socket was dislocated as he wrestled with him. And he [the man] said, "let me go, for the dawn is coming," and **Jacob** said, "I will not let you go unless you bless me." And he [the man] said to him, "what is your name?" and he said, "**Jacob**."

This translation reveals three points: (1) The attacker realized that he could not prevail against Jacob, so he struck Jacob's hip socket. (2) Despite his wound, Jacob demanded a blessing from the attacker who wants to be let go before dawn. (3) Because of his endurance, Jacob received a new name as a blessing from the attacker. In short, this reading underscores Jacob's unmatchable perseverance for obtaining a blessing.[8]

A Korean diasporic reading, however, poses questions that begin and end with name and identity in a precarious situation. If it were Jacob who demanded the blessing, what he asked for may not be the same as what he received. Note that Jacob was greatly frightened when he heard from his messengers that Esau was coming to meet him with four hundred men (Gen. 32:7). In this situation, what Jacob needed might well be God's protection from Esau, "deliverance" from him, even power to overcome him as indicated in his prayer (Gen. 32:9–12), but not a name change. Even if the change of name can be regarded as a blessing for his life, it is far from what Jacob anticipated in this encounter. In fact, the text says that Jacob received a blessing *after* his name had changed, though its content is not specified.[9] Then, the theme of blessing would not be constitutive for the encounter. Rather, it is part of God's master plan. Its role within God's plan will be discussed later. At present, if Jacob was blessed because of his insistence on a blessing and endless endurance, what significance is there for his name being changed? Should not his new name imply a radical transformation of identity and character, indicating that he is no longer the same Jacob who sought material blessings from whomever he encountered and employed whatever trickery to achieve his desires?

Furthermore, if the traditional reading is accepted, it is the opponent who could not prevail against Jacob and asked to be released because of the dawn-breaking. This interpretation would not be a problem if the opponent were not a divine figure. The text, however, testifies that the opponent possesses the ability to change Jacob's name. At the same time, this opponent refuses to reveal his own name to Jacob. Since a name represents the bearer's identity or essential nature in the Hebrew Bible, changing a name is understood as a divine prerogative. The opponent also has the power to bless Jacob at the end of the meeting. Even if these arguments are circumstantial, the opponent claims a divine involvement in Jacob's new name, Isra-**el**. And Jacob has no difficulty in confessing that the unidentified man with whom he wrestled all night long was indeed a divine being: "For I have seen God face to face, and yet my life is preserved" (32:30b).[10] If, then, the attacker is understood as a divine figure, why could he not prevail against Jacob, and does this open the possibility for any human to be able to prevail over a deity? Why did he ask Jacob to be let go because of the dawn? Does the divine fear the light, work only at night, or worry about the possible rescue operation for Jacob from his family as soon as the morning comes? And why did he not reveal his identity at the outset, as was the case in Jacob's first meeting with God (28:10–17)?

These questions warrant an alternative interpretation of the encounter. Since it is Jacob who was in excruciating pain due to his dislocated hip, it is logical and reasonable for Jacob, not the opponent, to ask for the release. Taking "the hollow of the thigh" as the scrotum[11] surely increases the unbearable pain afflicted to Jacob. From this vantage point, vv. 25–27 can be translated as follows:

> And **Jacob** saw that he could not prevail against **the man** since the man struck the hollow of his hip, and **Jacob's** hip socket was dislocated as he wrestled with **the man**. And **Jacob** said, "let me go, for the dawn is coming," and **the man** said, "I will not let you go unless you bless me." And **the man** said to Jacob, "what is your name?" and **Jacob** said, "Jacob."

By this translation, the other questions fall into their appropriate places and take on new significance. The motivation behind Jacob's mentioning of the dawn-breaking reflects his desire to return to his original plan to be alone before daybreak. His desired isolation does not simply indicate his fear or anxiety for an impending meeting with Esau, but is part of his master plan to deal with Esau. After sending messengers ahead to Esau, dividing his camp into two, praying for God's assistance, selecting attractive presents for him, and moving his family in front of him (Gen. 32:3–23), Jacob isolated himself purposefully apart from all his family and possessions *in anticipation of God's physical appearance as he experienced at Bethel*. The last thing he needed was an assurance from God. After all, Jacob's return was prompted by God's command (Gen. 31:3). His isolation represents his final trick intended to create a setting that compels God to appear. This is as cunning as Jacob gets. Based on his experience of God, who once appeared while Jacob was all alone, needing help, sleeping, and not controlling whatever might happen, Jacob thinks that if he were all alone at night, God should show himself. Jacob's begging for release because of day-breaking is his desperation for achieving this goal, meeting God. No doubt, he sees the possibility of meeting God slipping away as he was wrestling with the mysterious man all night long. Ultimately, this manipulative scheme worked, but not in a way that Jacob envisioned.

If Jacob is the one who asked to be released, then it is the opponent, the divine being, who demanded a blessing from Jacob as a condition for the release. This is part of *God's trickery* of Jacob, taking back the blessing that Jacob seized from Esau. Until the wrestling match, Jacob has acquired blessings through crooked, manipulative, and deceitful ways. He took away the birthright from his older brother with a lentil stew. He cheated his father for obtaining the blessing of the firstborn. Esau's crying out is telling the truth about him: "Is he not rightly named *Jacob*? For he has *supplanted* me these two times" (27:36a). Even after he was assured of God's presence, protection, and promise at Bethel, Jacob showed his real character in making a deal with this God (28:18–22): "If God will be with me … then …" He continued for twenty years to outsmart Laban for multiplying his possessions. Soon after calling the angels of God whom he met on the way of homecoming "God's camp," he names the place Mahanaim (two camps) as if one belongs to God and another for himself.

Moreover, his deceitful intention is evident in dividing his possessions; in case Esau takes one, there is another that is spared for Jacob. Even in his prayer (32:9–12),

Jacob reminds God of what God promised at Bethel ... but with a little twist (32:12) so that he can escape from any responsibility of the potential failure of reconciliation with Esau. Jacob has done everything he can to retain blessing without really dealing with Esau. His *situation* has been completely changed from being a poor unknown fugitive to being a prosperous person returning to his homeland. Still, he is the same man, a "deceiver/manipulator/trickster." Having emerged from the womb clutching his brother's heel (25:2), Jacob—the heel-grabber—lives out the meaning of his name. Now, unexpectedly and unknowingly, he had to confront God who disguises Himself as an unnamed man, attacks him in hand-to-hand combat, causes unbearable pain, and finally threatens to take all the blessings that he has acquired. This God determines to strip away all of Jacob's deceitful history by demanding a blessing from Jacob for the price of release.

With this understanding, the abrupt shift from the wrestling match to asking Jacob's name is now quite logical. God is interested ultimately in Jacob's identity, not his situation. By defeating Jacob's plan and deceiving the master of trickery, God forges Jacob's character anew. The heel-grabber is here reborn into one whose life will be ruled by God.[12] *It is not Jacob's perseverance that causes his name change. Instead, it is God's interest, elaborative scheme, and tenacity that create this transformation.* Unless his name is changed, Jacob cannot meet his estranged brother. What Jacob needs is not another blessing, but rather a new name.

This reading prompts a different translation of the new name, Israel. Unlike the traditional translation, the name could be read as "for you have striven with God, and with men have you prevailed." The syntax of the sentence, כי־שרית עם־אלהים ועם־אנשים ותוכל supports such a translation. The second conjunction *wāw* connects the second clause with the first clause so that the former begins with *wāw*.[13] Consequently, the two clauses are composed of the same elements, verb and prepositional phrase, which contains eight syllables and creates a chiastic pattern:

כי־שרית עם־אלהים
ועם־אנשים ותוכל

This rendering is much more appropriate in the present text as well as Jacob's cycle as a whole. From the text itself, Jacob struggled *only* with God, not with any other human beings, and he thoroughly failed. On the other hand, in a wider context, he struggled with others, including Esau, who had the advantage of the birthright; Isaac, who had the right to bestow a blessing; Laban, who demonstrated material power; Rachel, who blamed him for her barrenness; and children, who deceived the fate of his favorite son, Joseph. In the end, though, he overcame them all. Accordingly, his new name means "for you have striven with God, and with men have you prevailed."

Struggling with a New Name: Reflection on Gen. 33:1–17

How, then, should Jacob's behavior in meeting with Esau (33:1–17) be understood? After morning break, he seems to have embodied a lifestyle that aligns with his new name: he walked ahead of all his parties to meet Esau, who approaches with four hundred men (33:3), and claimed that seeing the face of Esau was like seeing the face of God (33:10). Still, he refuses to journey together with Esau, even if Esau is willing to accommodate his pace and supply additional assistance (33:12–17). This seemingly contradictory behavior poses a question. Brueggemann asks, "Has the whole notion of a transformed Jacob been a ploy without substance? Or is it serious?"[14]

Most commentators concentrate on the radical transformation of Jacob, arguing that he indeed acts appropriately to his new name. Others are more cautious, asserting Jacob's refusal to be a simple indication of his old selfish nature. Whether Jacob has changed completely or not, he shares his possessions with Esau and also keeps a separate share for himself. No profound meanings need be attributed to his behavior. Still, other scholars claim that Jacob deceives Esau again. Nothing has changed in Jacob. His behavior toward Esau is a disingenuous ploy. He meticulously tricks him as he did before.[15]

Korean diasporic social location bears another possibility as I struggle with the significance of a newfound name in a new land. Identity is fluid and contingent. Depending on the situation, one may construct an identity that is still tethered to being one's old self. Or one may identify anew accommodating the profound change of one's life. These two possibilities coexist in any given context. This is part of the challenge of diasporic life and 24/7 translatability. No single identity dominates while the other fades away. Both are real and operative. They are integrated and belong to each other simultaneously. This integration of two characters could explain Jacob's behavior in Gen. 33 in particular, and the use of the two names interchangeably in the rest of Genesis.

As the sun rose upon Jacob/Israel, he limped *on ahead of* all his party until he approached his brother Esau (Gen. 33:3). This contrasts with his behavior before the wrestling match. Jacob/Israel confessed that seeing his brother's face was like seeing the face of God (Gen. 33:10). Note the several uses of the term "face" in Gen. 32, especially in v. 20 where it states Jacob's intention to send gifts ahead: "I may appease him (lit. 'covering his face' [אכפרה פניו]) with the present that goes ahead of me (לפני), and afterward I shall see his face (אראה פניו); perhaps he will accept me (ישא פני)." This desire is challenged by meeting God in the wrestling match, which results in naming the place of struggle Penuel (פניאל). Within this context, Jacob's statement in 33:10 should be neither simple flattery nor deceptive ploy. It is rather an authentic confession that could be stated only by someone who went through a dramatic change of character. Moreover, when Jacob insists Esau take the gifts he prepared, he does not use the expected term "my gifts" (מנחתי). Instead, he abruptly switches to "my blessing" (ברכתי) in 33:11, upon which Esau accepts it. Perhaps Esau thought that it is the blessing that Jacob had stolen from him and now he is giving it back.[16] Or it could be the blessing that Jacob received after being given the name Israel (32:29). If this is the case, this special designation points out yet another aspect of his new character. Jacob's refusal to go to Seir with Esau is possibly deception at first. This refusal, however, leads him to settle in Succoth. From there, he moves to the land of Canaan, the land that God promised to Abraham. In a larger context, his refusal may have been a way to fulfill God's promise made at Bethel.

Revealingly, this new name, Israel, does not appear in this meeting with Esau. This phenomenon is peculiar compared to other incidents of name change in scripture, such as with Abraham, Sarah, and Paul. In these latter cases, the old names simply cease to be used right after the new names are given and assumed. By contrast, Jacob's two names are used interchangeably in subsequent narratives. Even after God appears to Jacob *again* and prohibits for the second time any further use of the name Jacob (37:9–10), it is used repeatedly alongside the new. The continual use of both names—Jacob and Israel—can be understood as the complex identity of a person navigating a new land. In some cases, using Israel is more preferable, such as when Jacob embraces the possibility of Joseph's dream (37:11—see the proximity of appearance of the two names), when God assures Jacob for the journey to Egypt (46:1–4, 28–34, which sets up for the eventual Exodus), or when Jacob blesses Joseph's sons (48:1–22, recalling the inversion that the younger brother shall be greater than the older). In most cases, no apparent reasons are given for using both names. This ambiguity possibly signifies the dual nature of Jacob/Israel, struggling to live the life of two names at once in a fluid context.

Concluding Remarks

In the story of Jacob, God appeared to him only three times. The appearance of God to Jacob at Jabbok is enveloped by appearance at Bethel. The first appearance comes right after Jacob left his father's house (28:10–22). The second is at Jabbok. And the third comes after his return home (35:9–15). Across these three appearances, Jacob's situation is fully reversed. At first, Jacob lived the life of a manipulative, opportunistic, and selfish heel-grabber, although he still received God's promises of the Abrahamic blessings, constant personal presence, and eventual homecoming. At the second meeting, God used an elaborate scheme to defeat Jacob's own plan to gain God's assurance for dealing with his estranged brother, Esau. God's deception is superlative, such that Jacob, the master of trickery, is completely unaware of it. God hid behind an unnamed man, entwined with physicality, inflicted great pain, threatened to take away his own blessings, and ultimately crushed the very spirit of Jacob. God did all these things to none other than his chosen one, to transform his identity altogether. Now, the chosen heel-grabber has been renamed Israel and is able to embark on a journey of challenges across new contexts but with renewed confidence.

As the second-born in a Hebrew family, Jacob's identity is one of marginality. He learns to contest with whomever he meets. After he receives a new name from God, he emerges a more complex man, a limping but forward-moving Jacob/Israel. As such, he must strive for obtaining and bestowing a divine grace to all victims, even a blessing for his angry brother.

This characterization of limping Jacob/Israel is not unlike the challenge engaged by the Korean diaspora (and all diasporas). They struggle in steadily translatable ways with their context. In doing so, they come to perceive humanity and God in particular ways. As Sanneh argues, the translatability of Christianity is core to the religion's identity; thus, it is incumbent upon diasporic biblical scholars to render fresh perspective that is gained by their struggle, their limp, their new name and identity in a new land. A pluralistic and contextualized Christianity depends on their contribution to the faith.

Notes

I am honored to contribute this chapter to the festschrift of Joel Carpenter. His generous support over the years made me more than an Old Testament scholar who happens to be a Korean American, but a Korean American who reads the Bible from his own social-cultural context. I am grateful for his gentle yet persistent nudge toward this reorientation.

1. Lamin Sanneh, *Translating the Message: The Missionary Impact on Culture* (Maryknoll, NY: Orbis Books, 1989).
2. Within the book of Genesis, the name Jacob has been used more frequently. On several occasions, however, the new name Israel appears (Gen. 35:21, 22[x2]; 37:13; 42:5; 43:6, 8, 11; 45:28; 46:1, 2, 5, 28, 29, 30; 47:27, 29, 31, 8, 10, 11, 13[x2], 14, 21; 49:2; 50:2). In a few incidences, these two names occur in very close proximity (Gen. 35:9–10, 21–6; 42:1–5; 46:1–7, 27–31; 49:33; 50:2).
3. Viet Thanh Nguyen, "The Flawed Fiction of 'Asian American,'" *New York Times*, June 6, 2021, Sunday Review Section, 3.
4. His seemingly overcharacterization of these living faiths raises many questions. Is the untranslatability of the Arabic Qur'an so rigidly accepted considering it being translated into other languages? Is it possible to separate religious creeds or tenants from their cultured expressions? Does Sanneh take seriously the correlation between Christian missions with Western cultural imperialism? Have the roles of missionaries/translators, such as their implied biases toward themselves and the receiving people, been taken sufficiently into account for translation activity? Is there any potential danger for altering the core of the gospel in the process of translating its scripture? Can a religion fundamentally be translatable? Cf. Marilyn Robinson Waldman, Olabiyi Babalola Yai, and Lamin Sanneh, "Translatability: A Discussion," *Journal of Religion in Africa* 22, no. 2 (1992): 159–72; Marianne Moyaert, "The (Un-)translatability of Religions? Ricoeur's Linguistic Hospitality as Model for Inter-Religious Dialogue," *Exchange* 37, no. 3 (2008): 337–64; Retief Müller, "The (Non-)translatability of the Holy Trinity," *Hervormde Theologiese Studies* 75, no. 1 (2019): 1–8.
5. See Lamin Sanneh, "The Significance of the Translation Principle," in Jeffrey P. Greenman and Gene L. Green, eds., *Global Theology in Evangelical Perspective: Exploring the Contextual Nature of Theology and Mission* (Downers Grove, IL: IVP Academic, 2012), 35–49.
6. Numerous theological/biblical studies have been published by Korean and Korean diaspora scholars. The pluralistic religious traditions, immigrant history, multi-social-political boundaries, intergenerational dynamic, and underlying ideological identity of Korean diaspora negotiate, relativize, and appropriate the Bible to meet emerging concerns. The concepts of marginality, liminality, heterogeneity, temporality, spatiality, cultural memory, solidarity, and interstitial integrity have helped read biblical texts to articulate their own experiences, as well as contribute to their respectable fields. See two recent publications that include a helpful bibliography: John Ahn, ed., *Landscapes of Korean and Korean American Biblical Interpretation* (Atlanta, GA: SBL Press, 2019),

and Won W. Lee, ed., *The Oxford Handbook of the Bible in Korea* (Oxford: Oxford University Press, 2022).

7. Numerous linguistic, stylistic, and conceptual ambiguities in the story have been discussed extensively over the years. For an extensive bibliography, see the three latest works: Jonathan Grossman, "Jacob's Struggle at Jabbok—A New Reading," *Scandinavian Journal of the Old Testament* 34, no. 1 (2020): 134–56; Bradford A. Anderson, "The Intersection of the Human and the Divine in Geneses 32–33," *ZAW* 128, no. 1 (2016): 30–41; John E. Anderson, *Jacob and the Divine Trickster: The Theology of Deception and YHWH's Fidelity to the Ancestral Promise in the Jacob Cycle* (Winona Lake, IN: Eisenbrauns, 2011).
8. F. C. Holmgren, "Holding Your Own against God! Genesis 32:22–32 in the Context of Genesis 31–33," *Interpretation* 44 (1990): 5–17.
9. Others argue that since the blessing is already given in the form of changing Jacob's name, 29b should be translated as "and he took leave of him there," or "he bid a farewell there," rather than "and he blessed him there." See E. A. Speiser, *Genesis* (New York: Doubleday, 1964), 255; Hamilton, *The Book of Genesis: Chapters 18–50* (Grand Rapids, MI: Eerdmans, 1995), 327. This translation makes a good ending for the encounter. However, this ending is too perfect for a text where inconsistencies and ambiguities are predominantly present. As the scene of the encounter begins with the unidentified man's initiation of a wrestling match without apparent reason given, it ends abruptly without saying anything about what happened to him afterward. And the term ברך is used both in v. 27b and v. 30b. If it is translated as connoting a blessing in v. 27b, then it should be translated similarly in v. 30b as well.
10. "In his manhood, he [Jacob] strove with God. He strove with the angel and prevailed" (Hosea 12:3–4).
11. כף־ירד refers to "the scrotum, the hollow pouch of skin holding the testicles." Hamilton, *The Book of Genesis*, 331.
12. Even the progress of time from night to daylight sheds a light on the very transition that Jacob had to undergo, that is, his name changes from Jacob to Israel. At surface level, this progress provides a narrative framework for the entire text, indicating that most of the events occurred during the night and that whatever happened during the night is not the end for Jacob. Jacob could not dwell in the night as the story begins, but he must move on as the sun rose upon him. Only to the dominant concept of the name change, the "night" represents the life that Jacob as heel-grabber has lived until his mysterious encounter, and the rising sun foreshadows what kind of life he should live with a new name. By contributing directly to the cohesiveness of the text as a self-contained unit, this time change points indirectly to its conceptual coherence by circumscribing Jacob's transformation.
13. In this case, the *wa* on *wattûal* may be understood as *wāw* emphaticum. See Hamilton's *The Book of Genesis*, 335. This is contrary to the more traditional translation, "for you have striven with God and men, and you have prevailed" in which the second conjunction *wāw* functions simply to connect the two prepositional phrases.
14. Walter Brueggemann, *Genesis* (Atlanta, GA: John Knox, 1982), 268.
15. Anderson, *Jacob and the Divine Trickster*, 160–6.
16. Many commentators take this position. See Claus Westermann, *Genesis 12–36* (trans. John J. Scullion) (Minneapolis, MN: Fortress, 1985), 526; Hamilton, *The Book of Genesis*, 346. If this were the case, Jacob is willing to return the blessing to the original

owner for the sake of mending the estranged relationship. This conclusion, however, may run the risk to nullify God's utterance to Rebekah altogether.

Bibliography

Anderson, John E. *Jacob and the Divine Trickster: The Theology of Deception and YHWH's Fidelity to the Ancestral Promise in the Jacob Cycle*. Winona Lake, IN: Eisenbrauns, 2011.

Assis, E. *Identity in Conflict: The Struggle between Esau and Jacob, Edom and Israel*. Winona Lake, IN: Eisenbrauns, 2016.

Clark, Merilyn E. K. "Mapping the Boundaries of Belonging: Another Look at Jacob's Story." In *Bible, Borders, Belonging(s): Engaging Readings from Oceania*. Atlanta: Society of Biblical Literature, 2014, pp. 109–23.

Hamilton, Victor P. *The Book of Genesis: Chapters 18–50*. Grand Rapids, MI: Eerdmans, 1995.

Holmgren, F. C. "Holding Your Own against God! Genesis 32:22–32 in the Context of Genesis 31–33." *Interpretation* 44 (1990): 5–17.

Lee, Won W., ed. *The Oxford Handbook of the Bible in Korea*. Oxford: Oxford University Press, 2022.

Sanneh, Lamin. *Translating the Message: The Missionary Impact on Culture*. Maryknoll, NY: Orbis Books, 1989.

Walls, Andrew F. *The Cross-Cultural Process in Christianity: Studies in the Transmission and Appropriation of Faith*. Maryknoll, NY: Orbis Books, 2002.

5

Contextualization, Social Science Insights, and the Interpretive Task

Melba Padilla Maggay

Introduction

In our time, we are seeing a reenactment of the Jew-Gentile social crisis of the church in the first century. As with the converts of those anonymous Jewish Christians who first brought the gospel beyond the borders of Judaism, believers outside of what we know as "Christendom" are experimenting on what it means to be followers of Christ within the structures of their own religious traditions, whether Muslim, Buddhist, or Hindu.

Similarly, there is a "resurgence" of religious interest among those modernists in "post-Christian" societies as well as among postmodern and "post-secular" youth who are seeking a relationship with a transcendent being outside the framework of traditional Christianity.[1]

The task of contextualization, or the effort to make sense and live out the Christian faith in contexts outside of the old Christendom, is not new. It has been happening since the gospel broke out of its Jewish wineskins.

Jewish followers of Jesus, like Peter, had to learn that while "salvation is from the Jews," it has to be understood in a far larger frame—the *Missio Dei* as nothing less than the creation of a "new heaven and a new earth," a cosmic project whose scope encompasses not only forgiveness of sins but also the redemption of the entire creation and the calling of nations beyond Israel.

Similarly, today we are faced with the challenge of surfacing a face of Christ that is outside the usual structures of what we know as Christianity. As Frank Laubach states, "If we can untangle Christ from the terrible handicap of Christendom, which has kept so many millions from Him, we will be doing the Moros [ethnic group in the Philippines] a priceless service."

The fact is that whether we are aware of it or not, we are always contextualizing, translating, adapting, or appropriating the gospel within the meaning systems of our own cultures. Some do it well, and some do it poorly. What makes the difference is our competency in the reading of our "texts"—both Scripture and the local context in which it is being read and applied. In this chapter, we zero in on what it takes to do a competent interpretive task. We shall then proceed to clarifying the contextual issues before us. In the last part we demonstrate the usefulness of the social sciences in communicating a culture-specific message.

Reading the Text

The Latin Americans have long brought up the need to be "hermeneutically suspicious," that is, to be aware of how we are reading "texts," and what lenses we use in reading those texts.

Contemporary scholarship holds up to us at least three hermeneutical approaches: the traditional approach, the grammatico-historical approach, and the contextual approach.[2]

The first is the *traditional* or *intuitive* approach.

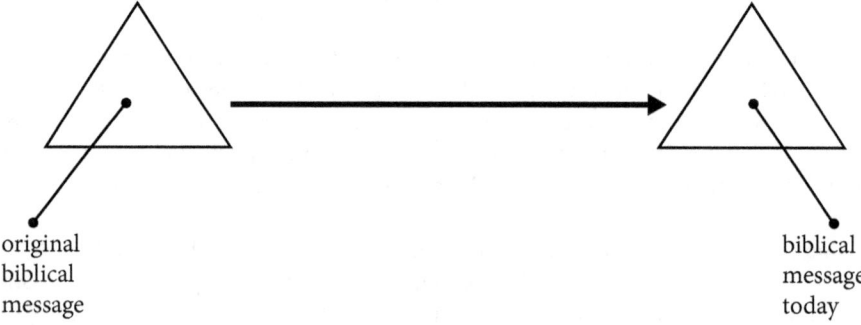

original
biblical
message

biblical
message
today

Figure 5.1

Source: Melba Padilla Maggay/Institute for Studies in Asian Church and Culture.

This approach assumes, quite rightly, that Scripture is meant for ordinary people. It highlights dependence on the Holy Spirit and immediately applies the Word on matters of personal obedience and submission to our Lord. However, this reading tends to be ahistorical and prone to fanciful allegorizations. The Bible is read as a quarry of culturally unconditioned truths.

Another approach is the *grammatico-historical* or *scientific* approach.

This approach appreciates that the text is embedded in the linguistic, cultural, and historical situations of the authors and their original audience, as far as these can be reconstructed. The problem, however, is in extracting the elements that are deemed to be normative and universal. Note the talk about "an irreducible minimum core" of the gospel, a project arising from the Greek cognitive habit of abstracting an "essence" out of the mere "accidents" of culture. The exegetical work tends to presume an "objectivity" that is neither possible nor desirable, given the interpreter's historical distance and cultural conditioning.

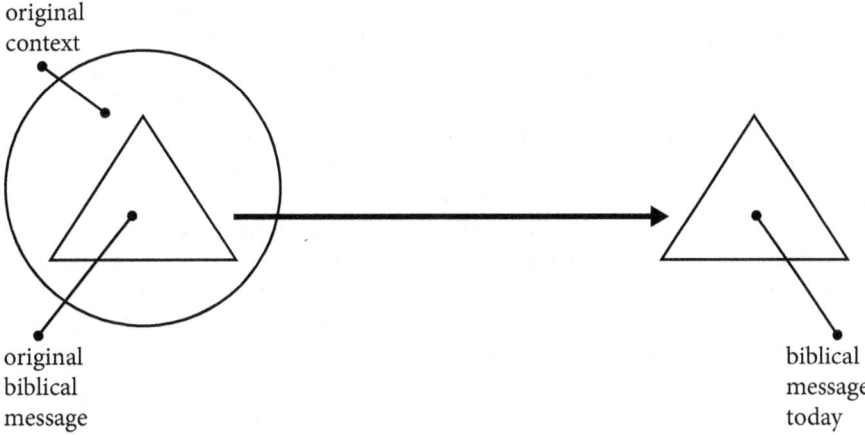

Figure 5.2
Source: Melba Padilla Maggay/Institute for Studies in Asian Church and Culture.

The third and most contentious are *contextual* or *reader-sensitive* approaches.

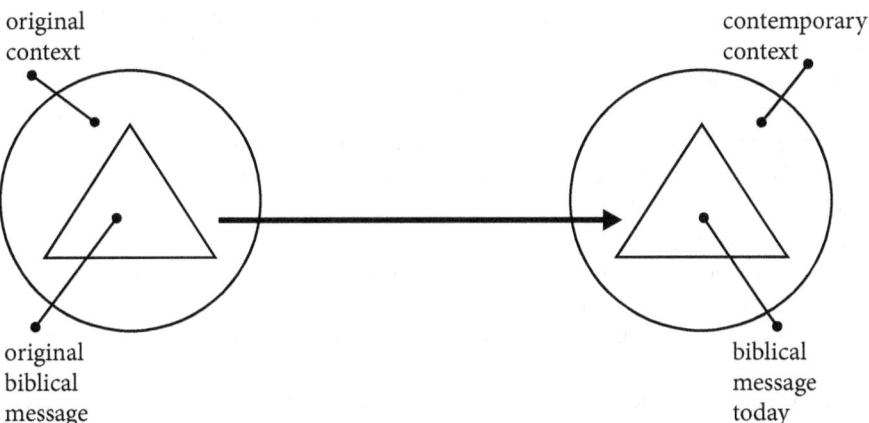

Figure 5.3
Source: Melba Padilla Maggay/Institute for Studies in Asian Church and Culture.

These approaches give due weight to the contexts of both text and reader, a complex and dynamic interpretive process in which the text and the interpreter's worldview, values, and historical situation are mutually engaged in what is now known as a "hermeneutical circle." Without the Holy Spirit, however, these contextual approaches run the danger of getting completely framed by nonbiblical meaning systems, whether ideologies, cultures, or religious traditions.

Perception studies tell us that "what we see is what we get," that is, what we see is what we are trained or conditioned to see. As the psychologist William James put it, "We have no eyes but for those aspects of things that have been labeled for us." Language—the things we are able to name—circumscribes the world we know: "The limits of our language are the limits of our world," says Suzanne Langer.

Eskimos have at least thirty variant words for snow—they can distinguish very fine gradations of what they call "snow," whereas for those of us in the tropics, it is just "snow"—this white flaky thing we see on television descending on the rooftops. In my Filipino culture, we have no Indigenous word for "privacy," which means we have no concept of a space that we fence in and beyond which no stranger can go. You can tell what people value simply by the absence or presence of words, as with the word "YHWH," which the Jews hardly pronounce out of deep reverence.

It is important to grasp that while we do have a universal faith encrypted in our Text, our perceptions and interpretations of it are limited because we perceive defensively—anything strangely outside of our usual frame of reference alerts our defense mechanisms to the possibility of error or "syncretism." We also perceive selectively. In its neutral sense, we do not intentionally censor a thing we do not wish to see—this is merely a function of our inability to see the big picture beyond our own limited universe of discourse.

The story of the Seven Blind Men and the Elephant illustrates this.

One blind man gets hold of the tusk and thinks it must be a sword; one gets to feel the tail and thinks it must be a whip; another touches the body and thinks it is a wall; one takes hold of the ear and thinks it is a fan, another the round legs and thinks it is a tree trunk, and so on.

Note that within their limited perception, each was accurate. It did feel like a sword, a whip, or a wall. But since no one was seeing the entire elephant, all were wrong.

Similarly, our theologies are only a piece of the whole; we all see through a glass darkly. We only know a part of the elephant; it is only at the end of time that we shall see it in its entirety.

In other words, the "manifold wisdom of God" is now being revealed through the churches, making known to the powers and to all men and women the unsearchable riches of Christ, the plan and mysterious purpose that has been hidden through the ages.[3]

There is not just one Theology, but many theologies arising from the Transcendent One revealing himself and engaging human cultures within their perceptual boundaries and constraints.

Contextualization and the Interpretive Task

The locus of controversy over contextualization is really this tension between "a faith delivered once for all to the saints," with its universal message, and the need to "incarnate" this faith as a living Word in particular cultures.

I wish to make us aware that when we contextualize, we are doing it in either of these two ways: *contextualization from without* and *contextualization from within*.[4]

Contextualization from without is a given gospel message that is unduly universalized and merely adapted to the structures of a recipient culture, formulated as "One Gospel, Many Clothes." The second way in which we contextualize is from within, where a culture-specific gospel message is surfaced from a conversation and engagement with the deep structures of a recipient culture.

From anthropology we learn that there are deep and surface structures to cultural systems. To illustrate:

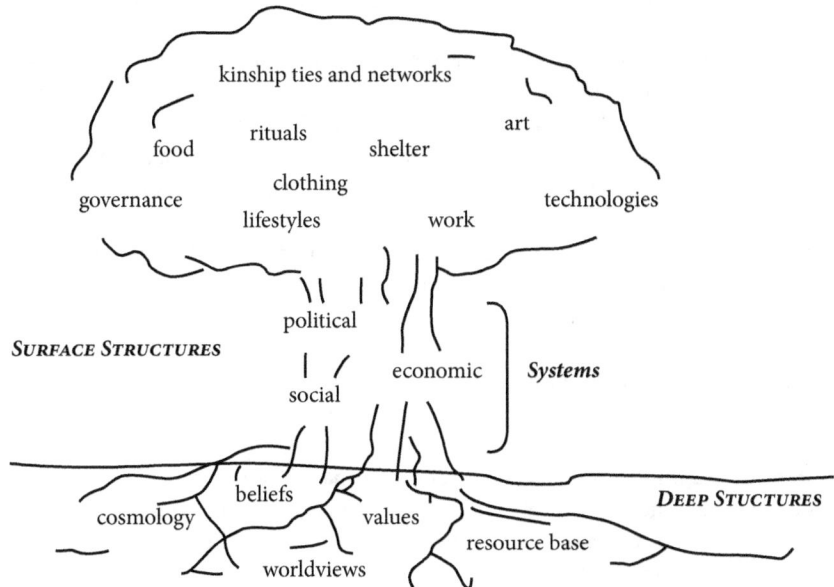

Figure 5.4

Source: Melba Padilla Maggay/Institute for Studies in Asian Church and Culture.

"Deep" structures are concepts such as worldview, cosmology, climate, and resource base that shape our beliefs and values. "Surface" structures are those systems we build on the deep structures.

How we organize our societies, our patterns of relationships, how we grow food, develop economies, invent technologies, and create art and rituals are things that through time and cultural diffusion can gradually change. But matters of consciousness, values, and mental models are deep structures that very rarely change, if ever, and sometimes, I ask myself if they need to be changed at all.

The failure to engage the deep structures of Asian cultures mostly accounts for the continuing resistance of our religious traditions. We live in a continent whose religions rival Christianity in comprehensiveness and philosophical depth.

A Roman Catholic scholar once pointed out to me that it took at least a thousand years for ancient Israel to shift from polytheism to monotheism, and even then not very successfully, as they were in constant danger of reverting to the religions of their surrounding neighbors.[5]

This brings up the question of what in our religious traditions needs changing, or whether in fact the gospel simply needs to make itself at home within the deep structures of our cultures and, within these structures, to carry out its transformative work.

Scripture—God's entire process of revealing himself in history—is instructive.

Many scholarly studies have shown that Israel, as a chosen nation, was forged out of the raw material already existing in the cultural norms and practices of the surrounding nations. The law and the covenant by which they were to live were similar in structure to the legal codes and social arrangements of other Near Eastern cultures.

Gerhard Von Rad, in his commentary on the primeval history that precedes the calling out of Abraham, notes the immersive continuity of Abram's origins from out of the nations. In Gen. 10, "The nations are represented for once without any regard for the deadly threat they posed for Israel." In fact, Israel was not in the table; it was not at the center of the nations, but represented by a name completely neutral—Arpachshad.

> That means Israel did not simply draw a direct line in time from the primeval myth to herself … . The line from primeval time does not lead lineally from Noah to Abraham, but it first opens into the universe of the international world.[6]

He says that there is a strangely new thing that now follows the comfortless story about the building of the Tower of Babel: the election and blessing of Abraham.

> From the multitude of nations God chooses a man, looses him from tribal ties, and makes him the beginner of a new nation and the recipient of great promises of salvation. What is promised to Abraham reaches far beyond Israel; indeed, it has universal meaning for all generations on earth.[7]

This is the "real testimony of the table of nations," says Delitzsch. There is this "invisible verdure of hope which winds through the barren branches of this register of nations, the hope, namely, that the widely separated ways of the nations will meet at last at a goal set by the God of revelation."[8]

Out of the womb of the nations will rise this royal priesthood, a holy nation prefigured first by Israel and culminating in that great throng of tribes, peoples, and nations in Rev. 7. It is coming out of an immensely rich multicultural world, yet bound by a unity that is accomplished by the Holy Spirit from Pentecost until today. It starts from a deep sense of cultural identity, then moves toward social critique and an awareness of the need for national cleansing and ethical purity. It goes through a process of solidarity and separation, as we have seen in the history of Israel.

The Old Testament scholar Chris Wright comments:

> It is a simple historical fact that in the transition from Bronze to Iron Age in Canaan a society emerged with some radically different forms of social, economic and political life, integrally linked to a clearly distinctive form of religious belief … they succeeded for centuries to prove, for example, that a theocracy could actually work without a human king, that land could be possessed and enjoyed

to the full without being treated merely as a commercial asset, to be bought, sold, and exploited through absolute ownership; that a broad equality of families with built-in mechanisms for the prevention or relief of poverty, debt and slavery could be maintained; that the people's spiritual needs could be met without a highly-consumptive, land-owning, cultic elite. [9]

In the New Testament, we see glimpses of the same affirmative and transformative process in Jesus' attitude toward his own religious tradition:

> On the one hand, Jesus gave no indication that his Jewish heritage was unimportant or that it was something that should now be discarded … there is no indication that Jesus intended his followers to start a new religion. To the contrary, Jesus was faithful in his visits to the temple, and he appeared to observe with his disciples the major Jewish holidays. On the other hand, it became clear in the course of his life and teaching that, with his appearance, the practice of this faith was being transformed."[10]

Contrary to the idea that Jesus' views were so divergent from rabbinical teaching, a Jewish scholar, Daniel Boyarin, argues that Jesus was in fact a conservative critic of the "traditions of the elders," pointing out the ways they had obscured the original intent of the law:

> The explanation that Jesus gives is to interpret the deep meaning of the Torah's rules, not to set them aside. And it is this deep interpretation of the Law that constitutes Jesus' great contribution—not an alleged rejection of the Law at all."[11]

Jesus' "authoritative reinterpretation" and fulfillment of the Law finds continuity in the writer to the Hebrews' prologue: "In many and various ways God spoke of old to our fathers by the prophets; but in these last days he has spoken to us by a Son."[12]

Similarly, in our day, we are to treat our ancient religions not so much as "wrong" but as "shadows" of the real thing that is to come. All cultures have sacrificial systems and shamanic visions that at their best are merely "dark speech." Like the blood of bulls and goats in the Old Testament, they cannot really take away sins and merely foreshadow the final sacrifice that is Jesus the Christ.

Our religions are, at bottom, longings for the transcendent as expressed in specific cultures. They are seedbeds of the Spirit's continual revelation, "deep structures" in which a hidden face of Christ is surfaced so that at the end of time we shall all behold him more fully.[13]

How then do we engage our deep structures such that we surface a face of Christ that speaks in a peculiar way and with force to specific peoples?

Let me explain this process in what I propose as a hermeneutical circle.

"Context" in this diagram is all the information we need to locate ourselves in a particular sociocultural context. It needs social science, research that is best done by professionals in the body of Christ who can more competently do this than clerics and theologians. Note that the Holy Spirit is at the center of this process.

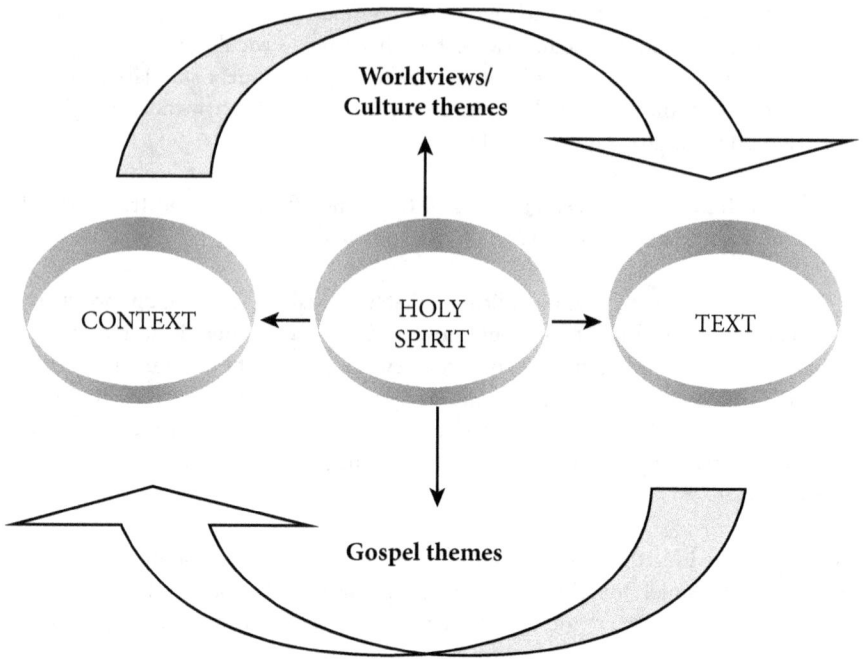

Figure 5.5

Source: Melba Padilla Maggay/Institute for Studies in Asian Church and Culture.

It is the Spirit that guides both the research and the identification of cultural themes and worldviews that need to be addressed. It is also the Spirit who leads us to the appropriate "text" and the formulation of gospel themes that can speak relevantly to the culture. The Word then addresses searching questions to the context and challenges us to transform it.

Notice that this is both a scientific and a pneumatic task. As a scientific enterprise, it requires the gifts and expertise of the entire Body of Christ, not just theologians. As a pneumatic task it requires sensitivity to the Spirit speaking through the Word and to what I call a "hermeneutical community."

During the epochal unrest that led to the overthrow of the Marcos regime in the Philippines, the Institute for Studies in Asian Church and Culture, which is mostly made up of social scientists, artists, and writers, discerned that Marcos no longer had the right to rule after the snap elections of February 1986. We were convinced that Marcos cheated and that it was Mrs. Aquino who won the elections. So we joined the movement that rose to unseat him.

The evangelical leadership at the time issued a series of statements calling for sobriety and reminding us of Rom. 13. Because the government is ordained by God, we are being rebellious in trying to overthrow Marcos as a duly constituted authority. As a small hermeneutical community, we thought that the relevant text, based on our own reading of the times and of Scripture, was not Rom. 13 but Rev. 13. There are moments historically when the state ceases to be a servant of God and instead apotheosizes and assumes the proportions of a Beast. That period was such a time. And the word to us was to resist, to stand up and be counted among those fighting for the restoration of the rule of law and not one-man rule.

This reading of the times and of the text is a process of discernment that requires the collective wisdom of an informed and biblically literate community.

Communicating the Gospel

It is important to understand that what we call the "gospel" is not unconditioned by culture—it has at least four canonical versions, is 2,000 years old, and is written within the categories of Semitic and Greek cultures, then translated into Latin and Roman forms, reinterpreted by Germanic and Anglo-Saxon tribes, and brought to us by Iberian and, later, American missionaries from what we call the "West."

Moreover, the actual religion of a people is a product of the interaction between the formal tradition and its historical and cultural appropriations. What we call "folk religion" is really this ongoing dialectical interaction between the people's reading of their formal texts and traditions and their culture and historical situation as controlling contexts.

In the case of the Philippines, for instance, one Filipino historian has done a study of the influence of the Pasyon narrative among millenarian movements around Mount Banahaw in Laguna in the latter half of the 1800s. His thesis was that this story of the sufferings of Christ, chanted by grassroots communities during Holy Week, provided a "grammar of dissent" against the abuses of the Spanish colonial regime and its friars and served as a motive force for the revolution.[14]

More recently, the language employed by Corazon Aquino and the "yellow army" during the days of "People Power" echoed that of Moses before Pharaoh: "Let my people go," she said to Marcos. And in the aftermath, her speeches celebrating the victory of the people had biblical resonances: in spite of the military might behind Marcos, God had intervened, she said, "the horse and his rider he has thrown into the sea." Some people felt this was bad hermeneutics, but who is to say that she cannot appropriate these stories as interpretive frames in the quest for the meaning of the events unfolding at that time?

Similarly, Arab Muslims have always looked down on Southeast Asian Muslims because the latter are considered not quite orthodox enough. Their brand of Islam looks "syncretistic" to more doctrinaire Islamists, an amalgam of their primal religious cultures and the traditions brought by Arab traders. Javanese Muslims are described thus:

> For most Javanese villagers, Islam was not a question of political legitimacy or doctrine but was simply part of their mentality—part of their attitude toward the world seen and the world unseen. Islam was not a religion or a sect in the sense of being an ideology and a defined social allegiance so much as a vocabulary by which people defined the sacred forces in everyday life.[15]

Among Filipino Muslims in the south, the Kalagan, one of thirteen Muslim ethnic groups, makes a distinction between "Muslim," which defines their identity, and "Islam," those who pray five times a day, fast during Ramadan, and live their lives according to the Quran.

This process of appropriation is a moving picture. The receivers of our messages are not passive recipients, but rather always hear the Word within their own interpretive frames as conditioned by culture and their historical location.

The Bible gives us glimpses of how we may proceed in communicating a culture-specific message. Some missional tools include the following.

The first is the "ladder of abstraction."

From communication theory, we know that the higher the generalization, the more abstract and less usable a particular message is for a specific context, as articulated by S. I. Hayakawa. Our message must go down the "ladder of abstraction."

Jesus as "savior" has lost its meaning for Christianized cultures like that of the Philippines. But if we get specific and talk of Jesus in Phil. 2 to a people utterly fearful of spirits—especially the monstrous *aswang*—it gains traction. We can invoke a name that is higher than any other name, more powerful than things in the heavens, things on earth, or things under the earth. This is good news to cultures oppressed by the fear of the spirit world. Yet we do not hear a message from this text, but only "God loves you and has a wonderful plan for your life." It is unsafe to presume that our gospel formulations will have equal effectiveness outside of their original cultural contexts.

A second approach is finding a point of entry as your "text." In Paul's preaching in various contexts, we see that he did not have one generic message, but he spoke to people within their own metanarratives and used these as his entry points.

To the Jews of the diaspora, as in Pisidian Antioch, he spoke of their being chosen as a people to bear the promise of the Messiah.[16]

To the pagans at Lystra, who mistook him for Hermes and Barnabas for the god Zeus, he went further back into creation and introduced the living God who made

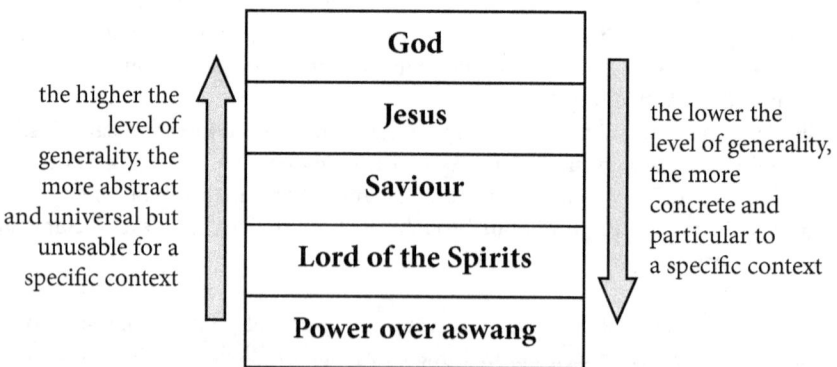

Figure 5.6

Source: Melba Padilla Maggay/Institute for Studies in Asian Church and Culture.

heaven and earth and who is not unknown to them through his provision of food and rain and fruitful seasons.[17]

To the sophisticated Athenians, he spoke of "the unknown God," the one who does not live in shrines made by artful imagination and human hands.[18]

Fulfilling the concepts that are already in the culture is another approach.

It is somewhat hard to imagine that Jesus' sacrifice would have been understood properly outside of the Jewish idea of sacrifice and priesthood. For centuries they were conditioned to be conscious that "without the shedding of blood, there is no forgiveness." This is something that other cultures could only half-grasp. Quite dimly, many cultures sense that when disaster strikes or some catastrophe happens, sacrifice must be offered to appease the wrath of the gods. The writer to the Hebrews tells us that Jesus is the final sacrifice and mediator between God and human beings; there is no need to offer sacrifices again and again. This is an example of what it means to take what is already there in the culture and bring it out of the shadows.

Similarly, Paul in his speech before the Areopagus quotes Greek poets to affirm what they already know—"in him we live and move and have our being."[19] God is already there, speaking through the literature and wise men of their cultures.

Proceeding from the familiar to the unfamiliar is another way. We notice that Paul moves from the idea of a creator who is immanent to one who is transcendent, a being who cannot be contained in shrines.

Paul builds on what is "hearable" to that which is dissonant.

While Paul begins with concepts that are familiar, he proceeds to talk of the unity of the human race—"From one man he made every nation of men, that they should inhabit the whole earth"—an idea that runs counter to the Athenian sense of their uniqueness, a race that is autochthonous or self-sprung from the Attic soil.[20]

He goes on with something more strange: "He has set a day when he will judge the world with justice by the man he has appointed. He has given proof of this to all men by raising him from the dead."[21]

The narrative tells us that at this point, some in the audience sneered, and others diplomatically said they wanted to hear him again on the subject.

The resurrection of the dead was so unfamiliar, perhaps even too untidy, for a Greek sensibility that could only imagine a disembodied soul coming out of a human body, and not a dead person rising bodily. The idea was too dissonant. They could not hear him anymore.

In communication they call this "theory of dissonance," that is, when a message is too negative or challenging, it creates an internal disequilibrium, an emotional and cognitive discomfort that drives people to block what is being said or seek information that will reinforce their position.

Another important approach is the move from affirmation to judgment. That is, in cross-cultural messaging we begin with what can be affirmed in the culture, even things that on the surface may look scandalously "syncretistic" or unbiblical.

For example, it is interesting that Paul began by saying "I see that in every way you are very religious." He could very well have said "you are very idolatrous." But he did not say so; instead, he was prepared to get behind this immense litter of idols around the city and understood that behind them was a deep religious longing. The Athenians even wanted to make sure no god was inadvertently missed: there was a shrine even for the "unknown god."

As outsiders to a culture, we have no right to judge what is before us until we have fully understood why people are doing what they are doing.

From affirmation, Paul moves toward some pointed "truth encounters": the "times of ignorance God has overlooked," he said. Now he commands all people everywhere to repent, for he has set a time of judgment. From a culture-specific message, we eventually move toward a more universal call for accountability of all nations and races.

Some Concluding Remarks

Contextualization is an ancient task that is rooted in the preparation that the Master Sower has already done and is doing in the soil of human culture. This is so that the seed of the Word can take root, transform the consciousness and structures of nations, and cause their societies to flourish.

We need to be aware that the Spirit is still speaking to the churches, revealing a face of Christ that we have yet to see and fully behold as diverse parts of the Body of Christ.

In communicating, we need to see to it that people are spoken to in their context and are in a condition to respond responsibly—what the French sociologist Jacques Ellul calls "respondability."

Otherwise, as the Lord Jesus says, we are merely "throwing pearls to the pigs."

Notes

1. Peter Berger and his colleagues have written a book titled *The Desecularization of the World, Resurgent Religion and World Politics* (Washington, DC: Ethics and Public Policy Center and Wm. B. Eerdmans Publishing, 1999). This could have been more accurately titled "The Desecularization of the West," since religion in non-Western cultures continues to be an integrating point for their societies. Their peoples have yet to secularize, a fact that has only now been noticed with the surfacing of Islam as a political religion. This is an example of how the "West" tends to universalize the interpretation of social phenomena, making their lenses an interpretive frame even for other contexts.
2. For this I am indebted to C. Rene Padilla's earlier work, "The Interpreted Word: Reflections on Contextual Hermeneutics," a paper read at the 10th General Committee of the IFES, July 1979, at Hurdal Verk, Norway, and published with permission in *PATMOS* (First Quarter, 1980), 19–22, 31–3.
3. Eph. 3.8–10.
4. For a fuller discussion of the distinction between "contextualization from within" and "contextualization from without," please see Chapter 13, "Contextual Communication," of my previous book, *A Clash of Cultures, Filipino Religious Consciousness and Early American Protestant Missions* (Metro Manila: Anvil and De La Salle University Press, 2011).

5. From a conversation with my esteemed colleague Ka Jose de Mesa, a Roman Catholic scholar known for his expertise in gospel and culture issues.
6. Gerhard Von Rad, *Genesis: A Commentary*, rev. ed. (Philadelphia, PA: Westminster Press, 1972), 144–5.
7. Ibid., 153–4.
8. Delitzsch as quoted in ibid., 144.
9. Christopher J. H. Wright, *Walking in the Ways of the Lord: The Ethical Authority of the Old Testament* (Downers Grove, IL: Inter Varsity Press, 1995), 59–61.
10. William A. Dyrness, *Insider Jesus, Theological Reflections on New Christian Movements* (Downers Grove, IL: Inter Varsity Press, 2016), 54.
11. Daniel Boyarin, *The Jewish Gospels: The Story of the Jewish Christ* (New York: New Press, 2012), 127.
12. Matt. 5.17, Heb. 1.1.
13. We see a similar pattern in Paul's speech before the Athenians in Acts 17, in which he affirms the longing of all peoples to seek after God within the limits of their cultural contours, in this case gropingly and provocatively expressed in the shrine "To an Unknown God."
14. Reynaldo Ileto, *Pasyon and Revolution, Popular Movements in the Philippines, 1840–1910* (Quezon City: Ateneo Press, 1979).
15. Lapidus, *A History of Islamic Societies*, 1988.
16. Acts 13:13–43.
17. Acts 14:8–18.
18. Acts 17:22ff.
19. Acts 17:27–8.
20. Acts 17:26.
21. Acts 17:31.

Bibliography

Berger, Peter. *The Desecularization of the World, Resurgent Religion and World Politics.* Washington, DC: Ethics and Public Policy Center and Wm. B. Eerdmans Publishing, 1999.

Boyarin, Daniel. *The Jewish Gospels: The Story of the Jewish Christ.* New York: New Press, 2012.

Dyrness, William A. *Insider Jesus, Theological Reflections on New Christian Movements.* Downers Grove, IL: Inter-Varsity Press, 2016.

Ileto, Reynaldo. *Pasyon and Revolution, Popular Movements in the Philippines, 1840–1910.* Quezon City: Ateneo Press, 1979.

Lapidus, Ira M. *A History of Islamic Societies.* Cambridge: Cambridge University Press, 1988.

Maggay, Melba Padilla. *A Clash of Cultures, Filipino Religious Consciousness and Early American Protestant Missions.* Metro Manila: Anvil and De La Salle University Press, 2011.

Von Rad, Gerhard. *Genesis: A Commentary*, rev. ed. Philadelphia, PA: Westminster Press, 1972.

Wright, Christopher J. H. *Walking in the Ways of the Lord: The Ethical Authority of the Old Testament.* Downers Grove, IL: Inter Varsity Press, 1995.

6

Crucial Lessons to Construct Democracy: From the Protestant Reformation to the Mexican Revolutions

Mariano Ávila Arteaga

In 2010, several Latin American countries celebrated two hundred years of independence from the Spanish empire. Other Latin nations claim at least one century since their birth as democratic countries. Yet, recent political experiences during the last two decades in Latin American countries (several legislative, judicial, and military coups d'état and the resurgence of neo-fascist rulers) are crucial reminders of the fragility of the democratic experiments in Latin American countries. The latest coup d'état on January 6, 2021, attempted in the US Capitol under the alleged instigation of the former president, is another clear demonstration of the vulnerability of and difficulties in building healthy democratic cultures.[1] Doing away with unethical power struggles, representing the people's interests, and cultivating democratic cultures at all levels of society and institutions are still fundamental and pending tasks. The Latin American dream of creating countries free from tyrannies, hegemonies, and plutocracies must continue to live and thrive.

This essay explores some crucial moments in history and a few essential thinkers that provide lessons that might be valuable for Latin American Christians committed to constructing democratic governments and institutions. We will make several historical connections that offer insights into Latin countries' political life and possible ways to strengthen their weak democracies. Our interest is to present a few grassroots movements and ideas that resulted in significant historical changes, small yet paradigmatic.

We start with the Calvinist Reformation of the sixteenth century. In its long itinerary, some landmarks provide us key lessons that may contribute to better governments and political life. We will consider the vision and actions of the Puritans—heirs of critical parts of the Calvinistic tradition—that revolutionized their world and contributed to the birth of political modernity.

Then this chapter considers two paradigmatic moments in Mexican history. One during the nineteenth century: the significant role of liberal associations, *sociétés de pensée* (Cochin), like the Freemasons, Liberals, and Protestants. They resisted the corporate and hierarchical structure of the traditional society of the *Ancien Régime*.

The influence such associations had in the Protestant schools and churches and the patient construction of alternative democratic models in those Protestant spaces left a paradigm for today's Protestants and Evangelicals that is urgent and essential for building democratic instances at all levels of society. Second, the Zapatista revolution in 1994 will be described as a recent and viable paradigm for democracy.

Historical Context: Traditional versus Modern Societies

Historical Protestantism in Europe from the sixteenth century onward had a secularizing character in the political arena (like in other areas, including the religious one).

The predominant worldview of fifteenth-century Europe was generally religious and Roman Catholic. Religion played a central role in the worldview, and it was the leading producer of meaning and social relations for collective life. Indeed, religion was responsible for building and preserving the world.[2] Politically, it meant a legitimation of kings' absolutism. The political doctrine *de jure Divino reges* asserted that kings derived their authority from God and could not be held accountable for their actions by any earthly power.

Politically, traditional societies were mainly hierarchical, and corporate people lived daily under vertical and authoritative systems. Such a pattern had direct implications for monarchies, absolutisms, fascisms, authoritarian regimes, and the hierarchical view of life still deeply embedded in Latin American societies until today.

The Protestant Reformation

On October 31, 1517, the Augustinian monk Martin Luther nailed a document on the door of All Saints' Church of Wittenberg. That seemingly insignificant protest set in motion a transforming movement with crucial political dimensions. Luther's single act contributed later to the release of thought and conscience, undermined the business of religion, debunked the dominant church's political control, and opened the possibilities for more democratic and egalitarian political church and social organization models.

Calvin's Thought and Its Contribution to Democracy

John Calvin (1509–64) also influenced spiritual and political thought. In Calvin's form of ecclesial government, authority rests in the presbytery, a group of elders elected by the congregation. It was a representative democracy inspired by old Israel's government by elders.[3]

In its development, Calvin's experience in Geneva moved from an aristocracy and overflowed into democracy. Socially and politically, Calvin's influence left a permanent imprint on the centuries that followed among the North Atlantic countries that applied his ideas.

Calvin scholars have highlighted that Calvin's political theology moves between the anarchic-like extremes of Anabaptist radicalism and Catholic hierocracy or theocracy. Calvin advanced greater church authority over political power. It provided the church with a remarkable ability to influence and control the political and social setting.[4]

Calvin articulated at least four fundamental concepts of theological-political thought. According to Carl Schmitt,[5] a renowned German jurist and political theorist, such ideas were later secularized in the theory of the state. Among them are

1. **Sovereignty in the political arena**. The Lordship of Jesus Christ in its secular form will become the sovereignty of the people.
2. **Loyalty and obedience to God** are a higher calling than loyalty and obedience to political authority. Calvin helped to relativize the political sphere by limiting its scope of influence. In a context of absolutism, the relativization of the power of the state was fresh air to a suffocating world.
3. **The rule of God's law** is the supreme standard of life and faith. This principle, later secularized, led to the rule of law as a key for democracies in which no one is above the law.
4. By calling the **ousting of tyrants** legitimate and necessary, Calvin developed a revolutionary doctrine. This thesis contemplated whether the responsibility for such action rested with the people, judges, or nobles.[6]

Calvin's ideas were seeds that germinated in democratic, constitutional, republican, and even revolutionary models. In the late sixteenth and seventeenth centuries, John Calvin's teaching was appropriated by Puritan ecclesial and political settings.

Puritans in the Seventeenth Century

In Scotland, John Knox led the Radical Calvinist Reformation and promoted the ideology that it was *the believers' duty* to remove tyrants from positions of power. Political scientist Michael Walzer documented English and Scottish Puritans' experience in the late sixteenth and early seventeenth centuries. He states, "The saints were responsible for their world—as medieval men were not—and responsible above all for its continual Reformation. Their enthusiastic and purposive activity was part of their religious life, not something distinct or separate: They acted out of their saintliness in debates, elections, administration, and warfare."[7] The Puritan's biblical convictions regarding the world and society held that "they were responsible for the structure of the social world in which they found themselves. That structure was not simply part of the order of nature; to the contrary, it resulted from human decision, and by concerted effort, it could be altered. Indeed, it *should* be altered, for it was a fallen structure in need of reform."[8]

Participation in church reformation set an example for reforming society. The Puritans questioned the divine right of the king and undermined the prevailing political structure.[9]

Abraham Kuyper (1837–1920) was prime minister of the Netherlands in the early twentieth century (1901–5). As a Calvinist, he expresses in a summary fashion what he considered the political implications of Calvin's democratic conception of life:

> Calvinism has derived from its fundamental relation to God a peculiar interpretation of man's relation to man, and it is this only true relation which since the 16th century has ennobled social life. If Calvinism places our entire human life immediately before God, then it follows that all men or women, rich or poor, weak or strong, dull or talented, as creatures of God, and as lost sinners, have no claim whatsoever to Lord over one another, and that we stand as equals before God ... Hence Calvinism condemns not merely all open slavery and systems of caste, but also all covert slavery of woman and of the poor; it is opposed to all hierarchy among men; it tolerates no aristocracy ... So Calvinism was bound to find its utterance in the democratic interpretation of life; to proclaim the liberty of nations; and not to rest until both politically and socially every man, simply because he is man, should be recognized, respected and dealt with as a creature created after the Divine likeness.[10]

Kuyper's theological ideas are a fine expression of the Calvinist heritage and undoubtedly capture the genius of such tradition. But we cannot separate theology from its imprint on history. In Kuyper's opinion, the maturing of democracy in the Netherlands, England, and the United States owes much of its original foundation to Calvin's religious worldview. Such nations, says Kuyper, in contrast to ancient and contemporary civilizations, are the ones that "achieved the highest development ever,"[11] and "Calvinism has *actually* ... ennobled the social life of the nations"[12] and "has yet a blessing to bring and a bright hope to unveil for the future."[13] Kuyper's messianism is still shared by many Calvinists today. In its secular form, it is ever present in the politicians' electoral discourses in the United States. It is indeed an integral part of the US ideology of "Manifest Destiny."

Why did a brilliant person like Kuyper not consider the colonial past of those nations that "achieved the highest development ever"? It was already evident in his day! We still need to ask ourselves: What can we say about the colonial heritage that such imperial nations left in the world? What about the dispossession and elimination of native Americans, trade of African slaves by Dutch merchants, inhuman slavery in the United States, Apartheid in South Africa, and the deterrence of democracy globally,[14] particularly in Latin America, until this day. While Kuyper's theological ideas may be valuable today for Latin Americans, we must keep a safe distance from its interpretations by "highly developed nations" that have led to such historical stigmata.

Political Modernity in Latin America

John A. Mackay provides an optimistic perspective to understand the Protestant arrival and presence on the continent. Mackay's central thesis is:

> The Christ who arrived in South America has put men at peace with life and has told them to accept it as it is, and things as they are, and the truth as it seems to be. But how about the other one? The one who makes men dissatisfied with life as it is, and with things as they are, and who tells them that, through Him, life

will be transformed, and the world will be defeated, and its followers will be put in agreement with reality, with God and with the truth? This other Christ wanted to come, but they prevented Him ... But today, again, *voices of spring are heard announcing His arrival.*[15]

These words summarize Mackay's assessment of the Spanish Catholic Christ who came to Latin America and, at the same time, introduce his optimistic opinion of the coming of the Protestant Christ. The Christ of Protestantism would transform the lives of men *and* the social reality of the subcontinent.

The following comment by Míguez Bonino regarding the attitude of Protestantism in its early stages in Latin America reflects Mackay's attitude.

> Roman Catholicism embodied a global system's ideology and religious structure, the outdated Hispanic royal order implanted in Latin America. As such, it had to disappear to give way to a new democratic, enlightened, dynamic liberal order that Protestantism has historically inspired ... In almost all Latin American countries ... a conflict takes place between the defenders of traditional society—the conventional native-born oligarchies—and the pioneers of "modernity," more advanced sectors of those same oligarchies, who wanted to reproduce in the new countries the conditions of the leading societies of the northern hemisphere. For them, "modernity" meant public education, representative democracy, economic liberalism, and the—somewhat diluted—Latin American version of the ideology of the French Revolution, the Encyclopedia, and, later on, Positivism.[16]

Unfortunately, Mackay's idealistic vision was mostly ignored by Protestant missionaries. The "voices of Spring" did not sing a pleasant song to Latin American countries. Mackay's dream became a reality of lights and shadows. His vision has inspired very few of the thousands of missionaries who have come to Latin America proselytizing for their denomination using marketing strategies. They have come forming disciples in the image and likeness of their culture, increasing the fragmentation of the Christian Church. But more troublesome is the fact that, for most missionaries, it is nearly impossible to distinguish between the Gospel of Jesus and the "American dream"; between the missionary task and the territorial, economic, cultural, and ideological expansion of the United States; and between the politics of Jesus and American politics.[17]

In addition, a significant part of the missionary legacy, predominantly from the United States, and visible in the political arena among Evangelicals, can be summarized in two terms: fundamentalism and cultural colonialism.

Fundamentalism

Fundamentalism crippled Protestants and became normative in most theological expressions of Latin Evangelical churches until this day. It has become "a sign of interdenominational identity."[18]

Evangelization in Latin America has been more particular than total, more with words than with concrete actions; it has preached a Gospel of offers and not a Gospel of obedience and discipleship. The false distinction between matter and spirit, body and soul, terrestrial life and eternal life, church and society, along with the dichotomy between world and church, has been a characteristic of evangelical preaching in many churches … there are no signs of change in such gnostic and partial tendency in the evangelistic work in Latin America.[19]

Cultural Colonialism

Powerful mass media (radio, TV, internet, Facebook, Instagram, etc.) has influenced people's habits, ways of thinking, needs, and tastes. They are shaped and molded according to the values and ideologies of the North Atlantic countries.

US lifestyle and culture permeate almost everything the average person reads, listens to, or watches every day. As Pablo González Casanova points out, the "spiritual conquest" of Latin America represents one of the greatest and best-orchestrated achievements of cultural colonization.

> The United States made an unprecedented cultural penetration in the history of Latin America. The values of "American civilization" spread and "internalized" far beyond mere "slogans." [It was] a politics of penetration geared towards influencing the theoretical frameworks and value scales of the elites and the masses, altering and alienating their "natural" styles of thinking and wanting … *The ontology of Hollywood became the common sense of much of the middle classes of Latin America* … Since the conquest of America by the Spanish and Portuguese, no culture penetrated so much south of the Rio Grande as the North American culture of the market.[20]

The legacy of the Calvinist Reformation can be still valuable today. In a continent where new forms of fascism (from the right and the left) are overrunning democracies (even in one of the oldest—the United States), we need to go back to the sovereignty of the people. When the heavy habitus of *caciques* (strong men) seems to perpetuate old monarchic regimes, it is urgent to maintain the spaces gained with blood and suffering. Protestant and Evangelical churches could reclaim the democratic heritage from the Calvinistic and Puritan practices. Latin Evangelicals need to appropriate the democratic institutional practices of those early protestants and their educational vision.

Nevertheless, to make such a crucial contribution, Latin American Protestantism needs to restructure itself, becoming a flexible and willing agent of change. A genuine *metanoia* (conversion) is required. José Míguez Bonino expressed it well, and his words are still relevant today:

> Our present ecclesial structures, theoretically and institutionally, bear the marks of our theological and ideological history. If we remain prisoners of the conditioning of that history, our fruitlessness will persist. In other words, Protestantism must undergo a conversion, returning to its origin, including a concentration on the

transforming power of the Gospel. Protestantism must also undergo a conversion toward a radically new beginning breaking from ideology, cultural dependency, economic and institutional alienation that has marked the life of Protestantism in our continent. This renewal must direct Protestant people to a new conscience, working to transform our institutions and the content of our plans. It should inform the way we develop ourselves and our societies. Reflection on our Latin American society's history, coupled with original theological reflection, can endeavor the necessary work to create these changes.[21]

Can Anything Good Come from Nazareth?

One of the direct results of colonialism by imperial nations, in the academic world (theology and social sciences), is the implicit disdain and neglect toward the South, or the so-called Majority world. In the fields of knowledge like the biblical sciences, theology, social sciences, and political thought (to name a few), the North Atlantic nations rarely take seriously the contributions of scholars or democratic models in the southern hemisphere. Yet, some of the most promising democratic ideas and models today are being developed and experienced in Latin America. Few, it is true, but highly significant. We will illustrate it with two examples from Mexico.[22]

Democratic Experiments in Mexico

In the days of the liberal oligarchy (1872–1910), Protestantism arrived in Mexico hand in hand with the liberal project and its modernization ideology. Ideas Associations, *sociétés de pensée*, Protestants, liberals, and Freemasons became a space where those who opposed the society's organization could meet: a corporate hierarchical organization favored by the *Ancien Régime* and the Roman Catholic Church. Protestants became bearers of political modernity and democratic models where education for everyone was a central goal.[23] Such associations "served as true laboratories ... where [democratic] social and political alternatives were crafted ... and represented a countermodel promoting education" for all social sectors, not only for the elites.[24]

In those days, and thanks to the centrality of education for those associations, Protestant schools became schools for democracy. They played a significant role in the formation of Mexican society following the revolution of 1910.

> In the schools, the goal of teachers was to facilitate learning of democratic practices. They wanted to convey a pure liberal ideology and transform students into representatives of an individualistic and egalitarian conception of social relations. Teachers transmitted civic values and democratic practices at the school level through games that symbolized republican forms of government, such as "school republic" and "school city." As described by a Methodist school teacher, the activity consisted of "a plan to instill the principles of true citizenship and to introduce children to the forms of government of their country." The school became a city where everyone could be elected to "positions of government, judge

or police." Teachers did these practices with a clear awareness of the social and political context of the moment. Then, Mexican people "were unaware of their right to sovereignty and left everything in charge of the highest class." The explicit purpose of the school's exercises was "the advancement of people … in their political life … in the way of thinking and voting of citizens."[25]

These early schools adopted liberalism and Protestant democratic views. They made a significant change in the early stages of the Mexican revolution (the 1910s) and contributed to crafting a new nation.

Along the lines of those Protestant teachers during the days before the Mexican revolution, Pablo Latapí Sarré, a prominent Mexican educator, proposes a curriculum that could inspire new models of *education for democracy*, even in Christian schools, colleges, and seminaries in the North Atlantic nations.[26] Among the issues proposed, Latapí mentions the consolidation of "civil society," the emergence of "social controllers," political parties in crisis, electoral issues, human rights violations, public and private corruption, impunity, and the growing and unstoppable dominance of organized crime (drug and human trafficking, etc.)

Whether any public or Christian education system responds to innovative suggestions like these, we need to ask ourselves: Is it possible that our educational institutions may be places where education for democracy can flourish? A flourishing democracy would bear the fruit of religious and ideological tolerance, responsibility, civic participation, and a genuine sense of solidarity with the growing population living in extreme and shameful poverty. Is it possible that our churches and educational institutions could provide examples of what democratic life means by their ecclesial practices?

A Revolution of the Other: Ethnicity as Revindication of Ancient Demands

Another model for grassroots processes of democratization is the Zapatista revolution (in which the Base Ecclesial Communities played a vital role), initiated by the Zapatista Army for National Liberation (EZLN) in 1994. In the last chapter of his magisterial first volume on *Política de la liberación*, Enrique Dussel provides an analysis of this paradigmatic movement.

The Zapatista revolution "clashed against the supposedly Western civilization, modernity, eurocentrism, creole-white and mestizo superiority."[27] It fought against the dominant homogeneity imposed by successive regimes, from the conquest in 1492 to the most recent Mexican governments.[28] They all had in common the denial of the Other, the original native Indigenous peoples.

Zapatismo survived "the genocide of European's modernity expansion during the conquest, the domination of the postcolonial liberal state, of the populist and even revolutionary welfare state, and lastly, the neoliberal globalizing project with its overwhelming homogenizing power to transform citizens into consumers of a global market."[29] The Zapatista revolution challenged Marxist analytical categories as well as dominant traditional paradigms in sociology[30] and political philosophy.[31]

Race, culture, politics, and religion came to the center of the debate, when the *indios Zapatistas*, with clear consciousness of their dignity, demanded self-determination and respect for their original culture and religion; for their political, judiciary, and economic practices, for their own techniques in agriculture, education, and sanitary issues. Finally, such claims came to the surface in the political arena after five centuries.[32] Here are some examples.

The revolution started internally. A year before the armed resistance, in March 1993, women demanded to the Indigenous Clandestine Revolutionary Committee (CCRI) to pass Women Laws by which "women were not going to be given in marriage against their will; they wanted to have as many children as they wanted and could take care of; they demanded the right to have political positions in their communities; they required the right to have voice and be respected in political assemblies; they wanted to have the right to education, etc."[33] These laws represented an internal revolution for Indigenous tribes and were passed unanimously. The process to fight external oppressors started with traditional internal ones.

A process started by exogenous intellectual agents from the mestizo Mexican class with an inherent messianism was reversed by the Mayan communitarian ways of understanding politics and change. The revolutionary vanguard became converted to the Chiapas Mayan Indigenous groups and their ancient democratic culture and practices: "Making vertical decisions in a unipersonal way, became a decision-making process that was collective and horizontal."[34] Instead of being a fight for power, the revolution became essentially a moral and ethical demand: "to begin the possibility that human beings have room for *dignity*."[35]

Another significant development in the practice of power by the Zapatista communities goes to the very essence of power, to its fundamental definition. For the Zapatistas, power originates in the communities, which is the sovereign authority. The exercise of power by those elected to wield it must be done as an act of obedience to the will of the people: "To govern, obeying."

> The person who exercises the delegated institutional power does it obeying the original power of the community and, thus, is a servant that rules, obeying. The delegated obedient authority serves the power of the community. This is an inversion of the definition of power from the origins of Modernity to the present. It has a different ontological and metaphysical origin.[36]

It is not difficult to see in these words an echo of the politics of Jesus, who made present a kingdom in which to be head is to be the last, a kingdom of mutual service and not domination, a kingdom in which the highest values are living to serve others without distinctions, giving our life for the sake of others, and loving our neighbors as ourselves.

Notes

This essay was developed out of a lecture given to commemorate the 500th birth anniversary of John Calvin at the Universidad de Chile, Salón de Honor, on June 10, 2009.

1. In a well-documented article in the *New York Times*, titled "The New Authoritarianism," Max Fisher and Amanda Taub speak of the "shifting nature of democracy worldwide" and summarize it as "more nationalistic, more restrictive, more illiberal, more dominated by strongmen and more, in a word, undemocratic" (*The Intercept*, April 2, 2021). The recent experience in the United States illustrates their indictment perfectly.
2. Against a Hellenocentric understanding of the origins of modern democracies, Enrique Dussel demonstrates that democracy was first experienced not in Greece, as it is the common assumption, but in the "Egyptian and Mesopotamian, Phoenician, and Semite worlds" (Dussel, Política de la liberación, 11 and chs. 1.2 and 1.3).
3. José María Mardones, *Postmodernidad y cristianismo. El desafío del fragmento* (Santander: Editorial Sal Terrae, 1988), 19–32; Peter L. Berger and Thomas Luckmann, *The Social Construction of Reality. A Treatise in the Sociology of Knowledge* (New York: Anchor Books 1967), 13–82.
4. "Calvin pursued power in Geneva with all the artfulness of a Machiavellian adventurer: the same might be said of his followers in England." Michael Walzer, *The Revolution of the Saints. A Study in the Origins of Radical Politics* (New York: Atheneum, 1972), 10.
5. See Carl Schmitt, *Political Theology. Four Chapters on the Concept of Sovereignty* (Chicago: University of Chicago Press, [1922] 1985).
6. Marta García Alonso, *La teología política de Calvino* (Barcelona: Anthropos editorial, 2008), 243.
7. Michael Walzer, *The Revolution of the Saints. A Study in the Origins of Radical Politics* (New York: Atheneum, 1972), 12.
8. Quoted by Nicholas Wolterstorff, *Until Justice and Peace Embrace* (Grand Rapids, MI: Eerdmans, 1983), 43.
9. In an unusual case of self-criticism, Wolterstorff makes the case for the importance of acknowledging that in their effort to establish an ideal state,

    > Calvinists very often resorted to intolerance and repression. The extent of their abuse was such that they made Calvinism intolerable everywhere. In time, and due to the pushback that Calvinists faced against their reforming plans and efforts, aside from other factors, the original worldview kept diminishing almost to the point of disappearance. Instead, it was replaced by a concern to create <u>ideas</u>, especially theological ideas. Calvinists devoted themselves to the formation of theology or philosophy. (*Until Justice*, 20–1; Orthodoxy without orthopraxis)

10. Other Calvinists, who Wolterstorff considers to be among "the most insufferable of all human beings," are what he calls the "triumphalist Calvinist." They believe to this day that the revolution to establish a Christian state has already taken place and their duty is to keep it as it is, or at best to make cosmetic renovations. Plenty of these examples can be found in the United States and the Netherlands. And he added, referring to Apartheid days: "South Africa today provides them in their purest form" (*Until Justice*, 21).
11. Wolterstorff, *Until Justice*, 34.
12. Ibid., 38–9.
13. Ibid., 40.
14. Noam Chomski's *Deterring Democracy* (New York: Hill and Wang, 1991). See also Howard Zinn, *A People's History of the United States* (New York: Harper Perennial,

1980), Eduardo Galeano, *The Open Veins of Latin America: Five Centuries of the Pillage of a Continent* (New York: Monthly Review Press, 1971), and the powerful story of Dutch colonial rule in Indonesia by Pramoedya Ananta Toer, *This Earth of Mankind* (New York: Penguin, 1982).
15. John A. Mackay, *The Other Spanish Christ: A Study in the Spiritual History of Spain and South America* (Eugene, OR: Wipf & Stock, [1933] 1969), 141, emphasis added.
16. José Miguez Bonino, "Historia y Misión," in *Protestantismo y Liberalismo en América Latina* (San José: DEI, 1985), 25–6.
17. Today's white supremacy ideology is held by the majority of white Evangelicals. According to the voters' surveys in Trump's first election (2016), 81 percent supported his platform, and in the last presidential election of 2020, according to Gallup's senior scientist Frank Newport, PhD, "The AP VoteCast survey shows that 81% of White evangelical Protestant voters went for Trump this year, compared with 18% who voted for Biden. The Edison exit polls estimate that 76% of White evangelicals voted for Trump, 24% for Biden." What kind of missionary work they do in Latin countries? What kind of Gospel are they preaching?
18. Pablo Deiros, *Historia del cristianismo en América Latina* (Buenos Aires: Kairos, 1992), 802.
19. Ibid., 241.
20. Pablo González Casanova, *Imperialismo y Liberación. Una Introducción a la Historia Contemporánea de América Latina* (México: Siglo Veintiuno Editores, 1979), 28, 29, 33, emphasis added.
21. Miguez Bonino, "Historia y mission," 34–5.
22. Other important examples are Bolivia and the movements that brought an Indigenous person to political power; Ecuador and its exemplary ecological laws; the government of Lula in Brazil and the significant ways in which poverty was reduced, and so on.
23. Jean Pierre Bastian, comp., *Protestantes, liberales y francmasones. Sociedades de ideas y modernidad en América Latina* (México: FCE, 1990), 7–14.
24. Ibid., 8, 13.
25. Bastian, *Los Disidentes: Sociedades Protestantes y Revolución en México, 1972–1911* (México: Fondo de Cultura Económica, El Colegio de México, 1989), 163–4.
26. Pablo Latapí, "Escuela y transición a la democracia," *Revista Proceso* 839, November 30, 1992, 34–6.
27. Enrique Dussel, *Política de la liberación. Historia mundial y crítica* (Madrid: Editorial Trotta, 2007), 499.
28. "These were States that pretended to be mono-ethnic, starting with the mestiza nationalist ideology and later with the ideologies of the universalist, pro-imperialist creole elites" (ibid., 499).
29. Dussel, *Política de la liberación*, 499.
30. The Zapatista demands are summarized in "roof, land, food, health, education, information, culture, independence, democracy, justice, liberty, and peace" for all. A new constitution must ensure that the rights and freedoms of people are acknowledged and that the weak are defended from the powerful.
31. Dussel, *Política de la liberación*, 499–500.
32. Ibid., 498.
33. Ibid., 500.
34. Ibid., 502.
35. Ibid.
36. Ibid., 503.

Bibliography

Bastian, Jean Pierre. *Los Disidentes: Sociedades Protestantes y Revolución en México, 1872–1911*. México: Fondo de Cultura Económica, El Colegio de México, 1989.

Bastian, Jean Pierre, comp. *Protestantes, liberales y francmasones. Sociedades de ideas y modernidad en América Latina*. México: FCE, 1990.

Berger, Peter L., and Thomas Luckmann. *The Social Construction of Reality. A Treatise in the Sociology of Knowledge*. New York: Anchor Books, 1967.

Chomski, Noam. *Deterring Democracy*. New York: Hill and Wang, 1991.

Deiros, Pablo. *Historia del cristianismo en América Latina*. Buenos Aires: Kairos, 1992.

Dussel, Enrique. *Política de la liberación. Historia mundial y crítica*. Madrid: Editorial Trotta, 2007.

Galeano, Eduardo. *Las Venas Abiertas de América Latina*, 56th ed. México: Siglo Veintiuno editores, 1989.

García Alonso, Marta. *La teología política de Calvino*. Barcelona: Anthropos editorial, 2008.

González Casanova, Pablo. *Imperialismo y Liberación. Una Introducción a la Historia Contemporánea de América Latina*, 2a edición Corregida. México: Siglo Veintiuno Editores, 1979.

Kuyper, Abraham. *Lectures on Calvinism*. Grand Rapids, MI: Eerdmans, 1931.

Mackay, John A. *The Other Spanish Christ: A Study in the Spiritual History of Spain and South America*. Eugene, OR: Wipf & Stock, 1969.

Mardones, José María. *Postmodernidad y cristianismo. El desafío del fragmento*. Santander: Sal Terrae, 1988.

Míguez Bonino, José. "Historia y Misión." In *Protestantismo y Liberalismo en América Latina*, 2nd ed. San José: DEI, 1985.

Schmitt, Carl. *Political Theology. Four Chapters on the Concept of Sovereignty*. Chicago: University of Chicago Press, [1922] 1985.

Toer, Pramoedya Ananta. *This Earth of Mankind*. New York: Penguin, 1982.

Walzer, Michael. *The Revolution of the Saints. A Study in the Origins of Radical Politics*. New York: Atheneum, 1972.

Wolterstorff, Nicholas. *Until Justice and Peace Embrace*. Grand Rapids, MI: Eerdmans, 1983.

Zinn, Howard. *A People's History of the United States*. New York: Harper Perennial, 1980.

7

Pathways for a Protestant Social Ethics in Latin America

Raimundo C. Barreto

The origins of social ethics as an academic discourse can be traced back to the movement known as the social gospel in late nineteenth century.¹ In *Social Ethics in the Making*, Gary Dorrien shows how this discourse was formed not only in the academy but also in the realms of church and society. Social ethics emerged as a successor to moral philosophy—standing, however, vis-à-vis theology and the social sciences. It focused on the study of social movements in relation to social problems, having as a central concern the understanding and effecting of meaningful change in the world.²

This chapter seeks to understand the rise of social ethics as a discourse and praxis among Latin American Protestants.³ It highlights key moments in the development of a Latin American Protestant social thought in the twentieth century, paying special attention to the socioreligious movements that shaped it. In addition, it briefly examines the present situation in the region from the point of view of two turns that have impacted Latin American Protestantism in the last few decades.

Richard Shaull proposed a dialogue between the Protestant Reformation and Latin American liberation theology.⁴ Behind such a project lay Shaull's hope to unsettle North American Protestant traditions, which he believed to be on the cusp of stagnation. For him, a tradition that repeats old answers in its response to new challenges in a constantly transforming world runs the risk of sclerosis and death.⁵ Shaull's concern with the ossification of religious traditions and the need for renewal is warranted. As Andrew Walls has shown, Christianity has experienced many deaths and resurrections in different parts of the world.⁶ Regions that were once centers of Christianity have been de-Christianized, while other regions where missionary efforts seemed fruitless for a long time later experienced a Christian boom, in some cases after the exit of missionaries. Although Christianity has the capacity to renew and recreate itself in new contexts and cultures, there is no law that guarantees its expansion or renewal.

Shaull's capacity to reinterpret his own faith tradition by looking into it through new lenses allowed him to envision new ways for its reinterpretation and innovation. By revisiting the Reformed tradition from a liberationist perspective, Shaull was able to understand the redemptive work of God as a continuous process of liberation through which people and communities victimized by violence and injustice acquired a new consciousness.[7] Such a new consciousness allowed them to reimagine their futures, envisioning an unprecedented possibility of self-determination.

For Shaull, the faith in a living God who is present and active in history creates conditions to promote profound transformations at different levels of human existence. But that has not always been the case in the Reformed tradition. In Latin America, for instance, Protestantism has been often associated with an exacerbated concern with the private realm of existence, thereby making concerns about social transformation irrelevant or, at least, secondary. In spite of that, there is a memory and legacy that attests to the transformative potential of Latin American Protestantism. In an effort to bring to mind the *ethos* that informs the development of a Latin American Protestant social ethic, this chapter highlights five moments in the history of Latin American Protestantism. The first moment identifies the emergence of Latin American Protestant consciousness on the continent. The second one brings attention to the search for autonomy in Latin American Protestantism. The third moment underscores a rupture with a reformist and developmentalist approach to social change, a move toward a liberationist social project. The fourth moment presents the formation of an evangelical social Christianity informed by the concept of *misión integral*. The last moment addresses the current challenges for Latin American Protestant social Christianity in a context characterized by Indigenization and Pentecostalization.

The Awakening of a Latin American Protestant Consciousness

The conquest and colonization of Latin America occurred around the same time the Protestant Reformation was taking place in Europe.[8] Nevertheless, Protestantism only established itself on Latin American soil from the nineteenth century onwards.

In the beginning of the twentieth century, the Protestant presence in Latin America was still small. Protestant immigrant churches in the nineteenth century focused on the preservation of ethnic identities and the pastoral care of their communities. Thus, for a long time they remained absent from the discussions seeking to discern the public role of Protestant churches in Latin America. José Miguez Bonino notes, for instance, that none of the immigrant churches was represented at the important Panama Conference of 1916.[9]

Mission-originated Protestantism, which spread in the region in the second half of the nineteenth century, represented only a small proportion of the population by the turn of the twentieth century. This kind of Protestantism (whose origins were predominantly North American) was often associated with the expansion of the political and economic influence of the United States in the region.[10] Despite its small numbers, though, the Protestant presence in Latin America began to impact the social reality in the region toward the end of the nineteenth century. With an emphasis on literacy, democracy, and progress, Protestant missionary initiatives created, among other things, an "extensive network of mission-run schools, clinics, hospitals, and literacy programs throughout the region."[11] However, it was not yet possible to speak of a Latin American Protestantism per se. What existed in the region at that point was a Protestant project guided by an external missionary agenda, which José Miguez Bonino described as being marked by "an ethic of withdrawal from the world accompanied by legalistic rigidity."[12]

Movements toward the formation of national churches in Latin American Protestantism began to take shape most since the Panama Conference (1916). This process is often referred to as the consciousness-awakening of a Latin American Protestant identity. While some sectors among Latin American Protestants began to work for the discovery of the "Latin Americaness" of the Protestant churches in the region, the task of understanding the Latin Americanization of the Protestant faith in the past century, its scope, and its limits remains both incomplete and crucial.[13]

At the same time as the field of social ethics was taking shape among North American and European Protestants, an autochthon Protestant social consciousness began to shape in Latin America. Such an identity construction took form within an emerging ecumenical movement, which can be traced back to the formation of the Cooperation Committee for Latin America (1913) and the subsequent realization of the Panama Conference (1916). That conference was organized by North American missionaries, in some way as a response to Latin America's basic absence from the Edinburgh World Missionary Conference in 1910. Strategies to evangelize Latin American intellectual elites and concerns as for how Protestantism could make a deeper impact upon Latin American culture and society dominated the conference's agenda.[14] The participation of a few young Latin American Protestant leaders in that conference, though, set off an irreversible process that over time led to the formation of a Latin American Protestant consciousness.

The Panama Conference was the starting point for a series of events that set in course a growing concern with the social dimension of the gospel in Latin America. Young Latin American leaders such as Erasmo Braga (1877–1932) became interested in the merging of the Protestant faith with the best of Latin American ideals, dreaming of a Protestantism capable of being a vital agent of social transformation and a channel of moral and political progress in the region.[15] Key for that ideal was a concerted emphasis on a Protestant education that contributed to the development of moral responsibility at the level of both the individual and the society.

People like Braga made important contributions to the quest for a Latin American Protestant identity. As part of that quest, Braga criticized the individualism and the sectarianism he saw in Latin American Protestant churches, urging them to overcome those attitudes. He challenged the Protestant churches to relate with Latin American society in all its dimensions:

> The tendency to church-centeredness raises a hedge around the evangelical communities, and this will inevitably result in their segregation from national life. Sharing in service to the community is a splendid means of witnessing to Christ in both private and public life.[16]

Braga contributed to create structures that enabled greater collaboration among the churches for the evangelization or Christianization of society based on two strategies: education and interdenominational cooperation.

Subsequent gatherings in Montevideo (1925) and Havana (1929)[17] contributed even more to the formation of Latin American Protestantism. The fact that those meetings coincided with the beginning of the Great Depression was of significance for the turn toward contextualization, as Jean Pierre Bastian explains:

> The Latin American Protestant leaders who emerged on the continent, and who made missionary societies proud, were [in fact] expressions of these [Pan-American] policies as their privileged interpreters. However, the economic crisis of 1929, and the constant attacks coming from the unions and nationalist governments against North American hegemony placed before this generation of evangelicals the question of their identity. The two conferences that occurred during this period were concerned with this awareness in relation to the necessity of articulating an evangelical Latin American response to the crisis.[18]

Braga chaired the Montevideo Conference in 1925, which adopted Spanish as its official language; the official language in the Panama Conference was English. This conference underscored Jesus' call for universal fellowship and the "growth of social idealism among university students in Latin America."[19]

The Search for an Autochthonous Protestantism

Other significant developments took place at the conference in Havana (1929), chaired by Mexican poet, writer, and journalist Gonzalo Báez-Camargo.[20] Four themes were central for that conference: evangelical solidarity, education, social action, and literature. Furthermore, the need for the "Latin Americanization" of Protestantism on the continent was widely debated, along with the question of the dangers brought about by the North American control of the churches.[21] In emphasizing the autonomy of the national churches, the Havana Conference became a watershed in the development of Latin American Protestantism.

Despite the limits of its impact on the local churches, this rising Latin American ecumenical movement stimulated the formation of ecumenical initiatives aimed at addressing the course of rapid social changes in the region, which attracted a number of young Christians.[22]

The Christian Student Movement (MEC) was one of initiatives that catalyzed those efforts to formulate a Protestant response to social, political, and economic problems in the region. Initially concerned with the evangelization of their peers, these Latin American students slowly began to reflect on their social responsibility as Christians in both the region and the world. These national Christian student bodies and the local groups they formed "acted as ideological incubators for the production of young Protestant Christians who were sensitive to the social and political implications of the Christian Gospel" and would take on important leadership roles in the Latin American Church and Society Movement.[23] The MEC embodied the Latin American ecumenical movement's ability to connect the demands of local, national, and regional realities with "socio-political perspectives, perceptions, and concepts" mediated through a global context.[24] Other similar ecumenical networks were formed during that period. In general, these organizations operated in tandem with one another, forming a manifold ecumenical network of emerging Protestant leaders throughout Latin America.

Engaging the Latin American Revolutionary Context

The First Latin American Conference of the World Student Christian Federation, held in 1952 in São Paulo, Brazil, was a watershed moment in such developments. For the first time, socialism was seriously considered by Latin American Protestants on theological terms.[25] M. Richard Shaull led reflections about the possible engagement between Marxism and Christian theology. While this kind of conversation was not necessarily new, what was fresh was the fact that the Latin American social reality was on the forefront of that reflection. For Shaull, the locus of such a conversation was the encounter with a revolution, the revolution of the disinherited.[26] Up to that point, efforts toward contextualization tended to merely recycle emphases generated in the North Atlantic, which were then digested locally. For instance, the emphasis on the social responsibility of the church, which became a household theme among ecumenical Protestants in Latin America in the 1950s, was brought to the continent by those who participated in the World Council of Churches assembly in Evanston (1954). Its theme, "Christ—The Hope of the World," guided theological reflection on Christian responsibility vis-à-vis the international economic development agenda. What the reflections taking place among Latin American Protestant students offered was a distinct starting point, which shed new light into the conversation and opened them up for new approaches and possibilities. As Shaull himself noted, one of the greatest contributions of that movement was that

> as small teams of lay persons and trained theologians worked together on the issues facing them in a revolutionary situation, they found themselves dealing with new questions and seeking new approaches. And they began to articulate theological and ethical positions that went beyond what they found in the books and study materials they were using.[27]

The MEC was just one of the multiple faces of a broader Church and Society Movement comprised by ecumenical Protestants willing to engage with social movements, workers' unions, secular student movements, the Catholic Left, and Marxists while not shying away from offering a Protestant perspective on the struggle for a more just society. They raised critical questions concerning the theological bases of their Christian commitment and began to reread the Bible with new eyes. The movement of Christian students, along with other sectors of the Latin American ecumenical movement, laid the groundwork for a new ethical and theological approach to the urgent questions that challenged Latin American Christianity during that important period. It provided the foundations for the development of a new method of theologizing in Latin America that emphasized the action of God in the world and encouraged Christians to unite in the struggle for life and justice. In that process, they moved from the earlier ecumenical concern with the Christianization of the social order, which rehearsed the social gospel ideal from the beginning of the twentieth century, to an emphasis on responsible society conceived by the global ecumenical movement and, finally—in the heat of the struggle against injustices that infused their communities—to the development of a theological language that recognized the revolutionary situation in Latin America as its *locus* of enunciation. This emphasis on the revolutionary situation evolved later to the language of liberation. Between the mid-1950s and the early 1970s, Latin American Protestants saw the rise of a theology in/of revolution as that expressed in the work of Sergio Arce Martinez (1924–2015), as well as of theologies of liberation as those seen in the works of Rubem Alves (1933–2014) and José Miguez Bonino (1924–2012). In each of these cases, these theologies emerged from within the Latin American historical condition and in dialogue with lay initiatives on the borders of church and society.

Despite its abrupt suppression in the mid-1960s,[28] the influence of this movement remained important. After Vatican II and the rise of a Catholic liberation theology in the Second General Conference of the Latin American and Caribbean Catholic Bishops in Medellin, Colombia (1968), fresh opportunities for collaboration between Catholics and Protestants arose, giving birth to a plurality of new ecumenical institutions in the 1970s and 1980s. These two decades were particularly difficult for many Latin Americans due to the grip of brutal military dictatorships and civil wars throughout the region. Many of those who participated in the multiple branches of the Church and Society Movement took on leadership roles in the new ecumenical organizations that emerged during this period. Others, forced to leave the ecclesiastical institutions they belonged to, joined nonreligious social movements to resist those criminal authoritarian regimes. A number of them were imprisoned and tortured, and few were killed by the military. Others embraced their political vocation, running for office when allowed.

This all happened at a time when new ecumenical structures like the Latin American Council of Churches (CLAI) were shaping up. While these developments represent an important aspect of the life of the church and its public witness, they remain a small sector of Latin American Protestantism. Since the 1960s, Evangelical and Pentecostal churches in the region have experienced a significant growth, offering new contributions to a Latin American social Christianity. The rise of new social actors—mostly evangelical and Pentecostal—contributed to the development of new theological language and organizations that can potentially renew and expand the impact of the ecumenical initiatives above.

The Rise of Progressive Evangelicalism

At the end of the 1960s, a movement emerged among evangelical Protestants dissatisfied with the anti-intellectualism and the individualism that reigned in that sector of Latin American Protestantism. René Padilla, one of the leading voices in that emerging movement, charged most Latin American evangelicals at the time of being a "Church without theology."[29]

A number of evangelical leaders had expressed dissatisfaction with what they perceived as a lack of evangelical zeal in the ecumenical movement. In response to that, they organized their own events and meetings, which held evangelization as a central concern. For many evangelicals in the late 1960s and 1970s, the ecumenical movement had reduced evangelization to social reform.[30] The first of those meetings, *Congresso Latinoamericano de Evangelización* (CLADE), happened in Bogotá, Colombia, in 1969.

CLADE I gave birth to a new evangelical theology, which addressed the social concerns of evangelicals who considered themselves theologically conservative, although socially progressive, setting the tone for the creation of a theological movement centered on the Spanish concept of *misión integral* (which indicates a sense of wholeness or comprehensiveness in the nature of the mission of the church). The Latin American Theological Fellowship (FTL), a progressive evangelical think-tank, emerged in the following year. Ever since, the FTL has played a crucial role in the production of an evangelical theology intent to be Latin American.[31]

CLADE I was organized by the Billy Graham Evangelistic Association following the World Congress on Evangelism in Berlin, 1966. Its main contribution to this new movement was to create an opportunity for evangelical Latin American leaders concerned about the relationship between the evangelical faith and social justice to meet. According to David Stoll, CLADE I made a public call "for Evangelicals to meet their social responsibilities, contextualizing their faith in the Latin American context of oppression."[32] A year later, a group of Latin American evangelicals founded the FTL in Cochabamba, Bolivia, choosing Samuel Escobar as its first president. Their purpose was to create a forum for theological reflection in response to the reality of poverty and injustice in Latin America.

C. Peter Wagner, a missionary in Bolivia at the time, sought to polarize the ecclesiastical landscape in Latin America, discrediting the missiological proposal of the Church and Society Movement, which he accused of denying the doctrine of personal salvation.[33] A group of theologians critical of Wagner's initiative worried that the Latin American evangelical community needed to develop its own theological expression. That episode contributed to the decision to form the FTL.[34]

Starting with CLADE II (1979), the FTL was in charge of organizing those congresses. Ever since, efforts have been made to depolarize the Protestant landscape on the continent. CLADE III (1992) included participants from the ecumenical movement and liberation theology. CLADE IV (2000) and CLADE V (2012) deepened the understanding of the existing pluralism within Latin American Protestantism by emphasizing concomitantly its unity and diversity. With an emphasis on the evangelical testimony in the new millennium, CLADE IV called on the evangelical community to be agents of transformation in a society marked by violence, poverty, and injustice.

Since its foundation half a century ago, the FTL has been a forum for theological conversation among evangelicals who share loyalty to biblical authority and who also take the social dimension of Christian mission seriously. Although assuming a distinct methodology and starting point, progressive evangelicals have reinforced some of the key features of Latin American liberation theology, including the centrality of praxis for theological reflection. As Orlando Costas once asserted, "Jesus not only challenged the universal claims of the Empire and underlined its corrupt moral nature. His political option also involved an identification with those who were victims of the powerful and the mighty. He took sides with the weak and destitute."[35] Costas warned against the danger of evangelical churches functioning as legitimators of the domination of Latin American peoples, arguing for a radical experience of social conversion for Latin American evangelicals.

In the past two decades, the movement known as theology of integral mission has diversified itself with the addition of women, Indigenous peoples, Black theologians, and Pentecostals in leadership roles. These new voices are reshaping the movement and renewing its theological agenda, but not without tensions. Among other things, this movement has opened new spaces for dialogue with emerging Pentecostal theologies in Latin America.[36] In a continent where evangelical churches are becoming increasingly visible on the social and political sphere, the contribution of progressive evangelical theologians to set a meaningful social agenda for theological reflection and praxis has become even more critical.

Despite the critiques it receives for its supposed elitism, the theology of integral mission has influenced social and political initiatives in evangelical churches throughout the region. At the end of the 1980s, for example, Robinson Calvalcanti, one of its founding members, created the Evangelical Progressive Movement (MEP) to support and mobilize left-wing evangelicals. Another symbol of this movement, Benedita da Silva, the first Black woman elected to the Brazilian senate, has made positive contributions as one of the few Black evangelical female politicians of national prominence. While her political training took place in the Catholic Base Communities, she has affirmed that her "faith and political militancy are aligned with the Spirit of the Lausanne Covenant."[37] A similar case has been made by Marina da Silva, an environmentalist from the Assemblies of God, who rose to national prominence due to her passionate commitment to protecting God's creation, having served as a senator and coming in third place in three consecutive presidential elections.

The MEP was formed to create an ethical alternative to evangelical political activism, in response to scandals involving evangelical politicians in the late 1980s. It identified itself as evangelical—theologically conservative, affirming the Bible, evangelization, personal conversion, and prayer—and politically progressive—committed to structural change in society. It encouraged membership in social movements, workers' unions, and political left-wing parties, promoting dialogue between evangelical leaders and politically progressive politicians. In the first decade of this century, the movement split due to the hardening of some of its leaders on matters of gender and sexuality. The split gave birth to *Evangelicos pela Justiça*, which, while affirming its evangelical identity, has not allowed its agenda to be kidnapped by narrow moral concerns.

Many other progressive evangelical movements have emerged in Latin America in recent decades. In Brazil only, *Rede Fale, Missão na Íntegra, Evangélicos pelo Estado de Direito, Evangélicxs pela Diversidade*, and the *Movimento Negro Evangélico* are some of the more recent organizations that catalyze evangelical public witness. Often in conversation with ecumenical networks and other social movements, these evangelical initiatives have assumed a politically progressive agenda, generally informed by the theology of integral mission.

Integral mission, however, does not have the monopoly on the evangelical involvement in popular and progressive political movements. Indigenous evangelicals have played an important political role of resistance in the Andes and other parts of the continent, relying on Indigenous knowledges to shape their evangelical theology. Likewise, a growing number of evangelicals are getting involved in grassroots movements in the region. In April of 2017, for example, Sebastião Ferreira de Souza, a pastor of the Assemblies of God, was tortured and killed on the order of ranchers, in a massacre that killed nine rural workers occupying unproductive lands in a landless workers' settlement in Taquaruçu do Norte, Mato Grosso. These individuals have found different theological inspiration for their sociopolitical engagement.

The affirmation from Michael Löwy that a Christianity of liberation preceded a theology of liberation[38] repeats itself in the case of the prophetic Pentecostal and Evangelical participation in the public sphere. Many of these initiatives are of a local character, spontaneous, and, in most cases, exist on the margins of the corridors of power that continue to co-opt a number of powerful evangelical pastors.

The Pentecostalization and Indigenization of Latin American Protestantism

Pentecostalism is a religious movement of the spirit, which, while having generated many independent churches, has also made its way into many evangelical denominations and the Catholic Church. The lines that separate these identities are tenuous. The question I want to briefly discuss in the final part of this chapter concerns the importance of not neglecting Pentecostalism as an important element in the Latin American Protestant *ethos*.

The Pentecostal face of Latin American Protestantism represents its most popular manifestation, aside from being its fastest-growing expression. While non-Pentecostal Protestant expressions struggle to legitimize themselves among the poor, Pentecostalism does not need this type of legitimation because it grows especially among the poor.[39] The Pentecostal presence among the poor in urban centers across Latin America is so significant that it can be said that the symbolic world of a great proportion of the most impoverished communities in the region has been pentecostalized.

At the beginning of this chapter, I brought attention to the process of Latin Americanization that was important in the formation of a Latin American Protestant social thought, a move toward indigeneity, when a Latin American Protestant identity began to take form. The intensification of that movement led to levels of identification of the social reality of the Latin American people, especially the most vulnerable ones, which resulted in the rise of a liberationist Latin American Christianity—Protestant, in the case of this chapter. Such a movement was particularly important for the Protestant insertion in the processes of nation-building at a certain historical moment. However, because there are new aspects of the quotidian reality of the Latin American people today that need to be taken more fully into consideration, that is no longer enough. To paraphrase the reference to Shaull in the beginning of this chapter, new realities require new responses, and the temptation to offer the same responses to different situations and challenges leads to sclerosis and death. This is not to say that many of the principles that informed the development of liberation theology or the Church and Society Movement have ceased to be important. The idea of the "eruption" of repressed and excluded voices, for example, which has become more current in the past couple of decades, can be seen as an update to Gustavo Gutierrez's emphasis on the "eruption of the poor in history."[40] While this liberationist tenet remains important for Latin American theologizing, it may be seen through a different lens, in light of the new subjects that have emerged as cultural and theological actors in the past decades.

Working on his major last contribution to the study of Christianity, a few years before his passing, Shaull and his old colleague and friend Waldo César spent a good amount of time doing fieldwork among Pentecostals in the *favelas* of Rio de Janeiro as a way to discern new approaches to the Latin American religious scene.

> In the face of this situation, Waldo and I realized that a new approach was called for, on the part of men and women whose faith was leading them to become involved in this social struggle: an approach that would combine *in-depth study of social reality from the perspective of our faith with theological and biblical reflection carried on in the midst of this struggle.*[41]

César was a sociologist, and Shaull a theologian. Their work was self-described as sociotheological. In his theological reflection on the continued interaction he and César had with those Pentecostal communities on the hills of Rio de Janeiro, Shaull affirmed that the Pentecostal response to the movement of the Spirit was consistent with the biblical testimony of God's special interest in the poor.

Pentecostals, he insisted, are in a privileged position to hear, understand, and respond to God's revelation, because of how they have become part of the thought-world of the poor. This assertion is an extrapolation of the liberationist principle of the hermeneutical privilege of the poor to include the worldview of the poor. Thus, listening to the Pentecostal voice has become a moral imperative for Latin American theology and social ethics, especially for those who take that understanding of the hermeneutical privilege of the poor seriously.[42] The encounter between those interested in social justice and these charismatic Protestants is crucial for the development of a social ethics that can speak to the daily life of the oppressed in a way that is meaningful to them, and which they can engage on their own terms.

Shaull also speaks of the potentially transformative impact of the encounter with the pentecostalized poor on non-Pentecostals. The spiritual transformation Shaull implies these encounters can produce has to do with the disposition of those who do not identify as Pentecostal to learn from the Pentecostal spirituality that informs a large number of impoverished communities in Latin America today. The understanding of their symbolic world can be a transformative experience for Christians of all stripes open for a renewed experience of the "Realm of the Spirit."[43] When we find ourselves inserted in such a context, our own lives and perspectives are changed, and we can legitimately join those communities in their struggle to change the dehumanizing conditions impacting their lives.

Instead of imposing foreign tools to interpret Pentecostal spirituality, this perspective of engagement shares visions and possibilities that are inherent to Pentecostal spirituality, although sometimes only latently. As Cheryl B. Johns shows:

> There are inherent within Pentecostalism characteristics which are themselves conducive to conscientization. Such elements as the roots of the movement from its holiness and black origins, its oral-narrative theologizing, its experiential, pneumatic hermeneutic create an ethos which gives dignity to the marginalized and a voice to the voiceless. These dynamics call for people realizing their ontological vocations as subjects of history. Such characteristics are themselves powerful means of liberation and humanization within the "free spaces" of Pentecostal communities, and they are pregnant with possibilities for the transformation of social structures.[44]

Pentecostalism, as a religious expression born among the poor, can provide its own responses to the plight of the poor and marginalized. However, like the other religious responses presented earlier, Pentecostalism is not self-sufficient. On the contrary, it can be significantly enriched as it flourishes in dialogue with non-Pentecostal traditions through the engagement of partners sincerely concerned with working together for a fuller realization of justice.

Latin American theologians were among the first to recognize that no theologizing is neutral, but always situated sociohistorically (and culturally). This chapter shows that Protestant sociopolitical involvement in Latin America is not new. What is new in the current situation is the emergence of new social actors, including Pentecostal Christians not previously associated with progressive political activism in the region. These new social actors have not appeared in the public arena in a historical and existential vacuum. There is a legacy of Protestant sociopolitical participation in the region to resort to and build upon. On the other hand, if the Latin American reality has been profoundly affected by economic imbalance and social injustice, Shaull reminds us that this reality has also become pentecostalized. Thus, the affirmation of God's preferential option for the poor now requires a concerted effort to understand the worldview of the poor, which is becoming increasingly Pentecostal. This pentecostality ingrained with Indigenous and African-derived cultural elements exerts an important role in symbolic resistance, insofar as it preserves and reinterprets cultural values of the less-favored classes and oppressed ethnic communities, including Indigenous and Afro-Latinx traditions.

Conclusion

In recent decades, we have learned more about the pervasive and persistent impact of the colonial matrix of power on the region. Decolonizing efforts have emerged in literature, philosophy, history, and most recently in theology.[45] It is no longer possible to ignore the popular ethos, which is profoundly informed by Indigenous and African-derived knowledges and traditions. In this scenario, the Pentecostal world-thought that has become increasingly prominent in the contemporary Latin American religious scene offers a social grammar that can potentially reorient the lives of the oppressed. The reform and reinvention of Protestantism in Latin America in the first decades of a new millennium requires more than ever the capacity to understand and include the many silenced voices in the region. Christian koinonias continue to be formed in which Shaull termed the new frontiers of social transformation. It is from those new frontiers that Latin American Christian communities are challenged to discern God's presence and action in the world and find innovative ways to continue resisting the powers of oppression and death.

Notes

1. Gary Dorrien, *Social Ethics in the Making: Interpreting an American Tradition* (Malden, MA: Wiley-Blackwell, 2011), 1.
2. Ibid., 2.
3. Max Stackhouse, *Ethics and the Urban Ethos: An Essay in Social Theory and Theological Reconstruction* (Boston: Beacon Press, 1972), 5.
4. Richard Shaull, *The Reformation and Liberation Theology: Insights for the Challenges of Today* (Louisville, KY: Westminster/John Knox Press, 1991).
5. Ibid., 15.
6. Andrew Walls, *The Cross-Cultural Process in Christian History: Studies in the Transmission and Appropriation of Faith* (Maryknoll, NY: Orbis Books, 2002).
7. Richard Shaull, "A Theological Perspective on Human Liberation," *New Blackfriars* 49, no. 578 (1968): 511.
8. Justo González and Ondina E. González, *Christianity in Latin America: A History* (Cambridge: Cambridge University Press, 2008), 184.
9. José Miguez Bonino, *Faces of Latin American Protestantism* (Grand Rapids, MI: W. B. Eerdmans, 1997), 84.
10. Virginia Garrard-Burnett, "'Like a Mighty Rushing Wind': The Growth of Protestantism in Contemporary Latin America," in Lee M. Penyak and Walter J. Petry, eds., *Religion and Society in Latin America: Interpretative Essays from Conquest to Present* (Maryknoll, NY: Orbis Books, 2009), 192.
11. Ibid.
12. Bonino, *Faces of Latin American Protestantism*, 41.
13. Richard Shaull, "Toward the Recovery of the Prophetic Power of the Reformed Heritage," in Denise L. Comody and John T. Carmody, eds., *The Future of Prophetic Christianity: Essays in Honor of Roberty McAfee Brown* (Maryknoll, NY: Orbis Books, 1993), 65.
14. J. Kessler and W. M. Nelson, "Panama 1916 y su Impacto sobre el Protestantismo Latinoamericano," in CLAI, ed., *Oaxtepec 1978: unidad y misión en América Latina* (San José: CLAI, 1980), 11–30.
15. Julio Andrade Ferreira, O Profeta da Unidade: Erasmo Braga, *Uma Vida a Descoberto* (Petrópolis: Vozes, 1975).
16. Erasmo Braga and Kenneth Grubb, *The Republic of Brazil: A Survey of the Religious Situation* (London: World Dominion Press, 1932), 130.
17. Dafne S. Plou, *Caminos de Unidad: Itinerario del Diálogo Ecumenico en América Latina 1916–1991* (Quito: CLAI, 1994), and H. Fernando Bullon, *Protestant Social Thought in Latin America* (Eugene, OR: WIPF & STOCK, 2015).

18. Jean-Pierre Bastian, *Breve História do Protestantismo en America Latina* (Mexico City: Casa Unida de Publicaciones, 1986), 11.
19. Webster Browning, *El Congresso Sobre la Obra Cristiana en Sud America* (Montivideo: CCLA, 1926), 226. Cited in Bullon, *Protestant Social Thought in Latin America*, 78.
20. Wilton M. Nelson, "En Busca de un Protestantismo Latinoamericano: De Montevideo 1925 a La Habana 1929," in CLAI, ed., *Oaxtepec 1979: Unidad y Misión en America Latina* (San José: CLAI, 1980), 31–44 (39).
21. Luiz Longuini Neto, *O Novo Rosto da Missão* (São Paulo: Ultimato, 2002), 104.
22. Roberto E. Rios, "Iglesias y Movimentos Ecuménicos," *Christianismo y Sociedad* 17, no. 61–62 (1979): 67–72.
23. See Alan Neely, "Protestant Antecedents of the Latin American Liberation Theology," PhD Dissertation, The American University, 1977, 185.
24. Ibid.
25. Paulo Grissolli, "Acampamento da ACAs do Rio, São Paulo e Campinas," *Testimonium* 1/3 (1953): 47.
26. Richard Shaull, *Encounter with Revolution* (New York: Association Press, 1955), 3.
27. Richard Shaull, "Theological Developments in Brazilian SCM, 1952," unpublished manuscript, Princeton Theological Seminary Library, November 2003.
28. Waldo César, interview with the author on July 18, 2003, Rio de Janeiro.
29. C. René Padilla, *Missão Integral: Ensaios Sobre o Reino e a Igreja* (São Paulo: FTL-B, 1992), 104.
30. Orlando E. Costas, "Una Nueva Consciencia Protestante: la III CELA," in OAXTEPEC 1978 (San José: Comité Editorial del CLAI, Consejo Latinoamericano de Iglesias, 1980), 92.
31. Oscar Campos, "The Mission of the Church and the Kingdom of God in Latin America," PhD Dissertation, Dallas Theological Seminary, 2000, 3.
32. David Stoll, *Is Latin America Turning Protestant? The Politics of Evangelical Growth* (Berkeley: University of California Press, 1990), 131.
33. Carlos Eduardo Brandão Calvani, "O Movimento Evangelical: Considerações Históricas e Teológicas," Master of Religious Sciences, Instituto Metodista de Ensino Superior, São Bernardo do Campo, 1993, 117.
34. Longuini Neto, *O Novo Rosto da Missão*, 159.
35. Orlando E. Costas, *The Church and Its Mission: A Shattering Critique from the Third World* (Wheaton: Tyndale, 1974), 243.
36. David Mesquiati de Oliveira, *Pentecostalismos em Dialogo* (São Paulo: Fonte Editorial, 2014).
37. Paul Freston, *Evangelicals and Politics in Asia, Africa, and Latin America* (Cambridge: Cambridge University Press, 2001), 34.
38. Michael Lowy, *The War of Gods: Religion and Politics in Latin America* (New York: Verso, 1996).
39. Alexandre C. de Souza, Pentacostalismo: De onde vem, para onde vai? *Um Desafio às Leituras Contemporâneas da Religiosidade Brasileira* (Viçosa: Ultimato, 2004).
40. Gustavo Gutierrez, *A Theology of Liberation*, 15th anniversary ed. (Maryknoll, NY: Orbis Books, 1998), xxi.
41. Richard Shaull and Waldo César, *Pentecostalism and the Future of the Christian Churches: Promises, Limitations, Challenges* (Grand Rapids, MI: William B. Eerdmans, 2000), ix.

42. Richard Shaull, "From Academic Research to Spiritual Transformation: Reflection on a Study of Pentecostalism in Brazil," *Pneuma* 20, no. 1 (2001): 71–84 (75).
43. Ibid., 77.
44. Cheryl B. Johns, *Pentacostal Formation: A Pedagogy among the Oppressed* (Sheffield: Sheffield Academic Press, 1993), 139.
45. See Raimundo C. Barreto and Roberto Sirvent, eds., *Decolonial Christianities: Latinx and Latin American Perspectives*, New Approaches to Religion and Power Series (New York: Palgrave Macmillan, 2019).

Bibliography

Barreto, Raimundo C., and Roberto Sirvent, eds. *Decolonial Christianities: Latinx and Latin American Perspectives*. New Approaches to Religion and Power Series. New York: Palgrave Macmillan, 2019.

Bastian, Jean-Pierre. *Breve História do Protestantismo en America Latina*. Mexico City: Casa Unida de Publicaciones, 1986.

Bonino, José Miguez. *Faces of Latin American Protestantism*. Grand Rapids, MI: W. B. Eerdmans, 1997.

Braga, Erasmo, and Kenneth Grubb. *The Republic of Brazil: A Survey of the Religious Situation*. London: World Dominion Press, 1932.

Browning, Webster. *El Congreso Sobre la Obra Cristiana en Sud America*. Montivideo: CCLA, 1926.

Bullon, H. Fernando. *Protestant Social Thought in Latin America*. Eugene, OR: Wipf & Stock, 2015.

Calvani, C. E. B. "O Movimento Evangelical: Considerações Históricas e Teológicas." Master of Religious Sciences, Instituto Metodista de Ensino Superior, São Bernardo do Campo, Brazil, 1993.

Campos, Oscar. "The Mission of the Church and the Kingdom of God in Latin America." PhD Dissertation, Dallas Theological Seminary, 2000.

CLAI, ed. *Oaxtepec 1978: unidad y misión en América Latina*. San José: CLAI, 1980.

Costas, Orlando E. *The Church and Its Mission: A Shattering Critique from the Third World*. Wheaton: Tyndale, 1974.

De Oliveira, David Mesquiati, ed. *Pentecostalismos em Dialogo*. São Paulo: Fonte Editorial, 2014.

De Souza, Alexandre C. *Pentacostalismo: De onde vem, para onde vai? Um Desafio às Leituras Contemporâneas da Religiosidade Brasileira*. Viçosa: Ultimato, 2004.

Dorrien, Gary. *Social Ethics in the Making: Interpreting an American Tradition*. Malden, MA: Wiley-Blackwell, 2011.

Ferreira, Julio A. *O Profeta da Unidade: Erasmo Braga, Uma Vida a Descoberto*. Petrópolis: Vozes, 1975.

Freston, Paul. *Evangelicals and Politics in Asia, Africa, and Latin America*. Cambridge: Cambridge University Press, 2001.

Garrard-Burnett, Virginia. "'Like a Mighty Rushing Wind': The Growth of Protestantism in Contemporary Latin America." In *Religion and Society in Latin America: Interpretative Essays from Conquest to Present*, edited by Lee M. Penyak and Walter J. Petry. Maryknoll, NY: Orbis Books, 2009, pp. 190–202.

González, Justo, and Ondina E.González. *Christianity in Latin America: A History*. Cambridge: Cambridge University Press, 2008.

Grissolli, Paulo. "Acampamento da ACAs do Rio, São Paulo e Campinas." *Testimonium* 1/3 (1953): 47.
Gutierrez, Gustavo. *A Theology of Liberation*, 15th anniversary ed. Maryknoll, NY: Orbis Books, 1998.
Johns, Cheryl B. *Pentacostal Formation: A Pedagogy among the Oppressed.* Sheffield: Sheffield Academic Press, 1993.
Longuini Neto, Luiz. *O Novo Rosto da Missão*. São Paulo: Ultimato, 2002.
Lowy, Michael. *The War of Gods: Religion and Politics in Latin America.* New York: Verso, 1996.
Neely, Alan. "Protestant Antecedents of the Latin American Liberation Theology." PhD Dissertation, The American University, 1977.
Padilla, C. René. *Missão Integral: Ensaios Sobre o Reino e a Igreja*. São Paulo: FTL-B, 1992.
Plou, Dafne S. *Caminos de Unidad: Itinerario del Diálogo Ecumenico en América Latina 1916-1991*. Quito: CLAI, 1994.
Rios, Roberto E. "Iglesias y Movimentos Ecuménicos." *Christianismo y Sociedad* 17, no. 61-62 (1979): 67-72.
Shaull, Richard. *Encounter with Revolution*. New York: Association Press, 1955.
Shaull, Richard. "From Academic Research to Spiritual Transformation: Reflection on a Study of Pentecostalism in Brazil." *Pneuma* 20, no. 1 (2001): 71-84.
Shaull, Richard. *The Reformation and Liberation Theology: Insights for the Challenges of Today*. Louisville, KY: Westminster/John Knox Press, 1991.
Shaull, Richard. "A Theological Perspective on Human Liberation." *New Blackfriars* 49, no. 578 (1968): 511.
Shaull, Richard. "Toward the Recovery of the Prophetic Power of the Reformed Heritage." In *The Future of Prophetic Christianity: Essays in Honor of Robert McAfee Brown*, edited by Denise L. Comody and John T. Carmody. Maryknoll, NY: Orbis Books, 1993, pp. 49-66.
Shaull, Richard, and Waldo César. *Pentecostalism and the Future of the Christian Churches: Promises, Limitations, Challenges*. Grand Rapids, MI: William B. Eerdmans, 2000.
Stackhouse, Max. *Ethics and the Urban Ethos: An Essay in Social Theory and Theological Reconstruction*. Boston: Beacon Press, 1972.
Stoll, David. *Is Latin America Turning Protestant? The Politics of Evangelical Growth*. Berkeley: University of California Press, 1990.
Walls, Andrew. *The Cross-Cultural Process in Christian History: Studies in the Transmission*. Maryknoll, NY: Orbis, 2002.

8

Christianity among the Nankani in Ghana

Rose Mary Amenga-Etego

Introduction

Christianity in Ghana has its roots in the fifteenth century. Historically, the arrival of the Portuguese at Edina of former Gold Coast, now Elmina in the Central Region of Ghana, in January 1482 marked the beginning of the Christian mission to the Indigenous population. However, the dominant discourse in the history of Christianity in Ghana is traced to the eighteenth-century Protestant missionary endeavor with its associated *tabula rasa* approach to evangelization, that is, an approach based on the notion that the African mindset could be reprogrammed to rid it of its Indigenous worldview so that Christianity could be planted.[1] This politically correct public narrative, however, not only narrows the historical experience and account of the Christian missionary enterprise in Ghana; its continuous dominance in scholarship in contemporary society is problematic. This is because it is a narrative based on fifteenth- to nineteenth-century missionary activities in the coastal and southern parts of the country. This narrative scarcely, if any at all, includes the early twentieth-century missionary endeavor in the northern part of the country.[2] The aim of this chapter is to draw attention to the fact that the current mission narrative, with its projection of the *tabula rasa* approach, does not fully account for the missionary experience in Ghana. Using the Nankani from the Upper East Region of Ghana as a contextualized example, I will show that, in fact, there were two different mission approaches in Ghana, and both have contributed to Ghana's contemporary religious scene.

Is the northern mission excluded because of its timeframe or because this contextual mission history does not neatly fit into the dominant *tabula rasa* narrative? The fact that the southern missionary enterprise did not extend to the north until after the arrival of the Roman Catholic missionaries—the Missionaries of Africa—from Burkina Faso in 1906 is significant enough to have been included in the Ghanaian Christian history. With its differently nuanced missionary approach, its inclusion would have provided two narratives giving insight into the contribution of the French-speaking West African states to the missionary enterprise in Ghana.

The dominant narrative is therefore problematic because it does not fully capture the diverse realities of the early missionary initiatives in Ghana. Largely based on the Evangelical and Protestant missionary endeavors in the south, this narrative's emphasis on *tabula rasa* glosses over the so-called failed Portuguese Catholic missionary attempt of the fifteenth century. Besides, any projection of the *tabula rasa* narrative, in relation to the entire mission field in Ghana, indirectly produces four viewpoints. As indicated, the first viewpoint glosses over the so-called Portuguese missionary era as insignificant, while the second deploys it as the basis for the stringent missionary approach—the *tabula rasa* approach. Likewise, the third view depicts mission as imposing Western culture alongside the gospel, while the fourth presents an underlying resistant and triumphant Indigenous agency.

Such a binary presentation has the potential of breeding not only a hypocritical complacency for Christians in Ghana but also a religio-cultural antagonism toward Christianity. While the former is attributed to the proliferation of churches in Ghana, the latter is embedded in some of the religio-cultural intolerance or violence in Ghana.[3] Yet, the religio-cultural scene in Ghana, especially with respect to the Indigenous religio-cultural systems and Christianity, speaks otherwise. This is because Ghana is generally described as a peaceful, accommodative, and tolerant religiously pluralistic country.[4] Of course, scholars attributed Ghana's functioning peaceful religious pluralism to the accommodative and pragmatic nature of the Indigenous religio-cultural systems to which all Ghanaians are still attached.[5]

As a Nankani with family members following the three major religions in the country (Indigenous religions, Islam, and Christianity), I am aware that in the context of religious pluralism, religious tolerance and interreligious coexistence as well as religious intolerance or boundary demarcations are vital not only for the nation but also for the multireligious family. The presentation of diverse historical narratives of the different religious endeavors is necessary for the establishment of peace and contentment of individual religious adherents, but also for the underlying understanding and the nurturing of peaceful coexistence in the family and community.

Mission among the Nankani

The northern mission, also known as the Navrongo mission, entered Ghana through Burkina Faso, a landlocked French West African country, in 1906.[6] It is also called the Navrongo mission because Navrongo was the first mission station in the north. Like the southern mission, it was a Catholic mission. Yet, unlike the Elmina mission in the south, which was by sea and predated colonialism, the Navrongo mission was by land and was circumscribed by the colonial administration. The missionaries arrived riding donkeys and with a mandate to engage the culture of the people.

According to McWilliams, "Lavigerie's master word was adaptation [to local conditions]: the missionaries must conform to every way except to vice and error."[7] With such a mandate from their leader (Lavigerie) and having been in the French-speaking nations of West Africa, the attitude and mission strategy of these missionaries were not as strict as those of the south. With help from the host community in Navrongo, the first missionaries built their residence, a single-room round mud hut with a grass roof. To honor this history, the mud hut is rebuilt at the same space whenever the previous building collapses.

It is significant to note that the first attempts to introduce Christianity to Ghana in both the south and north were from Catholic missions, but while the latter group were indeed missionaries, the former were explorers. Interestingly, the Portuguese of the southern mission arrived on a ship and stayed in the fort and later in a castle by the sea in Elmina, while the Canadians of the northern mission came riding a donkey and stayed in a single-room mud hut like those of their host community. In a discussion with Grace Mboya on the missionaries and their challenges in Ghana, she reflected on the above and asked, "Which of them were here to deliver a message?"[8] This is a profound question that goes beyond this chapter. This makes one wonder whether mission is simply a matter of taking up residence among an Indigenous people, or whether it points to a much deeper relationship and a way of doing mission.

Overgeneralization of *Tabula Rasa* in the Ghanaian Mission History

Historically, missionary Christianity in Ghana is classified into three phases. Constituting the dominant narrative from southern Ghana, the first phase is described as the advent/quarantine era (fifteenth century), the second (eighteenth century) as the Europeanization or convert isolation/segregation era, and the third phase (nineteenth century) as the indigenization of Christianity. In this chapter, I argue for a fourth phase (twentieth century), an accommodative era focused on the northern narrative.

Hans Debrunner records that on January 20, 1402, Don Diego D'Azambuja's search for a legendary West African King, known as Prester John, landed his party on the coastline of Edina (Elmina).[9] Upon arrival, the crew hoisted the flag of Portugal, and with a chaplain on board, the first Roman Catholic Mass was celebrated. With the discovery of gold, however, the search was abandoned. A new agenda was envisioned as they made friends with the locals, acquired land, and built their first place of residence, Fort St. Jorge. With booming trade and competition from other European nationals, the Portuguese built a more formidable castle known as the Elmina Castle. Although the castle had a chapel for the chaplain, the king of Portugal had to remind the chaplain of his duties as trade had eclipsed the mission. In other words, the presence of a chaplain, the celebration of mass, the chapel, and the statues of Mary and St. Anthony (the patron Saint of Portugal) are all that constituted the first phase of Christianity in Ghana. Originally undertaken with "the purpose of counteracting the growth and influence of Islam," the presence of gold had diverted their cause.[10]

It has been argued that despite this fifteenth-century encounter with the Ghanaian terrain, it was not until the eighteenth century that the faith started to take root.[11] Even so, Christianity was not firmly established until the nineteenth century. Captured by Debrunner as the "Rays of Hope, 1720–1780,"[12] the eighteenth century witnessed a turning point after the arrival of chaplains, though their mandate was to cater to the spiritual needs of their nationals in the colony. Notable among these mission chaplaincies were the Monrovian Brethren (1786) at the Elmina Castle and the Society for the Propagation of the Gospel (SPG) at the Cape Cast Castle. These were followed by the Basel Mission (1826) at the Christiansborg Castle in Accra, who were replaced by the Methodist Mission (1835) when the former moved to Akropong. These chaplains started what is known as the castle schools to cater to mulatto (mixed-race) children. These schools expanded to include other children and their products became formidable partners of the missionaries and colonial administrators.[13] Again, in his chapter on "Black Man's Religion, 1840–1870," Debrunner shows how a merger of factors, aided by T. F. Buxton's infamous "Let Missionaries and schoolmasters, the plough and the spade, go together. It is the Bible and the plough that must regenerate Africa," transformed missions in the nineteenth century.[14] Using education, agriculture, trading, and skills training in carpentry and masonry, the mission field expanded from the coastal to the forest zone. Among these, education, especially the boarding schools, were the most effective spaces for *tabula rasa*, accommodating both the cultural and intellectual forms of segregation.

Scholars have argued that this was because Christianity entered the scene with European worldviews, values, and attitudes. Consequently, the initial phase of Christianity in the south was stern, intolerant, and uncompromising, resulting in what is now theorized as *tabula rasa*, a common evangelization method of that time among missions to Indigenous people. This perspective is believed to have emanated from the view that the eighteenth-century missionaries saw nothing valuable in the Indigenous religio-cultural systems, hence the association of the gospel with civilization. By this, missionaries prevented Indigenous converts from participation in all aspects of their beliefs and practices.[15] When it became evident that it was quite impossible for the converts to completely withdraw or disassociate themselves from their traditions and customs, more stringent methods were adopted by some missionaries. Scholars[16] identified the measures undertaken as "convert segregation" and classified it into three interrelated categories: physical, cultural, and intellectual.

With physical segregation, the missionaries relocated the converts to mission areas variously known in the country as Christian village, Salem, Kpodzi, and Bethel. Indigenous converts were removed from their families, clans, and communities and made to resettle in new locations near the mission settlements. Thus, uprooted from their family and religio-cultural settings, they were more malleable to the new religio-cultural indoctrination (the civilizing mission [Europeanization] and the gospel).[17] It has been argued that the removal was to protect them from some of their angry families and kinsmen. Other arguments include the view that the missionaries were afraid that the unbroken relationship with non-Christian kinsmen was a source of constant recontamination and slow spiritual growth. Therefore, the segregation prevented them from reverting to their Indigenous beliefs and practices.[18] Culturally, conversion to Christianity meant a complete rejection of the Indigenous customs and practices. This was not limited to just the religious sphere, but also to the sociocultural and political spheres because it is difficult to isolate religion from culture.[19] With the translation of the Bible into local languages, however, this cultural barrier was broken to facilitate an engagement with the Indigenous religio-cultural worldviews.

For instance, Capitein's translation of the Bible into Fante, Protten's work on Ga, and Schelgal's work on Ewe inevitably forced the missionaries to engage the Indigenous societies and worldviews in a profound way that continues to impact Ghanaian society. Lamin Sanneh beautifully argues out how these translations broke down some of the barriers, sometimes introducing new relationships that are grounded on reciprocity.[20] Intellectual segregation was primarily linked to education, especially the boarding school system.[21] Even though the Bible was translated into various languages, children learned or spoke English and not their Indigenous languages, which constituted the foundation of the *tabula rasa* approach to the mission history in Ghana.

Although this narrative captures a very important part of the Ghanaian missionary experience, it is incomplete. It does not account for other contextualized experiences, for even if those are considered peripheral, they still occurred. The generalization of the strict southern *tabula rasa* missionary experience has not encouraged researchers and students in this area to explore and capture other nuanced forms of the mission histories in the country. The strict rejection of Indigenous religio-cultural views and resources in favor of the Euro-Christian worldview and lifestyle is just one narrative.[22]

Mission within an Indigenous Religio-Cultural System

Engaging Ghanaian mission history and its relationship with the Indigenous religio-cultural system of the northern missionary enterprise is essential, not only for providing a counternarrative but also for its contribution to the liberal nature of Ghanaian Christianity. From a historical and anthropological viewpoint, the northern mission immediately engaged the religio-cultural beliefs and practices of the people. These beliefs and cultural practices included names and naming ceremonies, myths and folktales, charms and amulets, symbols, music and praise singers, postharvest festivals, emissaries, and night rooftop announcers (town-criers), riddles, proverbs and sayings, mural art, motifs, and wall paintings.[23] These Indigenous beliefs and practices, also classified as Indigenous media, soon became useful resources and tools for the mission work. In the next two sections, I will discuss and illustrate how some of these media forms became crucial in the transfer of the new doctrines and subsequent social change.

Unlike contemporary Christian evangelism that has modern sophisticated media like TV, radio, internet, and social media as well as a variety of print media,[24] earlier mission endeavors faced serious difficulties, especially in communication.[25] Therefore, the use of the available Indigenous media forms became an essential source for drawing attention, gaining entrance, as well as stimulating and sustaining the interest of the Indigenous people in the new religion. This is because such media forms like myths, names and naming, music, proverbs, and sayings, which are part and parcel of Indigenous people's religio-cultural lifestyles and history, are not only sources for teaching and transmitting knowledge, but they also constitute an affectionate bond that facilitates easy reception, retention, and memorization. Expressing the accumulated Indigenous wisdom and knowledge forms that are passed down from generation to generation, these uniquely "woven" pieces are embedded with a strong sense of the people's religio-cultural identity; they are the conduits of Indigenous knowledge, culture, and history. In other words, the past and the present feed each other just as they are reinforced through the linkages in their re-employment. Therefore, when these media forms are creatively used, even in new contexts, they become a subtle but effective way of engineering understanding and reception at the ground level because they provide the platform through which the people can relate, share, and exchange information.

In the case of the northern mission, one of the ways the missionaries engaged the Indigenous people at the level of their beliefs and practices included the subtle subversive relationship they established with Indigenous rituals and prayers. Reminiscent of Paul in Athens (Acts 17: 16ff), some Indigenous sites like sacred groves and shrines (both evil and good) were gradually transformed into Christian sacred sites and reinterpreted as grottos, churches, mission settlements, or mission schools. Shrines were removed and replaced with statues of saints and Mary with Christian prayers of dedications and/or Catholic masses. While the above were at the community level, the individual and personal level embodied the exchange or replacements of talisman and amulets with crosses, rosaries, scapulars, holy water, and other approved Catholic religious resources or practices. The application of the sign of the cross on oneself or on one's food is still an important practice today in the area.

While conducting a field study on the religio-cultural roots of witchcraft beliefs among the Nankani in 2009,[26] some elders were worried about contemporary Christians. Described as Christians without any depth in faith, the elders noted that current Christians are preoccupied with unnecessary fear of witchcraft, demons, and ancestral curses, instead of seeking growth in their faith. The elders stated that with faith, making the sign of the cross on oneself, holding the crucifix, or wearing the rosary (around the neck) are powerful enough to dispel worry, anxiety, fear, or danger. They also noted that the recitation of 'The Lord's Prayer' and 'Hail Mary' counteracted such fear. Three elders demonstrated how the missionaries taught them to make the sign of the cross with such an enthusiastic upright, self-composed, and devout outlook. Another explained how they were instructed to pray over any food that was given to them before eating, even if the food was part of a ritual meal. According to Akuchisa, an old catechist of Naga,[27] in many of the communities at that time, there was sometimes no other means of getting food if one did not eat from the common or family meal. As a result, the missionaries made some of those provisions as exceptions for their early converts who continued to live with their families.[28]

Indigenous names, proverbs, sayings, and symbols provided an easy source for dialogue. Analogies, for example, were easily drawn from the names and naming systems in both religions. In the Indigenous cultures and practices, names were given in relation to honorable personalities, especially those that the society appreciated or acknowledged. This was meant to aid the individual child in emulating and perpetuating the same values. Known as one's *sigre* (sic. *segere*,[29] guardian spirit), the practice had ritual obligations. This medium found parallels in the Catholic naming system. Consequently, it was very easy to adopt, add, or substitute names of saints and the celebration of feast days of patron saints, while infant baptism served as the naming ceremony for those who wanted it. Similar analyses were made with certain injunctions and sanctions. Some taboos were substituted with some of the injunctions of the Bible or other doctrinal injunctions. The notion of what was sinful and righteous, good and bad, as well as reward and punishment was prevalent in the Indigenous culture. For instance, the catechesis on the Ten Commandments with respect to "thou shall not kill" (Ex. 20:13) was linked to, interpreted, and understood within the context of the spirituality of the land and human beings. Likewise, the analogy of the story of Adam and his sons, especially the imagery of Abel's blood crying out from the ground (Gen. 4:10), resonated with the people. Akuchisa explained how such collaboration in the narratives endeared the missionaries to the indigenes.

In as much as individual biblical passages or verses were concerned, the narrative interpretation of the Bible, whether as a story or a genealogy, resonated well with those who believed in similar accounts. Although there were no similar miraculous accounts of a virgin birth, there was belief in the interference of the spirit world; hence, some kinds of parallel narratives could be cited in relation to the biblical narratives on the birth of Samuel and John the Baptist. Again, even though it is difficult to understand some of the miracles and the passion narrative, the extensive use of parables and sayings by Jesus made him stand out as a special person who possessed the power and blessing of the Supreme Being/Creator Spirit. This is quite understandable since certain categories of people, including rainmakers and healers, were believed to have obtained their powers from the Supreme Being within the Indigenous religious context.

It is pertinent to note that the missionaries did not initiate all these things. Some of these practices revolved around Indigenous agency from some of the early converts, especially those who became community prayer leaders or catechists.[30] These converts, who were knowledgeable about their Indigenous beliefs and practices, continued to initiate and introduce changes that gradually contributed both to the mission work and to transformations in both the religio-cultural system and society at large. Although some of these substitutions led to misinterpretation and misrepresentation of Christian beliefs and practices and introduced some syncretic practices,[31] they nonetheless provided room for the initial interreligious dialogue even if that foundation was unconsciously initiated.

Having unearthed the northern missionary approach to the existing religio-cultural system, it is essential to understand how a sense of meaning-making and connectedness gradually emerged and nurtured, and how that unconsciously laid a foundation for peaceful interreligious coexistence among the Nankani. Yet, the question arising from this is how can such a narrative explain the emerging atmosphere of religious intolerance in Ghana?

Juxtaposing the liberal northern (Navrongo) mission and the *tabula rasa* approach of the southern (Elmina/Cape Coast) mission provides a lens through which we can explore the above question. Unlike the long-established identity of Christianity as the commercial, political, social, and civilizing project in the south, and the whole nation, one cannot be oblivious of the contribution of the northern mission to the accommodative and tolerant nature of Christianity in Ghana, especially the north. The chapter has pointed out how people with different religious persuasions (Indigenous, Islam, and Christianity) within a community or household in the Nankani traditional area are able to accommodate and adapt their routinized domestic, social, and religious practices to maintain peaceful coexistence. Christianity, based on the missionary encounter, flourishes in a context of appreciative and reciprocal engagement with one another, both in private and public, irrespective of the context (home, community, and/or nation). Nankani Christians have provided a reasonable foundation to draw the northern missionary narrative to the limelight.

Fundamentally contributing to interreligious dialogue and tolerance in the country, it is not uncommon for Christian heads of households and other title holders in the north to self-identify as members of Indigenous beliefs and practices while privately internalizing their Christian faith. In the Upper East Region of Ghana,[32] for instance, although much of the population are Christians, several of them identify with the Indigenous traditions of their people. It is also quite common to hear other Ghanaians label people from the north as Muslims without any resistance or denial. For many northerners, other peoples' perceptions of their religious identity are insignificant. This is in stark contrast to the religious landscape in the south where people tend to suppress and deny their Indigenous and other religious identities in favor of Christianity as the civilized and modern identity. Unfortunately, these discrepancies have had an impact on the disaggregated religious statistical data of Ghana at both regional and national levels.

For instance, in the 2021 census,[33] the national data on the three dominant religions were Christianity 21,932,708 (71.3 percent), Islam 6,108,530 (19.9 percent), and Traditional Religion 999,319 (3.2 percent). To understand this national data with respect to this chapter, one must note that the Upper East Region is one of the sixteen administrative regions in Ghana and had a population of 1,298,179 (4.2 percent) out of the national 30,753,327. From its regional population of 1,298,179 (4.2 percent), the disaggregated data were Christianity 641,818 (49.4 percent), Islam 385,020 (29.7 percent), and Traditional Religion 227,626 (17.5 percent). It must be noted that the regional data were not captured in percentages; however, the imputed percentages help clearly present the data on the Indigenous religion and Christianity from the regional data with respect to the national statistics. Thus, despite being (Upper East Region) 4.2 percent of the national population, the region has 22.8 percent of all adherents of the Indigenous religion and 2.8 percent of the total Christian population. This poses a challenge to the understanding of the distribution of Christians in Ghana and the certainty of the nation's religious demographic data. The latter is crucial because the Indigenous religion is marginalized in public religious discourse, though it undergirds the lived experiences of Ghanaians. Second, it does not account for the underlying problem of religious intolerance amidst a vibrant and publicly lived experience of religious accommodation and peaceful coexistence.

Conclusion

The issue at stake is that the highly publicized missionary narrative, symbolized by *tabula rasa*, is problematic. It does not adequately account for the two opposing lived experiences of religious adherents in Ghana's religiously pluralistic society. That is, a resistant Indigenous and Christian perspective that presents an antagonistic narrative, on the one hand, and a religiously tolerant society, on the other. This calls for a reexamination of the dominant narrative to reflect the multifaceted contextual situation in the country, hence the necessity of the inclusion of the Navrongo missionary account.

As exemplified in the chapter, the mission strategy employed among the Nankani and other peoples of the north not only promoted tolerance but also sustained and promoted the Indigenous religio-cultural system. This facilitated its expansion, which further assisted the repackaging of the new belief and doctrine (Christian faith) to the people and vice versa. This creative and dynamic negotiation skill, if even by means of an unconscious dialogue, illustrates some of the Indigenous people's agency in the advent of Christianity and social change. Besides, through these multiple representations, Indigenous media proved to be very potent in creating a significant model for social change and development. Today, it is argued that Indigenous African media and communication systems have endured in the face of Western forms of mass communication and their attendant technological advancement. At the same time, the story of the Christian mission cannot be left out.

The issue is that this type of social change draws its sustenance from within its religio-cultural environment. Hence, even though it adopts and adapts to the changes that are taking place within its midst and the global environment, it produces a unique blend of heritage that is able to speak to its past, present, and future. It is this unconscious compromise that gives each party its own narrative that is accommodative and inclusive enough for our contemporary multiethnic, multicultural, multireligious, and multigendered society.

Finally, I question the generalization of *tabula rasa* not simply because there are multiple narratives and pathways; this dominant narrative has served its purpose and will continue to do so, but also because it is time to make the narrative engage the different trajectories in our contemporary society like conflict, conflict management and peace-building, politics, and development. What are the intersections and how can we move forward in our contemporary African societies instead of nursing old wounds? As a student of religious studies,[34] I am not simply questioning the sustenance of this binary narrative; I am calling on both students and scholars to begin to engage this normative narrative with respect to the multifaceted dimensions embedded in it to provide new pathways for further discussions. Two issues are emerging in our contemporary Ghanaian society with regard to Christianity and religious tolerance, and it will be good for scholars to begin to investigate them. These relate to the current religious intolerance in the country, especially in the educational institutions,[35] and the Ghanaian Pentecostal/Charismatic public antagonist outlook on the Indigenous religio-cultural system. These issues call for critical examination not simply as new phenomena, but also in comparative analysis with the existing *tabular rasa* mission narrative.

Notes

1. Hans W. Debrunner, *History of Christianity in Ghana* (Accra: Waterville Publishing House, 1967), 198; Francis Anekwe Oborji, *Concepts of Mission: The Evolution of*

Contemporary Missiology (Maryknoll, NY: Orbis Books, 2006), 7; and Victor I. Ezingbo, *Re-imaging African Christologies: Conversing with the Interpretations and Appropriations of Jesus in Contemporary African Christianity* (Eugene, OR: Pickwick Publications, 2010), 15–16.

2. Remigius F. McCoy, *Great Things Happen: A Personal Memoir of the First Christian Missionary among the Dagaabas and Sissalas of the Northwest Ghana* (Montreal: The Society of Missionaries of Africa, 1988), and Allison M. Howell, *The Religious Itinerary of a Ghanaian People: The Kasena and the Christian Gospel* (Ghana: African Christian Press, 2001).
3. Brigid M. Sackey, "Charismatics, Independents, and Missions: Church Proliferation in Ghana," *Culture and Religion* 2, no. 1 (2001): 41–59. https://doi.org/10.1080/014383 00108567162; Kwabena Darkwa Amanor, "Pentecostal and Charismatic Churches in Ghana and the African Culture: Confrontation or Compromise?" *Journal of Pentecostal Theology* 18, no. 1 (2009): 123–40. https://doi.org/10.1163/174552509X442192.
4. Samuel Kofi Boateng Nkrumah-Pobi and Sandra Owusu-Afriyie, "Religious Pluralism in Ghana: Using the Accommodative Nature of African Indigenous Religion as a Source for Religious Tolerance and Peaceful Coexistence," *International Journal of Interreligious and Intercultural Studies* 3, no. 1 (2020): 79.
5. Ibid., 79–80, and Elizabeth Amoah, *African Spirituality, Religion and Innovation* (BASR Occasional Papers, 1998).
6. Rose Mary Amenga-Etego, *Mending the Broken Pieces: Religion and Sustainable Development in Northern Ghana* (Trenton: African World, 2011).
7. See H. O. A. McWilliam, *The Development of Education in Ghana* (London: Longman, 1959), 37.
8. Telephonic conversation (January 9, 2015) with Grace Mboya, a retired educationist and Catholic from Naga who lives in Bolgatanga.
9. Debrunner, *History of Christianity in Ghana*, 7–8.
10. Peter Clarke, "Christian Relations with Islam and African Traditional Religions in West Africa (c.1500 to the Present)," *Scriptura* 56 (1996): 69.
11. Brigid M. Sackey, *New Directions in Gender and Religion: The Changing Status of Women in African Independent Churches* (Lanham, MD: Lexington Books, 2006), 22.
12. Debrunner, *History of Christianity in Ghana*, 60–83.
13. Ibid., 154.
14. Ibid., 103–73.
15. Clarke, "Christian Relations with Islam," 78.
16. See Patrick S. J. Ryan, "Is It Possible to Conduct a Unified History of Religion in West Africa," *Universitas* 8 (1984): 104; Debrunner, *History of Christianity in Ghana*, 147–8; and Ralph M. Wiltgen, *Gold Coast Mission History 1471–1880* (Techny: Divine Word Publication, 1956), 111.
17. Max Assimeng, *Religion and Social Change in West Africa: Introduction to the Sociology of Religion* (Accra: Woeli Pubishing Services, 2010), 85; and Sackey, *New Directions in Gender and Religion*, 13, and Debrunner, *History of Christianity in Ghana*, 69.
18. Assimeng, *Religion and Social Change in West Africa*, 85.
19. Therefore, current arguments advanced for the contemporary phenomenon of Christian chiefs in Indigenous Ghanaian communities are problematic. See Debrunner, *History of Christianity in Ghana*, 267–8, 351–2; and Samuel Yeboah, "Christian Beliefs and African Indigenous Rituals in Ghana," Master of Philosophy Dissertation, University of Ghana, 2016.

20. Lamin Sanneh, *Translating the Message: The Missionary Impact on Culture* (Maryknoll, NY: Orbis, 1989), 172–4, 206; and Lamin Sanneh, *Encountering the West: Christianity and the Global Cultural Process, The African Dimension* (London: Marshall Pickering, 1993), 73–92.
21. Wiltgen, *Gold Coast Mission History*, 111.
22. See William Bascom, "African Culture and the Missionary/Les Missions et la Culture Africaine," *Civilisations* 3, no. 4 (1953): 491–504. www.jstor.org/stable/4137757.
23. Ian McDonald and David Hearle, *Communication Skills for Rural Development* (London: Evans Brothers, 1984).
24. Paul Gifford, *Ghana's New Christianity: Pentecostalism in a Globalizing African Economy* (Bloomington: Indiana University Press, 2004), 30–40.
25. McCoy illustrates this in *Great Things Happen*.
26. This field study was funded by an ACLS/AHP fellowship grant in 2009/10.
27. Vincent Akuchisa, an old catechist of Naga, Out Station of the Our Lady of Seven Sorrows Parish, Navrongo.
28. It was noted by some people, including the catechist, that the era is over, hence contemporary elders in their respective communities and local churches should not only desist from that practice but also stop talking about it.
29. R. S. Rattray, *The Tribes of the Ashanti Hinterland*, vol. II (Oxford: Clarendon Press, 1932), 293–7.
30. Akumbiligi Zoyah, the first Christian convert from Naga.
31. Howell, *The Religious Itinerary of a Ghanaian People*.
32. This is one of the sixteen administrative regions in Ghana.
33. Government of Ghana, *Ghana 2021 Population and Housing Census*, vol. 3C (Accra: Ghana Statistical Service, 2021), 58.
34. A student because I have come to understand the wisdom and logic of my field respondents (interviewees) who see me as such. For them, I am a student not because I work within the classroom setting but because I am constantly returning to them to ask questions (field studies), some of which they claim are so basic even those younger than I will not ask. Yet, that is the foundation of my discipline and fieldwork, to start afresh with every new study where possible.
35. Charles Wereko-Brobby, "Religious Intolerance, Christian Fundamentalism and the Ghana Constitution," March 5, 2015. https://citifmonline.com/2015/03/religious-intolerance-christian-fundamentalism-and-the-ghana-constitution. See also "Keep Education and Religious Devotion Separate in Ghana," *Ghanaweb*, March 3, 2015.

Bibliography

Amanor, Kwabena Darkwa. "Pentecostal and Charismatic Churches in Ghana and the African Culture: Confrontation or Compromise?" *Journal of Pentecostal Theology* 18, no. 1 (2009): 123–40. https://doi.org/10.1163/174552509X442192.

Amenga-Etego, Rose Mary. *Mending the Broken Pieces: Religion and Sustainable Rural Development in Northern Ghana*. Trenton: African World, 2011.

Amoah, Elizabeth. *African Spirituality, Religion and Innovation*. BASR Occasional Papers, 1998.

Assimeng, Max. *Religion and Social Change in West Africa: Introduction to the Sociology of Religion*. Accra: Woeli Publishing, 2010.

Bascom, William. "African Culture and the Missionary/Les Missions et la Culture Africaine." *Civilisations* 3, no. 4 (1953): 491–504. www.jstor.org/stable/4137757.

Clarke, Peter. "Christian Relations with Islam and African Traditional Religions in West Africa (c.1500 to the Present)." *Scriptura* 56, no. 1 (1996): 69–78.

Debrunner, Hans W. *History of Christianity in Ghana*. Accra: Waterville Publishing House, 1967.

Ezingbo, Victor I. *Re-imaging African Christologies: Conversing with the Interpretations and Appropriations of Jesus in Contemporary African Christianity*. Eugene, OR: Pickwick Publications, 2010.

Gifford, Paul. *Ghana's New Christianity: Pentecostalism in a Globalizing African Economy*. Bloomington: Indiana University Press, 2004.

Government of Ghana. *Ghana 2021 Population and Housing Census*, vol. 3C. Accra: Ghana Statistical Service, 2021.

Howell, Allison M. *The Religious Itinerary of a Ghanaian People: The Kasena and the Christian Gospel*. Ghana: African Christian Press, 2001.

McCoy, Remigius F. *Great Things Happen: A Personal Memoir of the First Christian Missionary among the Dagaabas and Sissalas of the Northwest Ghana*. Montreal: The Society of Missionaries of Africa, 1988.

McDonald, Ian, and David Hearle. *Communication Skills for Rural Development*. London: Evans Brothers, 1984.

McWilliam, H. O. A. *The Development of Education in Ghana*. London: Longman, 1959.

Nkrumah-Pobi, Samuel Kofi Boateng, and Sandra Owusu-Afriyie. "Religious Pluralism in Ghana: Using the Accommodative Nature of African Indigenous Religion as a Source for Religious Tolerance and Peaceful Coexistence." *International Journal of Interreligious and Intercultural Studies* 3, no. 1 (2020): 73–82.

Oborji, Francis Anekwe. *Concepts of Mission: The Evolution of Contemporary Missiology*. Maryknoll, NY: Orbis Books, 2006.

Rattray, R. S. *The Tribes of the Ashanti Hinterland*, vol. II. Oxford: Clarendon Press, 1932.

Ryan, Patrick S. J. "Is It Possible to Conduct a Unified History of Religion in West Africa." *Universitas* 8 (1984): 98–112.

Sackey, Brigid M. *New Directions in Gender and Religion: The Changing Status of Women in African Independent Churches*. Lanham, MD: Lexington Books, 2006.

Sackey, Brigid M. "Charismatics, Independents, and Missions: Church Proliferation in Ghana." *Culture and Religion* 2, no. 1 (2001): 41–59. https://doi.org/10.1080/014383 00108567162.

Sanneh, Lamin. *Encountering the West: Christianity and the Global Cultural Process, The African Dimension*. London: Marshall Pickering, 1993.

Sanneh, Lamin. *Translating the Message: The Missionary Impact on Culture*. Maryknoll, NY: Orbis, 1989.

Wereko-Brobby, Charles. "Religious Intolerance, Christian Fundamentalism and the Ghana Constitution," March 5, 2015. https://citifmonline.com/2015/03/religious-intolerance-christian-fundamentalism-and-the-ghana-constitution.

Wiltgen, Ralph M. *Gold Coast Mission History 1471–1880*. Techny: Divine Word Publication, 1956.

Yeboah, Samuel. "Christian Beliefs and African Indigenous Rituals in Ghana." Master of Philosophy Dissertation, University of Ghana, 2016.

9

Pyongyang and Protestantism: Imaged as Sodom, Jerusalem, and Babylon, 1866–1945

Sung Deuk Oak

This historical study overviews three images and discourses of Pyongyang from the Christian and anti-Christian perspectives—Pyongyang as the Sodom in Korea (1866–1905), Pyongyang as the Jerusalem of Korea (1906–34), and Pyongyang as the Babylon of Korea (1935–45). These three images represent a thick history of the drastic vicissitude of Protestantism in the city. Pyongyang has been known through two things—the great revival in 1907 and the notion of the "Jerusalem of Korea"—which represent that Pyongyang was one of the largest mission stations in Asia and the capital of Korean Protestantism. This essay challenges such a conventional and monolithic image of Christianity in Pyongyang until 1945. As there has been no study on the topic, this essay examines historical occasions and discourses that made those images—the most wicked pagan city, the holiest Christian city, and the imperialist city of the anti-Christ. This essay focuses on the second image and its dark side. It reveals the rapidly changing faces of Protestantism in Pyongyang; the complex dynamics of the contesting images anticipates its muddled history under the communist regime since 1945.

Pyongyang as the Sodom of Korea, 1866–1905

Pyongyang was the ancient capital of Korea. It was the capital of the Old Chosŏn of legendary emperors Tan'gun and Kija; Chinese Han's colony in the second century BCE and the final capital of Koguryŏ Empire (37 BC–668 AD); the Western capital of Koryŏ Empire (912–1392); and the second largest city of Chosŏn Kingdom from the fifteenth century. It had around 60,000 citizens in 1894 when the Methodists and Presbyterians opened their mission stations.

The image of Pyongyang as Sodom, an immoral and unfriendly city, was formulated by four incidents—the General Sherman Incident and the "martyrdom" of Robert Thomas in 1866; the persecution of Korean Christians in 1894; the death of William J. Hall, the first Methodist medical missionary to the city after the Sino-Japanese War in 1895; and the Japanese occupation of the city during and after the Russo-Japanese War in 1904–5—in other words, the international wars of modern imperialism. Pyongyang gained notoriety as a Christian-persecuting city. The other factor was the immorality of the city, mainly due to kisaengs (dancing girls or entertainment slaves) and their schools. Most yangban officials and influential families in Seoul had at least a concubine kisaeng from Pyongyang.

The General Sherman Incident and the Death of Robert Thomas, 1866

The first disastrous encounter between Protestantism and Pyongyang was the General Sherman Incident in 1866. The heavily armed American schooner left Chefoo for Pyongyang on August 9 and made an experimental trading voyage with a cargo of cotton, glass, tin, and needles. As the distance between Chefoo and the mouth of the Taedong River was 150 miles, the steamship could reach there after a week's voyage. Heavy rains enabled the vessel to go up along the river toward Pyongyang. Initially Korean officials provided the ship with water and food, yet refused any commercial trade and warned against the ship's illegal inland invasion. Approaching the city, however, the ship fired guns and cannons and killed seven Koreans and injured five. When the river fell, General Sherman was grounded and burned down by the attack of fire-rafts. Most of the crew members—five Westerners, thirteen Chinese, and three Malay sailors—were drowned. Some were arrested and killed. As there was no treaty between Korea and any Western empire, Korea regarded the inland trip of Westerners as an unpardonable invasion. Robert Thomas (1840–66) of the London Missionary Society, who visited an island of Hwanghae Province for two months in 1865 and worked as an interpreter of the General Sherman, was arrested and executed on a sand island near Pyongyang on September 5. Alexander Williamson (1829–90), an agent of the National Bible Society of Scotland in Chefoo, appointed Thomas, a colporteur, who distributed Chinese Scriptures among Koreans along the river. After visiting the Corean Gate in Manchuria in 1867, Williamson wrote that the crew invoked their sad fate by means of violent acts toward the natives.[1] Such a realistic evaluation of the ill-fated vessel and a young missionary's unnecessary death had dominated the Protestant missions and Bible societies up to 1910.

In 1871, American marines made a "punitive expedition" and invaded Kanghwa Island near Incheon. This American–Korean War (Sinmi Yangyo) led the Korean government to shut down the kingdom against Western powers until 1882 when the Korea–US treaty was signed. Pyongyang, however, gained the image of a Sodom that maltreated, brutally murdered, and cruelly massacred foreign visitors through newspaper reports in England, Australia, France, and the United States in 1860s and 1870s.[2]

Persecution of Korean Christians, 1894

Samuel A. Moffett (1864–1939) of the Presbyterian Church in the United States arrived in Seoul in January 1890. He planned to open a mission station in Pyongyang, which was relatively free from political muddle and thus suitable for the application of the

Nevius' Three-Self principles. Moffett visited Pyongyang eight times from 1890 to 1893. Korean denizens refused the religion of Western barbarians who invaded in 1866. Police officials and mobs threw stones at Moffett and his temporary house in 1893. Moffett thought if the General Sherman Incident had not happened, people would have been more open to Christianity. William J. Hall (1860–94) of the Methodist Episcopal Church came to Pyongyang to open its mission station in April 1894.

The conflict began when Moffett and Hall purchased Korean houses under the name of Korean helpers. International treaties did not allow foreigners to buy property out of the open port cities, and Pyongyang was not such a city. When Korean Christians refused to donate money to the town shrine worship, government officials put them into prison stocks. Dr. Hall's helper Kim Ch'ang-sik and other Koreans were tortured and threatened to death. Kim refused to renounce the name of God and kept his faith. Dr. Hall sent telegrams to the British legation in Seoul to save Koreans' lives. The foreign department of the Korean government ordered the governor of Pyongyang to release Koreans. William B. Scranton (1856–1922) and Moffett in Seoul came down to Pyongyang and got compensation from the governor for Korean Christians' persecution and the damage of mission houses.

Missionaries proved their superiority over the legislation of the Korean local government in the name of the international law and foreigners' extraterritoriality. After the stoning of Stephen, more Koreans joined the church.[3] On the other hand, the persecution revealed the social class struggle between the merchant class and the local government clerks and officials. A newly rising middle class in the city—innkeepers, herbal doctors, and merchants—gathered at the church, expecting missionaries to protect their wealth and lives from corrupt local officials.

The Sino-Japanese War and the Conversion of Kil Sun-ju

In July 1894, the Sino-Japanese War started. The Japanese defeated the Chinese decisively at the battle of Pyongyang in September 1894. When most people fled to the mountains and remote villages, the city was devastated by the fight. Dr. Scranton, superintendent of the Korea Mission of the Methodist Episcopal Church, said that the city deserved divine punishment.

> Sodom in Korea and most inhospitable of all its towns has met the vengeance of Heaven for its wickedness and inhumanity. The Chinese army—a mob of some 20,000—took possession of the city for some two months, robbed the people of their homes, their rice and rice kettles, and their wives even, until, when the Japanese army took possession, a city of some 80,000 inhabitants had been diminished to a few hundred ... A letter just received from Dr. Hall at his post is of a most encouraging nature, and the whole story, as we review the year, calls forth a *Te Deum laudamus*. The church in "Sodom," as we call it, is growing up in the fire. It will unquestionably be a strong one.[4]

The scattered Christians spread the gospel. The infant church was growing up in the fetters of the prison and then in the fire of the war. *Te Deum laudamus* ("God, We

Praise You"). Such triumphal praise against Pyongyang's appalling image as "Sodom in Korea" was shared with other missionaries in Seoul.⁵

Kil Sŏn-ju, an herbal doctor and a Daoist practitioner in Pyongyang, had to flee to a remote mountain village during the war like most of the 80,000 people of the city. When he returned to his house, he found that it was burnt down, and the lot was taken by a Roman Catholic French missionary who purchased adjacent lots for the church building. Kil was helpless against the powerful French priests. His religious crisis and material failure led him to be interested in Protestantism and American missionaries. After reading *The Pilgrim's Progress*, he prayed to the Daoist Jade Shangdi god every day, and finally, he heard the divine voice calling his own name. His lifelong search for the mystic union with God was accomplished. He was baptized on August 15, 1897. He became a nationwide revivalist since the great revival of 1907. However, the Korean government and American missionaries could not help him get the land back for another ten years.

Pyongyang as the Jerusalem of Korea, 1907–36

The discourse of "Pyongyang as the Jerusalem of Korea" started with the Great Revival in 1907. The Conspiracy Case (1911), the March First Independence Movement (1919), and the rapid growth of Protestantism in the early 1920s made the city the capital of Christianity in Korea. In 1926 Protestant Christians made Robert Thomas the martyr of Pyongyang. Socialists counterattacked such a hagiographic project. They coined a pun— "Korea of Jerusalem," where spiritual reductionism ignored real issues of the people.

The 1907 Great Revival and Contesting Images

Methodist revivals, which started in Wonsan in 1903, spread to the Presbyterians in 1904. The peak was the Pyongyang revival in January 1907. Christians publicly repented sins of unfaithfulness, lying, stealing, sexual immorality, and even killing. Explosive church growth followed.⁶

The great revival created two contesting images of Korea. American journals carried the negative image continuously. A pro-Japanese war correspondent, George Kennan, described Korea as a desperate state and Koreans as a product of decayed civilization.⁷ Professor G. T. Ladd of Yale University visited Seoul in 1907 as a guest of Resident-General Ito Hirobumi. Ladd argued that the sins confessed at the revival meetings showed how Koreans were uncivilized, primitive, superstitious, and hopelessly corrupt. He endorsed the Japanese colonization of Korea for its civilization and enlightenment,⁸ which was the Japanese pan-Asian version of the white man's burden. Methodist bishop Merriam C. Harris agreed to Ito's idea of politics by the Japanese government and morality by Christianity.

Missionaries propagated the positive image of Korea. They witnessed the best of Korean character.⁹ John Moore in Pyongyang confessed that he was liberated from the "contemptible notion that the East is East and the West is West and that there can be no real affinity or common meeting ground between them."¹⁰ Once, they had believed it was impossible to lead Koreans to the higher ground of Christian life; now they confessed, "We have seen, and know that we can pray them down to the depths and up to the heights."[11] W. A. Noble compared the Korean churches' philanthropic activities of the Pyongyang district with those of the Wyoming Conference. He concluded that perseverance, self-denial, intelligent activity, and Christian fervor of the Pyongyang churches were second to none.[12] Missionaries refuted the Japanese notions of Korea as a hopeless nation. They praised the Korean church as "the Christian lamp that is to lighten the Eastern world."[13] Pyongyang was known as an ideal mission field that reminded Western visitors of the apostolic church and "the center of the most remarkable missionary work now underway anywhere on the earth."[14] Koreans began to say, "The only lights in Korea's black sky are the churches."[15]

From this positive image of Korea, a new discourse emerged—Korea as a new Israel of the East. Some conservative or pro-Japanese missionaries produced such an image of Korea as the old Israel—a small and politically weak nation surrounded by strong empires, yet a country of spirituality, arts, and literature. Some argued that Koreans were originally the Semites. They believed in the monotheistic God Hanăŏmin from the ancient times and that many aspects of Korean culture and customs had similarities with Jewish culture.

Church Growth, 1911–19

In 1915 most shops in Pyongyang closed on Sundays. Around 6,000 Christians (10 percent of the city's population of 60,000) kept the Sabbath and attended Bible classes and worship services.[16] In 1916 the city had a Roman Catholic church (560 members with a French priest), a Congregational church (ninety-four members with a Japanese pastor), five Methodist churches (2,296 members in total), and six Presbyterian churches (3,982 in total).[17] Two megachurches had 1,376 and 1,800 average attendants each. Eight hundred and sixty-five women registered at a Presbyterian Bible class held in March 1917. The rapid expansion of the church began to make Pyongyang the center of Protestantism in Korea.

In 1917 intellectuals however began to criticize Korean Protestantism's conservatism, stratification, and anti-intellectualism. Yi Kwang-su's novel, *Mujŏng: The Heartless*, depicted that elders of the church did not understand the essence of Western Christianity and civilization but blindly believed in its superiority and imitated appearance. He enumerated the defects of the church—the caste system (hierarchy between pastors and laypeople), ecclesiastical supremacy (the distinction between believers and nonbelievers), anti-intellectualism (despising worldly learning), and superstition (blind faith) of the congregation.[18]

Christian Political Nationalism, 1911–19

During the first decade of Japanese colonial rule, the government persecuted Protestant Christians in Pyongyang. In 1911 the Japanese colonial government fabricated the Conspiracy Case. They arrested more than seven hundred nationalists in northwestern provinces and accused 123 men of assassination attempts against Governor-General

Terauchi. Most of the accused were Christians—ninety-eight Presbyterians, six Methodists, two Roman Catholics. They were teachers (thirty-one) and students (twenty), businessmen (fifty), and urban intellectuals (ten). Forty-six (37 percent) were from Sŏnchŏn and twenty-seven (22 percent) from Pyongyang. During the time of detainment, defendants were tortured, and the secret nationalist society Sinminhoe was detected. One hundred and five people were convicted. They spent one to three years in prison. After release they developed underground networks and prepared for the independence movement.

Korean nationalists launched the nationwide independence movement on March 1, 1919. At 1:00 p.m., an hour earlier than in Seoul, Presbyterians and Methodists in Pyongyang, Sŏnchŏn, Chinnampo, and Wonsan held a public meeting and declared the independence of Korea. Kil Sŏnju went to Seoul as one of the thirty-three signatories of the declaration of the independence and was imprisoned. Three other senior pastors of the Presbyterian churches and thirteen elders were arrested in Pyongyang. Sunday worship was forbidden for a few months. The police punitively burnt down nineteen churches in P'yŏng'an provinces, and twenty-six schools were closed for three months. Japanese police officers and gendarmes flogged, bayoneted, and shot unarmed people. Christian students of Soongsil Academy published an underground weekly newspaper, *The Independent*, in April and May to encourage people and warn the pro-Japanese groups.

Kim Ik-Tu Revival Movement, 1920-5

Although the March First Movement had not achieved the goal, it improved the ecclesiastical image, for the church suffered for the nation. The Japanese government adopted the so-called cultural rule and loosened an oppressive attitude toward the church. The mission schools could teach the Bible and conduct the chapel service. The churches launched the forward movement to gain more members among the people who had a friendly attitude toward Protestantism. But the primary reason for its rapid expansion was Kim Ik-tu's revival movement, whose characteristics were miraculous healings and colloquial style of sermons. Daily newspapers reported marvelous cases of healings. A society for proving miraculous healing published a book that showed the before and after pictures of patients. His revival gave new hope for the suffering people. It provoked the debate, however, between traditional cessationism and novel continuationism. It also prompted socialists to criticize him as a high-class shaman trickster and his revivalism as unscientific superstition. The Japanese government watched his revivals with suspicious eyes, for the considerable offering of the meetings could be sent to the provisional Korean government in Shanghai.

Christian Notion of "Pyongyang, Jerusalem of Korea," 1925-32

As a result of propagating campaigns and revivals, northwestern Protestantism grew explosively and became the majority of Korean Christianity. Around 1925, people began to call Pyongyang "the spiritual capital of Korea,"[19] whereas Sŏnchŏn was called "the Kingdom of Christianity" and Chaeryŏng "the World of Christianity."[20]

In the late 1920s, the primary adversary of Protestantism was not the colonial government but atheist socialists and their anti-Christian movement. The Christian neologism of "Pyongyang, Jerusalem of Korea" rivaled the socialist pun of "Korea of Jerusalem." Christians in Pyongyang made Robert Thomas "the martyr of Pyongyang," whose blood became the seed of the church of Pyongyang. Inspired by the Roman Catholic canonization of martyrs at the 60th anniversary of the 1866 persecution, Protestant Christians began to define the death of Thomas as martyrdom. The promoter of this project was Oh Mun-hwan (1903–62), an English teacher of Soonggŭi Girls' School. In August 1926, he published *The Westerners Disturbance in Pyongyang: A Watershed Event of the History of Korean Christianity*. He incorrectly argued that Robert Thomas (of the London Missionary Society) was martyred as a Presbyterian and that he was the father of the Korean Presbyterian Church. When Christians celebrated the sixtieth anniversary of the death of Thomas, Oh's book popularized the image of Thomas as the first martyr of Korean Protestantism. Oh published a biography of Robert Thomas in 1928. As the anti-Christian movement reached its zenith in 1925-8, Pyongyang Christians and missionaries launched the Thomas memorial project as a countermovement. They removed the stigma of a foreign invader from Thomas and restored him as the founder of the thriving churches in Pyongyang. In May 1927, Pyongyang Christians organized the Thomas Memorial Society and held a memorial service on the sand island where Thomas was executed. They believed that the righteous blood of Thomas was the seed of Protestantism in Korea. Presbyterians in Pyongyang built the Thomas Memorial Church in 1932, representing Pyongyang as the starting site of Korean Protestantism and as its capital.

Socialist Anti-Christian Movement and "Korea of Jerusalem"

After the Russian Revolution in 1917, some Korean nationalists and Christians became communists. They organized the communist parties in China and Korea. Influenced by the Chinese socialist anti-Christian movement, Korean socialists attacked Christian revival meetings. The Protestant Church became the target of criticism for its failure in keeping pace with both the thinking of the people and improved education of the younger generation.[21]

In 1924 six Presbyterian churches had 4,000 believers in Pyongyang. One hundred and twenty churches surrounding the city had 21,000 adherents with thirty schools. Sixteen Methodists had 2,300 followers. When they disregarded the colonial reality and the sufferings of the people, socialist reporters of *Kaebyŏk* (New Creation, published by Chŏndogyo and which is one of the most influential and popular monthly magazines) criticized corrupt pastors and elders. They could see pastors and elders everywhere, "even at retired kisaeng houses." An adultery case litigator and a usurer were pastors or elders.[22] Another article criticized the hypocritic Protestant discourse of Pyongyang as Jerusalem of Korea with a pun of "Korea of Jerusalem" in 1925.

> I do not know whether it came from missionaries in Chosŏn or the mouths of globe-totters, but some Westerners who are interested in Chosŏn call it Chosŏn of Jerusalem. It seems correct because high-rising red-brick churches are appearing from the cloudy hill in every city and the church bells sound of the country's peace regularly, and every town and marketplace has a large church building where loud

hymn singing echo down the streets. More than 400 large or small schools managed by the churches are busy day and night to produce the children of the heavenly kingdom. Carrying the red Bible, young people flock to churches every Sunday. It does not seem strange, therefore, to call it the Jerusalem of Chosŏn, a hometown of Christianity. Yet when we look again at the boasting Chosŏn of Jerusalem, it is just like the castle of Jerusalem under the colonial rule of the great Roman Empire about 1,900 years ago, which was full of hypocrite scribers, wicked Pharisees and Sadducees, violent Roman soldiers, and power seekers. Look at the rampancy of the pretenders treading down the poor, the blind hypocrites guiding the blind, and the group of wicked serpents in the Chosŏn of Jerusalem, a colony of the Japanese empire. So how cannot one realize that the so-called Chosŏn of Jerusalem is like a whited sepulcher. Jesus, a patriot of Judea, lamented over the castle of Jerusalem that stoned the righteous to the death, "O, Jerusalem, Jerusalem, your house is left unto you desolate." Then what can we say over the Chosŏn of Jerusalem?[23]

The article twisted the phrase "Jerusalem of Korea" into "Korea of Jerusalem." That meant Christianity in Korea reduced political issues to religious ones. Such a severe criticism against the reductionism of Korean Protestantism continued in the magazine in the 1920s. Pak Hŏn-yŏng (1900–55), who later became the head of the communist party in southern Korea, argued that imperialist Anglo-Saxon missionaries invaded the heathen lands with the weapon of the bible and opened the way for the business of Western capitalists. He condemned Christianity as deceptive superstition and a religion for the wealthy.[24]

Triumphalist Jubilee: "Jerusalem of Korea," 1934

Korean Presbyterians and Methodists celebrated their first jubilee in 1934. Methodists commemorated Robert S. McClay's scout trip to Seoul in June 1884, and Presbyterians remembered Horace N. Allen's arrival in Seoul in September 1884. Fifteen thousand Presbyterians participated in the street parade triumphantly for hours in Pyongyang and showed off their force. The *Donga Daily* reported Pyongyang as "the Jerusalem of Korea."[25] Northwestern cultural nationalism, theological fundamentalism, and spiritual triumphalism made such an image. A member of the Christian Endeavor Society who participated in the crusader parade described, "Pyongyang is originally the center of Protestantism and called the second Jerusalem. We cannot separate Pyongyang from Protestantism."[26] That was the zenith of Pyongyang as a Christian city. What was waiting for the churches was the apocalyptic persecution and suffering and apostasy and blasphemy under the militaristic Japanese colonial government that waged the wars.

Pyongyang as the Babylon of Korea, 1935–45

Kil Sun-ju's Prophecy of the Fall of Pyongyang, 1935

After the Manchurian Incident in 1931, the Japanese established the Japanese-dominated state of Manchukuo. Kil Sun-ju, as a nationwide revivalist, delivered the message of the imminent Second Coming of Christ. The current events revealed evidence for the end-time—a great earthquake in Japan, wars in Manchuria, the apostasy of the church, and the rise of atheist communism. The preacher raised his prophetic voice against the deteriorating world and church. Based on the *Book of Revelation*, his eschatology anticipated Pyongyang's imminent apostasy and its transformation into the Babylon of Korea, a city of the anti-Christ. When the city of Pyongyang fell, he prophesied, it would be the time for Jesus to come again. After the benediction at a revival meeting in Kangsŏ on November 26, 1935, he collapsed and died of a cerebral hemorrhage at sixty-six. His final words were, "Don't enter Pyongyang."

Shinto Shrine Worship, 1936–45

In January 1936, three Presbyterian schools, including Soongsil Christian Union College, were closed, rejecting Shinto shrine worship. The Japanese government required all the students and teachers to attend the Shinto shrine worship not as a religious ceremony but as a civic duty of the loyal subjects of the empire. Most Presbyterians in Pyongyang rejected such a lenient position and regarded the ceremony as idolatry. But all the presbyteries yielded to governmental enforcement and pressure one by one. After the Second Sino-Japanese War in July 1937, the Japanese strengthened the policy of the Japan-Korea-One-Body and mobilized all sources of the Korean peninsula for the war. Finally, the General Assembly of the Presbyterian Church decided to accept the Shinto shrine worship as a civic duty on September 10, 1938. However, many churches in Pyongyang protested the decision and closed the churches. The conformists took the buildings. Nonconformists held family worship services on Sundays and waited for the fall of the Japanese Emperor.

Supporting the Wars, 1937–45

During these seven years of wars—the second Sino-Japanese War and the Pacific War—Christianity in Pyongyang suffered four things: Shinto shrine worship, the Japanization of the church, support for the wars, and the rapid decline of the church. In January 1941, the churches of northern P'yŏng'an province abolished sabbath-keeping. The governor-general expelled the missionaries in 1939. Church membership fell more than 30 percent in 1941. Inspired by the Japanese occupation of Singapore in January 1942, 552 among 560 churches in southern P'yŏng'an province donated their church bells to make bullets and cannonballs to kill Americans. They offered money for the airplanes. From August 1943, they had only an early morning Sunday service. Many churches were closed in 1944. They became town meeting centers, factories for the war supply, or dormitories for the workers.

Aforementioned Oh Mun-hwan, a promoter of martyrdom faith of Thomas, became a pro-Japanese collaborator in 1937. He organized the Pyongyang Christian Fellowship in April 1938 and went to Manchuria to comfort the Japanese soldiers with twelve pastors and elders. He wrote a booklet, *The Emergency State and Christianity*, and advocated the Japanese imperialist idea of the Great East Asia Co-prosperity Sphere. Oh regularly attended Shinto shrine ceremonies and prayed for the victory of Japan. He donated two automobiles to the Japanese army as a representative of the General Assembly of the Presbyterian Church in Korea. When the Pacific War started in 1941, the government staged two dramas—*The Taedong River* and *Naknang*—in Pyongyang and criticized the late Thomas as the pioneer of American imperialism. (The Kim Il-sung regime revived this distorted interpretation after the Korean War in 1950–3.)

Chu Ki-ch'ŏl's Martyrdom and the Theology of the Cross, 1944

Chu Ki-ch'ŏl (1897–1944), minister of the Sanjŏnghyŏn Presbyterian Church in Pyongyang, launched a campaign against Shinto shrine worship. He knew through the newspapers that the German Lutheran Church was yielding to Hitler's Nazism. Chu was convinced that the existential mode of the Korean Church under the same fascist system was the eschatological prophetic faith. He continued to fight against the enforced Shinto shrine worship despite being imprisoned five times. His fighting was not just spiritual biblicism against idolatry but nationalistic resistance against militaristic imperialism. He was tortured so badly in prison that he was almost dead when released. He died as a martyr. Through his martyrdom, the Korean church escaped annihilation and survived as a true church.

Conclusion

The three discourses of Pyongyang as Sodom, as Jerusalem, and as Babylon dramatically evolved with international wars, missions, ideologies like nationalism, colonialism, capitalism, and communism for eighty years from 1866 to 1945. To name a few, Robert Thomas, Sŏ Sang-nyun, William Hall, Samuel Moffett, Kim Ch'ang-sik, Kil Sun-ju, Oh Mun-hwan, and Chu Ki-ch'ŏl played significant roles. Their historical roles changed for better or for worse over time. The fluid images of Pyongyang and its agents are the sources of historical alert and theological imagination.

This essay found the following new historical facts. (1) The discourse of Pyongyang as the Jerusalem of Korea was sandwiched between Sodom and Babylon. Therefore, Jerusalem can quickly deteriorate into Sodom or Babylon at any time. (2) People did not use the term "Pyongyang as the Jerusalem of the East" before 1945. (3) The image of Pyongyang as the Jerusalem of Korea coexisted with the socialist discourse of "Korea of Jerusalem." The latter criticized the spiritual reductionism of Pyongyang Christianity in the 1920s. (4) Primary sources mentioning Pyongyang as the Jerusalem of Korea are minimal. This fact implies that refugee Christians, who fled to South Korea from Pyongyang and the northwestern region after the liberation in 1945, popularized the discourse, hoping to return to the old territory and recover the good old days.

The present and future meanings of the discussion are threefold. In 2007, the Korean Protestant churches adopted the slogan "1907 Pyongyang Again." Such a crusader spirit, armed with geomantic piety, pictured Pyongyang as the holy property to possess. They anticipated that the North Korean regime would collapse sooner or later. This greedy triumphalism regarded Pyongyang as the other to be occupied, and the land for expanding the church. Now, however, church growthism has been utterly defeated. Korean Protestant churches are rapidly declining, like in the 1920s. Seoul deteriorated from Jerusalem to Sodom or Babylon. Seoul Christianity needs to learn from the history of Pyongyang Christianity. Finally, Pyongyang is vital for World Christianity and Korean Christianity. The peace of Pyongyang is indispensable for that of the Korean peninsula and East Asia. Pyongyang has been Babylon under the communist party since 1945. That image has existed almost for eighty years. Rapidly changing situations and creative human imagination can change Babylon into a new Jerusalem.

Notes

1. William E. Griffis, *Corea the Hermit Nation* (New York: Charles Scribner's Sons, 1882), 391–5.
2. For American newspapers' reports of the General Sherman Incident, see James P. Podgorski, "Korean and American Memory of the Five Years Crisis, 1866–1871," MA Thesis, Purdue University, 2020.
3. Samuel A. Moffett, "The Work of the Spirit in North Korea," *Missionary Review of the World* (November 1893): 831–2.
4. "Missionary Report; Korea," in *Seventy-Sixth Annual Report of the Missionary Society of the Methodist Episcopal Church for the Year 1894* (New York: Society, 1895), 241.
5. William B. Scranton, "Missionary Review of the Year," *Korean Repository* (January 1895): 17.
6. The Central Presbyterian Church in Pyongyang swarmed three times within four years and retained membership of 914 members and 334 catechumens in early 1907. The church building, which seated 1,200 persons on its floor, was crowded every Sunday. The attendance at the midweek prayer meetings ranged from 700 to 1,300. Communicants increased from none to 6,640 in fifteen years, and new baptisms numbered 2,207 in a year from 1907 to 1908. See William L. Swallen, "Korean Christian Character," *Assembly Herald* (November 1908): 510.
7. George Kennan, "Korea: A Desperate State," *Outlook* (October 15, 1905): 307–15; "The Korean People: The Product of a Decayed Civilization," *Outlook* (October 21, 1905): 307–15.
8. George T. Ladd, *In Korea with Marquis Ito* (New York: Scribner, 1908), 296–7.
9. John Z. Moore, "A Changed Life," *Korea Mission Field* (hereafter *KMF*) (October 1907): 160.
10. Moore, "The Great Revival Year," *KMF* (August 1907): 118.
11. Edith F. McRae, "For Thine Is the Power," *KMF* (March 1906): 74.
12. W. A. Noble, "Korean Decadence," *KMF* (July 1906): 176.
13. John Z. Moore, "The Vision and the Task," *KMF* (April 1906): 108; "A Changed Life," *KMF* (October 1907): 159.
14. William T. Ellis, "On the Trail of the American Missionary: Ideal Mission Field in Northern Korea," *Evening Star* (February 17, 1907): 21.
15. William T. Ellis, "Church Federation Makes Long Strides: Investigator Finds Missionaries of Different Creeds Working Hand in Hand in Corea," *New York Tribune* (February 4, 1907): 54.

16. Presbyterians had five churches with 3,068 members (the Central Presbyterian Church had 1,158; the Seminary Church 770; the Ch'angjŏnni 408; the Sanjŏnghyŏn 385; and the South Gate 348); Methodists had four churches with 1,631 members (see "平壤과 基督敎 [Pyongyang and Christianity]," *Kidok sinbo* [February 19, 1915].)
17. "平壤 耶蘇敎 近況 [Present Situation of Protestantism in Pyongyang]," *Maeil sinbo* (August 2, 1916).
18. Yi Kwang-su, "Defects of the Korean Church Today," *KMF* (December 1918): 256–7.
19. Hugh H. Cynn, "The Korean Young Men's Christian Association," in *Christian Movement in Japan, Korea and Formosa* (Tokyo: Japan Times, 1925), 601.
20. "巡廻探訪 13: 宣川地方 大觀 3 [Itinerating Visiting 13: Overview of Sŏnch'ŏn Region 3]," *Donga Ilbo* (July 14, 1926).
21. Edmund Brunner, "Rural Korea," in *The Christian Mission in Relation to Rural Problems: Report of the Jerusalem Meeting of the IMC* (New York: International Missionary Council, 1928), 156.
22. Kim Ki-jŏn and Ch'a Sang-ch'an, "朝鮮文化 基本照查—平南道號 [Korean Culture Basic Investigation—Issue on Southern P'yŏng'an Province]," *Kaebyŏk* (September 1924): 66.
23. Kyŏnjidongin, "예루살넴의 朝鮮을 바라보며: 朝鮮耶蘇敎 現狀에 對한 所感 [Looking at Korea of Jerusalem: Thought on the Present Situation of Korean Protestantism]," *Kaebyŏk* 61 (July 1925): 54–5.
24. Pak Hŏn-yŏng, "歷史的으로 본 基督敎의 內面 [Inside of Christianity from the Historical Viewpoint]," *Kaebyŏk* 63 (November 1925): 69.
25. "朝鮮의 예루살렘 平壤에: 十字軍의 閱兵式 [In Pyongyang the Jerusalem of Korea: The Parade of the Crusaders]," *Donga Ilbo* (September 5, 1934).
26. Unsŏng, "敎十字軍의 大行進: 基督敎勉勵靑年大會 後記 [The Great Parade of the Crusaders: Postscript of the Conference of the Christian Endeavor Society]," *Samch'ŏlli* 6–11 (November 1934): 82.

Bibliography

English

Brunner, Edmund. "Rural Korea." In *The Christian Mission in Relation to Rural Problems: Report of the Jerusalem Meeting of the International Missionary Council*, vol. VI. London: Oxford University Press, 1928, pp. 100–208.
Cynn, Hugh H. "The Korean Young Men's Christian Association." In *Christian Movement in Japan, Korea and Formosa*. Tokyo: Japan Times & Mail, 1925, pp. 597–601.
Ellis, William T. "On the Trail of the American Missionary: Ideal Mission Field in Northern Korea." *Evening Star*, February 17, 1907.
Ellis, William T. "Church Federation Makes Long Strides: Investigator Finds Missionaries of Different Creeds Working Hand in Hand in Corea." *New York Tribune*, February 4, 1907.
Griffis, William E. *Corea the Hermit Nation*. New York: Charles Scribner's Sons, 1882.
Kennan, George. "Korea: A Desperate State." *Outlook* (October 15, 1905): 307–15.
Kennan, George. "The Korean People: The Product of a Decayed Civilization." *Outlook* (October 21, 1905): 409–16.
Korea Mission. "Missionary Report: Korea." In *The Seventy-Sixth Annual Report of the Missionary Society of the Methodist Episcopal Church for the Year 1894*. New York: Society of the MEC, 1895, pp. 240–50.

Ladd, George T. *In Korea with Marquis Ito*. New York: Scribner, 1908.
McRae, Edith F. "For Thine Is the Power." *Korea Mission Field* 2, no. 5 (February 1906): 73–4.
Moffett, Samuel A. "The Work of the Spirit in North Korea." *Missionary Review of the World* (November 1893): 831–7.
Moore, John Z. "The Vision and the Task." *Korea Mission Field* 2, no. 6 (April 1906): 107–8.
Moore, John Z. "The Great Revival Year." *Korea Mission Field* 2, no. 8 (August 1907): 113–18.
Moore, John Z. "A Changed Life." *Korea Mission Field* 3, no. 10 (October 1907): 159–60.
Noble, William A. "Korean Decadence." *Korea Mission Field* 2, no. 9 (July 1906): 176.
Podgorski, James P. "Korean and American Memory of the Five Years Crisis, 1866–1871." MA Thesis, Purdue University, 2020.
Scranton, William B. "Missionary Review of the Year." *Korean Repository* 2, no. 1 (January 1895): 15–19.
Swallen, William L. "Korean Christian Character." *Assembly Herald* 14, no. 11 (November 1908): 510–12.
Yi, Kwang-su. "Defects of the Korean Church Today." *Korea Mission Field* 14, no. 12 (December 1918): 256–7.

Korean

"平壤과 基督教 [Pyongyang and Christianity]." *Kidok Sinbo* [Christian Newspaper], February 19, 1915.
"平壤 耶蘇教 近況 [Present Situation of Protestantism in Pyongyang]." *Maeil Sinbo* [Daily Newspaper], August 2, 1916.
"巡廻探訪 13: 宣川地方 大觀 3 [Itinerating Visiting 13: Overview of Sŏnchŏn Region 3]." *Donga Ilbo* [Donga Daily], July 14, 1926.
"朝鮮의 예루살렘 平壤에: 十字軍의 閱兵式 [In Pyongyang the Jerusalem of Korea: The Parade of the Crusaders]." *Donga Ilbo* [Donga Daily], September 5, 1934.
Kim, Ki-jŏn, and Ch'a Sang-ch'an. "朝鮮文化 基本照查—平南道號 [Korean Culture Basic Investigation—Issue on Southern P'yŏng'an Province]." *Kaebyŏk* [Creation] 51 (September 1924): 67–75.
Kyŏnjidongin. "예루살넴의 朝鮮을 바라보며: 朝鮮耶蘇教 現狀에 對한 所感 [Looking at Korea of Jerusalem: Thought on the Present Situation of Korean Protestantism]." *Kaebyŏk* [Creation] 61 (July 1925): 54–5.
Pak, Hŏn-yŏng. "反基督教 運動에 關하야: 歷史的으로 본 基督教의 內面 [On Anti-Christianity Movement: Inside of Christianity from the Historical Viewpoint]." *Kaebyŏk* [Creation] 63 (November 1925): 64–9.
Unsŏng. "教十字軍의 大行進: 基督教勉勵青年大會 後記 [The Great Parade of the Crusaders: Postscript of the Conference of the Christian Endeavor Society]." *Samch'ŏlli* [Three Thousand Li] 6, no. 11 (November 1934): 82.

10

Rediscovering Women Leaders in the History of Chinese Protestantism

Li Ma

Introduction

From Bible women in late Qing to today's Chinese women in a globally integrated economy, women have always been the majority of Protestants in China. Nevertheless, scholarly efforts in documenting the history of Chinese Christian women have been scant. Instead, two narratives have dominated the history of Chinese Protestantism. First, many have written that it is the foreign missionaries, including men and women, who have made history.[1] Second, even scholars who include Indigenous leadership into this history tend to mention only well-known male leaders of Chinese origin.

Nevertheless, a careful survey of this history reveals that many well-known male leaders from the Indigenous Chinese church had female mentors. For example, the famous evangelist John Sung, before becoming known as a popular charismatic preacher in all of Southeast Asia, was first recruited by Shi Meiyu (Mary Stone) into her Bethel Mission team near Shanghai in the early 1920s. Watchman Nee's conversion in 1920 was the fruit of female evangelist Dora Yu's ministry. China's premier Indigenous theologian T. C. Chao (Zhao Zichen) was influenced by female educator and Confucian scholar Zeng Baosun. Christian scholar Wu Ningkun, who returned from the University of Chicago to teach at Yenching University, was recruited by leading English literature scholar Lucy Chao (Zhao Luorui). While the names of these men were later elevated to fame in the history of Chinese Protestantism, the stories of their female mentors lapsed into obscurity.

Toward an Inclusive History

In recent decades, scholarship of Chinese Christianity has been dominated by a masculine perspective, which finds binary frameworks, such as church–state relations and civil society, appealing. Some male scholars have been motivated by an illusion of Christian nationalism, hoping for the growth of Christianity in China to usher in the next Christian nation. Driven by this impulse, their critical lens is often directed at the communist regime while ignoring the power structures within the church itself. Moreover, with Western readership favoring a "persecution" narrative when it comes to churches in China, Western media and scholarship find it more convenient to mold male figures of the Chinese church into China's Apostle Pauls and Bonhoeffers. By 2020, this outlook has given way to an activistic trend for Trumpism among Chinese evangelicals both in mainland China and in diaspora Chinese communities.[2] These developments require a sober reexamination of the history of Chinese Protestantism, for as long as the stories of women leadership are not integrated into this history, narratives and traditions codified by men will remain oppressive.

The lapse of women leadership into history has much to do with the shame around the discussion of power abuse at the hands of famous men in the Chinese church. From missionary advocates such as Katherine Bushnell in late Qing to Tiananmen movement participant Chai Ling in the 2000s, women leaders who have exposed sexual abuse in the church (at great costs to themselves) have been sidelined by historians until recently.[3] Given the record of evangelical Christianity in this post-#MeToo era, we now have an enhanced awareness of the necessity to look at church history from the perspective of the abused and silenced. Often these women and their sister advocates are found in local faith communities.

Lastly, a common understanding of women's leadership in the church has yet to expand beyond the four walls of church buildings. Traditional historiography limits female leadership in the Chinese church to the roles of evangelism-oriented tasks. This narrow conceptualization of "mission" and the "church" has thus excluded women leaders who serve in all walks of life, including scientists, social reformers, and writers.

In the next section I will introduce five generations of women leaders in the Chinese Protestant church who have created change in the church and in broader society. Each of the women selected occupied a unique position in a specific historical phase and left a legacy with a wider social impact. In their explorations of selfhood, gender roles, nationalistic consciousness, and Christian identity, many became cross-cultural synthesizers and formulated their own distinct expressions of the faith. Their stories also reveal both the promises and perils of Protestant Christianity in Chinese society.

Late Qing and Early Republic (1880s–1920s)

The history of modern China is incomplete without Christian women leadership. Since the missionary expansion in the 1880s, the challenge of modernity in China began with "Chinese womanhood." As historian Jessie Lutz argues, although missionary education projects, particularly schools for girls, emerged out of the needs of Western missionaries rather than the demands of the Chinese,[4] these projects happened at an important historical juncture when China's local gentry class found the role models of single-women missionaries from the West inspiring for their young daughters. Two Chinese women, Shi Meiyu (1873–1954) and Zeng Baosun (1893–1978), forged a path not yet taken by studying abroad and returning to China. They were the ones advocating for progressive experiments, including Western-style medicine and education.

In the treaty port city of Jiujiang in 1879, a local gentry-turned-pastor Rev. Shi led his seven-year-old daughter Shi Meiyu to learn from American medical missionary Katharine Bushnell. He pleaded with Bushnell to help train this young girl so that one day she could also live an independent life in the service of others. After helping missionaries as a translator and medical assistant for years, Shi Meiyu obtained a medical degree in 1896 from the University of Michigan. She then returned to her hometown of Jiujiang to found the Women and Children's Hospital. In the 1910s, structural obstacles to incorporating Chinese women in leadership roles increased from her Western women mentors.[5] Hoping to train more Indigenous women as nurses, Shi Meiyu raised funds in the United States and advocated for their roles as "active healers," partly rebuking the often used stereotypical image of victimhood of Chinese women.[6] By insisting on all-Chinese medical work, Shi Meiyu intentionally challenged missionary dominance by "white" women.[7] In 1920, the tension between Shi Meiyu and the Women's Foreign Mission Society worsened amid the larger fundamentalist-modernist controversy in America. To further promote Chinese leadership, Shi parted ways with her mission board and began the Bethel Mission in Shanghai.

Another prominent woman leader of the same era—Zeng Baosun—was born into the clan of Confucian scholar Zeng Guofan (or Marquis Tseng Kuo-fan). Her progressive-minded father, a trained Confucian scholar-official, also raised Zeng with natural feet and did not arrange an early marriage for her. Educated in a missionary school, Zeng later became interested in Christianity. Her conversion to Anglicanism marked a paradigm shift for China's privileged gentry class—the guardians of Confucianism. Female figures like Zeng's grandmother, a Confucian matriarch in the family, modeled a benevolent womanhood in the Confucian tradition. Throughout her life, Zeng Baosun defended traditional values as being compatible with Christianity. As Zeng wrote in her memoir, "I saw no conflict between Confucianism and Christianity and that Christianity could awaken China from its lethargy."[8] In 1916, she graduated from the University of London and the University of Oxford. Zeng returned to China and founded Yifang Girls' Collegiate School, an institution to materialize her progressive and traditional ideals together. Different from other mission schools, Yifang School gave students the right of self-government in community affairs.

Both Shi Meiyu and Zeng Baosun witnessed drastic social change as China passed from a declining empire to a fragile republic. Meanwhile, Protestant missions in China saw "the proliferation of women's societies" involving both Western women and Chinese women.[9] The first roadblocks for Indigenous Christian women included footbinding, concubinage, and female illiteracy. Shi and Zeng not only became role models in meeting these challenges but also excelled in establishing all-Chinese institutions. While this social progress was being made, they also became disillusioned with the existing power structures within the Western missionary community.

Civil War and Missionary Decline (1920s–40s)

A century after the first Protestant missionary, Robert Morrison, arrived in China, missionary education projects and institution-building have dominated Chinese society, especially in economically developed regions. As historian Jonathan Spence writes, "Through their texts, their presses, their schools, and their hospitals, the efforts of foreign Christians affected Chinese thought and practice."[10] Among the missionary institutions built to promote gender equality for Chinese women, the Young Women's Christian Association (YWCA), founded in 1890, played a prominent role in urban social reform through their adult literacy classes, hygiene and nutrition classes, vocational training, physical education, and overseas scholarships.[11] During its heyday among educated Chinese women, the YWCA also provided women with leadership training that sustained women's rights movements in the 1920s.

In 1922, *The Christian Occupation of China* was published by Milton Stauffer, surveying on a large scale all of China's Protestant Christian churches and ministries. Although Chinese translators gave it a less militant title (*zhong hua gui zhu*, meaning "China Belongs to the Lord"), many non-Christian intellectuals in China viewed this document as highly offensive. Historian Daniel Bays describes the release of this massive five-hundred-page document with such a provocative English title as "a public relations disaster,"[12] triggering a wave of anti-Christian campaigns in China.[13] The movement was so influential that it forced the Republican government to begin a "Claim Back Education Rights" campaign against the domination of missionary education institutions. Missionaries exploited their extraterritorial legal status and monopolized the "Sino-Foreign Protestant Establishment," as termed by Bays, leading to an increased resistance among Indigenous Chinese against missionary presence in China.[14]

It was within this broader environment of antiforeign and anti-Christian activism that the YWCA decided to transfer leadership to Indigenous Chinese women. In 1925, the YWCA appointed Ding Shujing to head its first Indigenous leadership. Ding had been an active member of the YWCA since 1913 after her parents converted to Christianity and sent her to missionary schools. After Ding Shujing became the YWCA's first Chinese woman general secretary, she pioneered a strategic expansion of the institution's reach to women from working classes and peasantry demographics.[15] In a time of civil unrest and labor protests, she was determined to include even radical labor groups as long as they shared common ideals for women's rights. For example, the YWCA opened night schools for women workers in Shanghai's factories. Although Ding Shujing never intended these programs to become an incubator for fledgling communist groups, they effectively nurtured the latter's mobilization. Later, many core cadres of the Chinese Communist Party confessed that it was the YMCA and YWCA that trained them to mobilize grassroots participation. After the 1930s, the YWCA in China faced a massive financial decline as the United States entered the Great Depression. It was during this leadership vacuum that male independent leaders such as John Sung, Wang Mingdao, and Watchman Nee grew their Indigenous influence.[16] But even in the midst of radical politics and Japanese invasion, Ding Shujing remained a calm voice for peace-making. In 1935, when she attended a YWCA assembly in Japan, Ding openly discussed the current affairs with Japanese women delegates.

By the late 1920s, China boasted thirteen private Christian universities, compared to the Republican government's two publicly funded universities. Among the first generation of Indigenous leadership in Christian higher education, there were three prominent figures: T. C. Chao of Yenching University, Francis Wei of Huazhong

University, and Wu Yifang, the female president of Ginling College.[17] Wu earned a reputation that ranked her side by side with China's foremost secular educator Cai Yuanpei, president of Peking University. After obtaining a doctorate in biology from the University of Michigan, Wu returned to China in 1927 after receiving an invitation to become the first president of a women's college. Before she accepted the job offer, Wu challenged the school to change its rules to reflect Indigenous practices and to end a culture of elitist superiority. In Wu's twenty-three-year presidency of Ginling College from 1928 to 1951, she accomplished bold reforms in teaching and administration.[18] Wu also stressed diversity by opening up recruitment to non-Christian students. Wu also created the Department of Home Economics to train young women in helping rural families. Students taught in rural schools, set up service stations, and experimented ways to enhance agricultural productivity.

Wu's attitude toward emerging communist activism in China shifted through different phases. She was initially critical of the Chinese Communist Party when serving as the executive committee member of Madam Chiang Kai-shek's women's relief project in 1938. But she was also equally critical of corruption within Chiang's government. For example, she protested the violence of the Nationalist Party against students and civilians in the Xia Guan incident and resigned from the National Congress. But unlike Zeng Baosun, who came to an anticommunist view because of her conservative social background, Wu was willing to lend some trust to the communists who also did much rural emancipation work. Her leadership won positive appraisal from US president Roosevelt who commended her by calling her a "Goddess of Wisdom." In 1945, Wu became the only women leader among the Chinese delegation at San Francisco where she advocated for women's rights and ensured their inclusion in the founding document of the United Nations.[19] Wu was also one of only four women delegates to sign the original UN Charter.

Militant Communism and Persecution (1950s–70s)

In the spring of 1949, many Western-trained Chinese Christians yearned to return and serve a new China that was on the horizon. Although some had reservations about the communist regime, the predominant sentiment was a strong patriotic devotion with rosy optimism. After all, many embraced Christianity because they viewed it as a religion to "save China." Tragically, nobody foresaw how the outbreak of the US–Korean War (1950–3) would soon throw the entire nation into antiforeign hysteria. China's thirteen Christian colleges would become the first casualties of the communist takeover.[20]

Before English literature scholar Zhao Luorui (1912–98) returned to China in 1949 at the request of her father, the renowned Chinese theologian T. C. Chao, she was working on her doctoral dissertation on Henry James at the University of Chicago. As a well-known translator of works by T. S. Eliot and Walt Whitman in her own right, Zhao Luorui had enjoyed a respected status among educated Chinese even before she went to Chicago. Zhao and her husband, Chen Mengjia, left for the United States upon the invitation of Harvard historian John Fairbank in 1944, where Chen taught Chinese paleography and archaeology at the University of Chicago. When T. S. Eliot visited the United States in

1946, he invited Zhao and her husband for dinner and thanked Zhao for her translation of *The Waste Land*. After Zhao Luorui became chair of the Western Language Department at Yenching University, she also actively recruited more alumni from the United States. Zhao's outlook on Chinese politics was much influenced by her father, T. C. Chao. Although Chao had expressed doubt about the use of violence by communists, he still trusted the new regime to be a providential platform for global ecumenical solidarity.

Things took a dramatic turn in 1951 after the US–Korean War broke out. While Mao Zedong himself praised American soldiers for embodying democracy in 1949, he and other communist rulers began to propagate nationalist fervor against "American imperialism." A movement to reform US-trained intellectuals began, leading to the nationalization of Christian higher education institutions. In the radical populist campaigns that followed, academic disciplines in all higher education institutions underwent an overhaul, with humanities and social sciences being abolished.[21] Chinese intellectuals who had obtained overseas degrees in these disciplines were ostracized. Soon, in a literary reform to simplify Chinese characters, Chen Mengjia became the target of public criticism and humiliation after he spoke up against the "unscientific" plan.[22] He lapsed into mental instability and later committed suicide in 1966 when Mao's cultural revolution began. This tragedy devastated Zhao Luorui, who sank into chronic depression. It was not until after the cultural revolution ended that Zhao Luorui resumed her research, specializing in American literature.

Writer and scholar Xie Wanying (1900–99) was among the many Western-trained Christian intellectuals who survived China's harshest season of political suppression. In fact, she was able to rise to the center of public life, and her pseudonym, Bing Xin, became a household name in China. Xie first gained fame through her feminist novels after the May Fourth Movement in 1919. By the time she passed away at the age of ninety-nine, Xie Wanying had earned the reputation of "grandmother" of modern Chinese literature.[23] She graduated from Peking Union College for Women and obtained a master's degree from Wesleyan College in the United States. Among China's literary critics, Xie's unique approach was dubbed "Bing Xin style," which combined poetic expression with narrative realism. After she began teaching as a professor of Chinese literature at Yenching University, Xie published more essays and short stories that were later included in China's elementary school textbooks. Her writing career was truncated for two decades by the political movements during the 1960s and 1970s. At the age of seventy, she was sent down to rural China for reeducation through harsh labor. Her last volumes of work showed a writer who carefully participated in the nation's public life through writing on noncontroversial themes such as motherly love and childhood innocence.

Market Reform and Global Mission Reboot (1980s–2000s)

Nearly a decade after the market reform, China's legalization of Bible printing in 1987 marked a turning point when the regime's religious regulations lightened. The following two decades saw a growth in the population of Christian converts, both domestic and in the Chinese diaspora. For example, even Three-Self churches saw an unprecedented growth. By 2003, in addition to the 45,000 registered official churches, around 40,000 groups affiliated with the Three-Self system were still waiting to be registered.[24] The demand had exceeded the supply of worship space and pastoral resources, leading to problems with overcrowding in local congregations. Another milestone occurred in 2004 when China rewrote private property rights into its constitution, leading to a housing market boom. More commercial space opened up for urban churches to expand in membership. By 2005, China's official statistics reported more than 18 million Protestant believers, a twenty-fold growth compared to the figure for 1949.

In an attempt to improve the image of official Chinese Protestantism overseas, the China Christian Council organized a Chinese Bible exhibit in Los Angeles in 2006[25] with Cao Shengjie as the lead delegate. Her career within the Three-Self establishment was one of turbulence before 1980. Later, when the Shanghai Academy of Social Sciences set up an Institute of Religion, Cao Shengjie was invited to join as a research fellow. She conducted research in Zhejiang Province, where Protestantism was booming. On her own merit as a feminist theologian, Cao has been a long-standing voice advocating for women's rights as defined by the communist ideology. In her writings for many Three-Self publications, Cao also cautioned against a direct importation of Western feminist theology. In 1995, Cao gave a speech at the United Nations' Fourth World Conference of Women, in Beijing, affirming the communist regime's advancement of women's status in society and the church.[26] Because of her writings and public speeches on this issue, many consider Cao Shengjie "one of the most important female leaders in the mainland Chinese church" who continues to emphasize the importance of women's work.[27] In 2005, through a good relationship with the Billy Graham Evangelical Association, Cao Shengjie and two other Chinese women leaders were invited to a presidential breakfast at the White House.

Around the same time, a Chicago-based ministry held a Gospel for China Conference in Hong Kong to commemorate the two hundredth anniversary of Robert Morrison's mission in China. At this house church-learning platform, over 5,000 participants were introduced to hymn-writer and evangelist L Xiaomin, who soon gained rare celebrity status through her famous collection of Chinese hymns. L wrote an original collection of Chinese praise music known as the *Canaan Hymns* despite her minimal education and lack of music education. These hymns became widely popular among an expanding Christian population, both domestic and overseas.

L Xiaomin's life story as an uneducated peasant girl, her inspiring musical experiences, and her evangelistic ambition became inseparable parts of her public persona. At one point, the *Canaan Hymns* became so widely used that even China's official Three-Self churches began to include L's hymns into their official publications, although not without criticism.[28] In the early 2000s, L Xiaomin became widely known among a growing wave of new Chinese converts, both domestic and overseas, through a documentary *The Cross: Jesus in China* (2003) produced by China Soul for Christ Foundation established by Yuan Zhiming, a Tiananmen movement participant-turned-pastor living in the United States. This widely popular documentary promoted L Xiaomin to a saintly pedestal. By then, L had composed over nine hundred hymns. Those who took pride in this young female oral musician applauded her as the most prolific hymn-writer in China and an epitome of deep house-church spirituality. In addition, she was given the title "China's songbird."[29] Her hymns are considered "the pulse of seventy million Chinese Christians"[30] and "a gift from God to the Chinese church."[31] However, those who scrutinized the theology of *Canaan Hymns* claimed that these were dotted with nationalistic fervor, predicting China to be the next Christian nation after America.

Controversies and Consumerism (2010s)

By the 2010s, Chinese evangelicalism has formed its own power structures, iconic figures, and a subculture of conservative masculinity. In 2014, former Tiananmen dissident and later Christian antiabortion advocate Chai Ling released a public statement about her alleged rape by a famous evangelist and Tiananmen leader Yuan Zhiming. By then, both Yuan and Chai were "two of the highest-profile Christian leaders among the world's 50 million overseas Chinese."[32] The Chinese Christian diaspora community considered Chai Ling and Yuan Zhiming to be of the same camp; they both led the Tiananmen movement, later fled China and converted to Christianity, and both became famous representatives of God's work among Chinese dissidents. A Pulitzer-winning journalist even describes Yuan as "one of the country's most influential figures through his documentaries and videotaped sermons."[33] Due to Yuan's fame, the controversy "roiled the Chinese Christian community."[34] Eighteen Chinese American pastors wrote an open letter to Yuan Zhiming calling him "to respond to Chai Ling's allegations responsibly in order to protect the image of the church."[35] They also convened a collaborative effort to commission a professional third-party investigative agency GRACE (Godly Response to Abuse in the Christian Environment) on Yuan's case.[36] According to the report, three other women also came forward with sexual abuse allegations. These incidents happened in France and Germany where Yuan Zhiming attended evangelistic meetings.[37] During this time, Yuan Zhiming denied all allegations but resigned from his position at China Soul for Christ Foundation.[38]

Long-term observers of the Chinese church are reminded of a similar sexual abuse allegation that emerged in 2011 when retired Chinese American medical physician Lily Hsu published a book titled *The Unforgettable Memoirs: My Life, Shanghai Local Church and Watchman Nee*. Through interviews with the victims of sexual abuses by Watchman Nee, Hsu revealed the truth of Nee's crimes for which he was once indicted by the communist government, but the charges were dismissed by the house church community as an attempt to frame him. Readers' passionate and divided responses to Hsu's books are revealing. Some church leaders listed Hsu's past record of "always standing on top of things" and accused her book of similar gimmickry for public fame. They even verbally attacked her as a modern "Judas Iscariot" and "Cain who shed the blood of Abel and persecuted the Lord."[39] Though these exchanges were highly visible among the Chinese Christian community, they became mere noises in English-speaking media.

In mainland China, the widespread use of social media has boosted the visibility of a subgroup of Christian celebrities who have become vastly popular, actress Yao Chen being an example. With more than 80 million followers on Weibo, she is considered China's highest-profile celebrity, "Queen of Weibo," and the country's own Angelina Jolie.[40] As the media describes, Yao Chen is "one of the top five most followed microbloggers in the world after the likes of Lady Gaga and Justin Bieber, and ahead of President Obama."[41] In 2014, *Time* magazine included Yao Chen in its "Time 100" list.[42] *Forbes* magazine also listed her as the world's most powerful woman. From time to time, Yao's Christian identity was revealed by her subtle tweeting of biblical passages on Weibo (China's Twitter). The tone of her Christian messaging has always been welcoming and inclusive. Her nonluxurious wedding in a church setting enhanced many young people's positive perception of Christianity. After giving birth, Yao Chen advocated against the motherhood penalty in the Chinese entertainment industry.[43] In the area of charity, Yao Chen was named the UN's Honorary Patron for China. In this capacity, she has visited refugees in places including the Philippines, Thailand, Somalia, Sudan, and Ethiopia. She was again named by the UNHCR as goodwill ambassador in China.[44] In 2016, Yao received the World Economic Forum's Crystal Award for raising awareness of the refugee crisis.

Another notable celebrity figure is Yuan Li, who enjoys the household name as China's "Audrey Hepburn." When she once spoke as a guest at one of China's top higher education institutions, Yuan confessed that her once privileged life as a celebrity used to make her utterly indifferent to the suffering of the poor and marginalized in society. After her conversion, Yuan began to care about the suffering of other people. She began helping migrant workers suffering from pneumoconiosis. Yuan Li found a way to engage with the public through her Weibo presence, as she had over 15 million followers.[45] She showed admirable boldness and courage in rebuking government policies and state-sponsored nationalism. At the same time, however, Yuan's fundamentalist and biblicist outlook on world affairs and her judgmental tone often led her to comment on matters that stirred up anti-Christian sentiments.

Conclusion

The short biographies in this chapter allow us to consider the complicated facets regarding the relationship between women and Chinese Protestantism. Writing their stories into history can help us gain a more nuanced understanding about the interplays of Christianity, gender, power, and modern Chinese history. At times, Christianity presented hopes of emancipation for Chinese women. In the midst of these changes, Chinese women face the task of exploring what it means to be both Chinese and Christian. They are inspired by Western missionary women, rituals in their culture, and, for some, their experiences of living in the global community.

But history has also recorded many time-bound moral ambiguities. The history of modern China changed drastically over more than a century of imperial collapse, nation-building, foreign invasion, civil wars, revolutions, Maoism, and neo-capitalist globalization supervised by the Chinese Communist Party. These macro-structural changes have shaped the history of Chinese Protestantism and women's place in that history in significant ways. Theological trends also play an important role; for example, in today's Chinese churches, rising social problems, including marriage and family issues, have created a precondition that welcomes a comeback of conservatism. The globalization of the Christian Right through various brands of American evangelicalism came at an opportune time of a strained US–China relationship, but also strengthened this subculture of masculinity.[46] These recent developments await more historical research.

Notes

1. Jane Hunter, *The Gospel of Gentility: American Women Missionaries in Turn-of-the-Century China* (New Haven, CT: Yale University Press, 1984); Kristin Du Mez, *A New Gospel for Women: Katharine Bushnell and the Challenge of Christian Feminism* (New York: Oxford University Press, 2015).
2. Li Ma and Jin Li, "Why Did Chinese American Evangelicals Advocate Voting for Trump? Trauma, US-China Tensions and Christian Nationalism," unpublished manuscript.
3. Kristin Du Mez, *A New Gospel for Women: Katharine Bushnell and the Challenge of Christian Feminism* (New York: Oxford University, 2015); Li Ma, *Christian Women and Modern China: Recovering A Women's History of Chinese Protestantism* (Lanham, MD: Lexington Books, 2021).
4. Daniel Bays, *A New History of Chinese Christianity* (Hoboken, NJ: Wiley-Blackwell, 2012), 69.
5. Connie Anne Shemo, *The Chinese Medical Ministries of Kang Cheng and Shi Meiyu, 1872-1937* (Bethlehem: Lehigh University Press, 2011), 143.
6. Ibid., 6.
7. Ibid.
8. Zeng Baosun, *Confucian Feminist: Memoirs of Zeng Baosun, 1893-1978* (trans. and adapted by Thomas L. Kennedy) (Philadelphia, PA: American Philosophical Society, 2002), 30.
9. Ibid., 31.
10. Jonathan D. Spence, *The Search for Modern China* (New York: W. W. Norton, 1991), 208.
11. Alison R. Drucker, "The Role of the YWCA in the Development of the Chinese Women's Movement, 1890-1927," *Social Service Review* 53, no. 3 (September 1979): 421–40.
12. Ibid., 109.
13. Li Ma and Jin Li, "Divergent Paths of Protestantism and Asian Nationalism: A Comparison of Two Social Movements in Korea and China in 1919," *International Bulletin of Mission Research*, May 29, 2018.
14. Bays, *A New History*, 108.
15. YWCA of China, *Introduction to the Young Women's Christian Association of China, 1933-1947* (Shanghai: The National Committee of the YWCA of China, n.d.), 1.
16. Bays, *A New History*, 124.
17. Li Ma and Jin Li, "The Tragic Irony of a Patriotic Mission: The Indigenous Leadership of Francis Wei and T. C. Chao, Radicalized Patriotism, and the Reversal of Protestant Missions in China," *Religions* 11, no. 4 (2020): 175–95.

18. Helen M. Schneider, "Mobilizing Women: The Women's Advisory Council, Resistance and Reconstruction during China's War with Japan," *European Journal of East Asian Studies* 11, no. 2 (2012): 217.
19. Rebecca Adami, *Women and the Universal Declaration of Human Rights*, vol. 32 (New York: Routledge, 2019), 35.
20. Peng Deng, *Private Education in Modern China* (Westport, CT: Praeger, 1997), 67–8.
21. Han, Minghan, *The History of Chinese Sociology* (Tianjin: People's Press, 1987), 172.
22. Chen Mengjia, "Two Hopes," in *Collected Works of Cheng Mengjia* (Beijing: Shang Wu Shu Ju, 2006), 241–2.
23. Mao Chen, "In and Out of Home: Bing Xin Recontextualized," in Philip F. Williams, ed., *Asian Literary Voices: From Marginalized to Mainstream* (Amsterdam: Amsterdam University Press, 2010), 63–70.
24. Erik Burkiln, "The Greatest Need in the Chinese Church: The China Christian Council Confronts the Task of Theological Education," *ChinaSource* 5, no. 1 (Spring 2003): 8–9.
25. Eunice Or, "Interview with President of China Christian Council Rev. Cao Shengjie," *Gospel Herald*, May 1, 2006. www.gospelherald.com/article/church/9815/interview-with-president-of-china-christian-council-rev-cao-shengjie.htm.
26. Cao Shengjie, "Chinese Christian Women in Education and Development: Understanding the Compatibility of Faith and Action for Women in a Changing Society," *Church and Society* 86, no. 5 (May–June 1996): 76–81.
27. Yifan Lu, "Equal Discipleship: Exploring Chinese Feminist Theology," *Ecumenical Review*, April 22, 2019.
28. The typical hymns in the Chinese New Hymnal of China Christian Council are more formal because most are translated from Western liturgical hymns.
29. Ruth Wang, "You Are the Light of the World, Song for Preachers, Created by China's Songbird, Lv Xiao Min," *China Christian Daily*, December 15, 2015. http://chinachristiandaily.com/news/category/2015-12-15/you-are-the-light-of-the-world--song-for-preachers--created-by-china-s-songbird--lv-xiao-min349.
30. Xiao Min, "Women of Christianity." https://womenofchristianity.com/hymn-writers/xaio-min.
31. C. Michael Hawn, "Landscapes and Soulscapes: How Place Shapes Christian Congregational Song," in Stanley Brunn, ed., *The Changing World Religion Map: Sacred Places, Identities, Practices and Politics* (Dordrecht: Springer, 2015), 2665.
32. Timothy C. Morgan, "China Soul's Yuan Denies Rape Accusation, Resigns from Preaching," *Christianity Today*, March 9, 2015. www.christianitytoday.com/ct/2015/march-web-only/update-chai-ling-yuan-zhiming-rape-accusation-china-soul.html.
33. Ian Johnson, "Jesus vs. Mao? An Interview with Yuan Zhiming," *New York Review of Books*, September 4, 2012. www.nybooks.com/daily/2012/09/04/jesus-vs-mao-interview-yuan-zhiming.
34. Ian Young, "Tiananmen Dissident Quits Church over Extramarital Sex; Denies Raping Activist Chai Ling," *South China Morning Post*, March 3, 2015.
35. IanYoung, "Tiananmen Dissident Quits Church over Extramarital Sex; Denies Raping Activist Chai Ling," *South China Morning Post*, March 3, 2015. Reposted in "Q&A about the Yuan Zhiming Incident," *Christian Life Quarterly*, no. 80 (December 2008). www.cclifefl.org/View/Article/5257.
36. "Report on Chai and Yuan, Signed and Released by 18 Chinese-American Pastors," *Chinese Christian Life Fellowship*, February 23, 2015. www.cclifefl.org/View/Article/3900.

37. Timothy C. Morgan, "Prominent Chinese Christian Convert Accuses Another of Rape," *Christianity Today*, February 27, 2015; "Independent Investigation Reveals Sexual Abuse of a 23-Year-Old Female College Student by Yuan Zhiming," *Christian Times*, July 21, 2016; Timothy C. Morgan, "Chinese Dissident-Evangelist Accused of Sexual Misconduct," *Religion News*, July 12, 2016; Timothy C. Morgan, "Allegations of Sexual Misconduct by Famous Chinese Evangelist Span 24 Years," *Christianity Today*, July 15, 2016.
38. "Chai-Yuan Report Is Released. Yuan Resigned but Denied All Allegations," *Christian Times*, March 3, 2015.
39. "What Crimes Did Lily Hsu Commit?" *Shi Dai Zhi Shi*, July 8, 2019. http://nlsdzs.net/post/401.html.
40. "Yao Chen Interview: Meet China's Answer to Angelina Jolie," *The Telegraph*, August 24, 2014.
41. James Beech, "Actress Marries at St Peter's," *Otago Daily Times*, November 23, 2012.
42. Daniel Eagan, "Chinese Actress Yao Chen on Motherhood and Her Career: 'I Couldn't Get the Same Roles Any More,'" *South China Morning Post*, May 19, 2019.
43. Ibid.
44. Jane Onyanga-Omara, "Chinese Actress Yao Chen Uses Huge Weibo Following to Help Refugees," *USA Today*, January 21, 2016.
45. Zhang Yu, "Actress Yuan Li Turns to Activism after Successful Screen Career," *Global Times*, October 9, 2015.
46. Jennifer Butler, *Born Again: The Christian Right Globalized* (London: Pluto Press, 2006), 14; Lee Marsden, *For God's Sake: The Christian Right and US Foreign Policy* (London: Zed Books, 2008), 101; Li Ma, *Religious Entrepreneurism in China's Urban House Churches* (London: Routledge, 2019).

Bibliography

Adami, Rebecca. *Women and the Universal Declaration of Human Rights*, vol. 32. New York: Routledge, 2019.

Baosun, Zeng. *Confucian Feminist: Memoirs of Zeng Baosun, 1893–1978* (trans. and adapted by Thomas L. Kennedy). Philadelphia, PA: American Philosophical Society, 2002.

Bays, Daniel. *A New History of Chinese Christianity*. Hoboken, NJ: Wiley-Blackwell, 2012.

Beech, James. "Actress Marries at St Peter's," *Otago Daily Times*, November 23, 2012.

Burkiln, Erik. "The Greatest Need in the Chinese Church: The China Christian Council Confronts the Task of Theological Education." *ChinaSource* 5, no. 1 (Spring 2003): 8–9.

Butler, Jennifer. *Born Again: The Christian Right Globalized*. London: Pluto Press, 2006.

Cao, Shengjie. "Chinese Christian Women in Education and Development: Understanding the Compatibility of Faith and Action for Women in a Changing Society." *Church and Society* 86, no. 5 (May–June 1996): 76–81.

"Chai-Yuan Report Is Released. Yuan Resigned but Denied All Allegations." *Christian Times*, March 3, 2015.

Chen, Mao. "In and Out of Home: Bing Xin Recontextualized." In *Asian Literary Voices: From Marginalized to Mainstream*, edited by Philip F. Williams. Amsterdam: Amsterdam University Press, 2010, pp. 63–70.

Chen, Mengjia. "Two Hopes." In *Collected Works of Cheng Mengjia*. Beijing: Shang Wu Shu Ju, 2006, pp. 241–2.
Deng, Peng. *Private Education in Modern China*. Westport, CT: Praeger, 1997.
Drucker, Alison R. "The Role of the YWCA in the Development of the Chinese Women's Movement, 1890–1927." *Social Service Review* 53, no. 3 (September 1979): 421–40.
Du Mez, Kristin. *A New Gospel for Women: Katharine Bushnell and the Challenge of Christian Feminism*. New York: Oxford University Press, 2015.
Eagan, Daniel. "Chinese Actress Yao Chen on Motherhood and Her Career: 'I Couldn't Get the Same Roles Any More.'" *South China Morning Post*, May 19, 2019.
Han, Minghan. *The History of Chinese Sociology*. Tianjin: People's Press, 1987.
Hawn, C. Michael. "Landscapes and Soulscapes: How Place Shapes Christian Congregational Song." In *The Changing World Religion Map: Sacred Places, Identities, Practices and Politics*, edited by Stanley Brunn. Dordrecht: Springer, 2015, p. 2665.
Hunter, Jane. *The Gospel of Gentility: American Women Missionaries in Turn-of-the-Century China*. New Haven, CT: Yale University Press, 1984.
Johnson, Ian. "Jesus vs. Mao? An Interview with Yuan Zhiming." *New York Review of Books*, September 4, 2012.
Lu, Yifan. "Equal Discipleship: Exploring Chinese Feminist Theology." *Ecumenical Review*, April 22, 2019.
Ma, Li. *Christian Women and Modern China: Recovering a Women's History of Chinese Protestantism*. Lanham, MD: Lexington Books, 2021.
Ma, Li. *Religious Entrepreneurism in China's Urban House Churches*. London: Routledge, 2019.
Ma, Li, and Jin Li. "Divergent Paths of Protestantism and Asian Nationalism: A Comparison of Two Social Movements in Korea and China in 1919." *International Bulletin of Mission Research* (May 29, 2018): 316–25.
Ma, Li, and Jin Li. "The Tragic Irony of a Patriotic Mission: The Indigenous Leadership of Francis Wei and T. C. Chao, Radicalized Patriotism, and the Reversal of Protestant Missions in China." *Religions* 11, no. 4 (2020): 175–95.
Ma, Li, and Jin Li. "Why Did Chinese American Evangelicals Advocate Voting for Trump? Trauma, US-China Tensions and Christian Nationalism." Unpublished manuscript.
Marsden, Lee. *For God's Sake: The Christian Right and US Foreign Policy*. London: Zed Books, 2008.
Morgan, Timothy C. "Allegations of Sexual Misconduct by Famous Chinese Evangelist Span 24 Years." *Christianity Today*, July 15, 2016.
Morgan, Timothy C. "China Soul's Yuan Denies Rape Accusation, Resigns from Preaching." *Christianity Today*, March 9, 2015.
Morgan, Timothy C. "Chinese Dissident-Evangelist Accused of Sexual Misconduct." *Religion News*, July 12, 2016.
Morgan, Timothy C. "Prominent Chinese Christian Convert Accuses Another of Rape." *Christianity Today*, February 27, 2015; "Independent Investigation Reveals Sexual Abuse of a 23-Year-Old Female College Student by Yuan Zhiming." *Christian Times*, July 21, 2016.
Onyanga-Omara, Jane. "Chinese Actress Yao Chen Uses Huge Weibo Following to Help Refugees." *USA Today*, January 21, 2016.
Or, Eunice. "Interview with President of China Christian Council Rev. Cao Shengjie." *Gospel Herald*, May 1, 2006.

"Report on Chai and Yuan, Signed and Released by 18 Chinese-American Pastors." *Chinese Christian Life Fellowship*, February 23, 2015. www.cclifefl.org/View/Article/3900.

Schneider, Helen M. "Mobilising Women: The Women's Advisory Council, Resistance and Reconstruction during China's War with Japan." *European Journal of East Asian Studies* 11, no. 2 (2012): 217.

Spence, Jonathan D. *The Search for Modern China*. New York: W. W. Norton, 1991.

Wang, Ruth. "You Are the Light of the World, Song for Preachers, Created by China's Songbird, Lv Xiao Min." *China Christian Daily*, December 15, 2015.

"What Crimes Did Lily Hsu Commit?" *Shi Dai Zhi Shi*, July 8, 2019. http://nlsdzs.net/post/401.html.

"Yao Chen Interview: Meet China's Answer to Angelina Jolie." *The Telegraph*, August 24, 2014.

Young, Ian. "Tiananmen Dissident Quits Church over Extramarital Sex; Denies Raping Activist Chai Ling." *South China Morning Post*, March 3, 2015. Reposted in "Q&A about the Yuan Zhiming Incident." *Christian Life Quarterly*, no. 80 (December 2008).

YWCA of China. *Introduction to the Young Women's Christian Association of China, 1933–1947*. Shanghai: The National Committee of the YWCA of China, n.d.

Zhang, Yu. "Actress Yuan Li Turns to Activism after Successful Screen Career." *Global Times*, October 9, 2015.

11

A Dream Deferred? The Lingering Effects of White Supremacy on Christian Young Adults in South Africa Today

Nadine Bowers Du Toit

Introduction

Former South African president Thabo Mbeki once paraphrased the poet Langston Hughes to refer to the crisis that was building in terms of the slow pace of change in South Africa: "What happens to a dream deferred? It explodes." Almost three decades after the advent of democracy, this quote remains as relevant as ever with reference to the ways in which racism continues to linger, and the dream of the so-called rainbow nation has become a nightmare. Young adults who were born either shortly before the advent of democracy or shortly thereafter continue to be affected by the ways in which race and class, largely still against the legacy of colonialism and apartheid, continue to intersect and operate. White supremacy is not a word often used in the South African context, but it is indeed what undergirds the history and much of the present, in that there remains a belief in South African society that "whiteness is a position of status—invisible and subliminal" and which as "a structural power" continues to privilege white people.[1] Resane further notes that it continues to pervade South African society and that "there is resistance to abandoning it and little or no resilience to fight it, both politically and ecclesiastically." During a recent empirical study of Christian young adults in the town of Stellenbosch, conducted under the auspices of the Nagel Center for World Christianity, the intersection between racism and inequality—both fruits of white supremacy—appears to linger in the lived experiences of Christian young adults.[2] As a theological educator, it has also been alarming to me in recent years to witness a rise in the type of fundamentalism by white students rear its ugly head, which rejects issues of race and class as real or relevant to theological reflection. This chapter seeks to explore these intersections, the manner in which theology and white supremacy have and continue to collude and the possible ways that young adults—in their own words—can begin to engage hopefully with the "principalities and powers."

White Supremacy and the Church in South Africa: Roots and Fruits

South Africa has a prolonged history of white supremacy, beginning with colonialism and reinforced by apartheid, but seemingly firmly rooted despite the dawn of what has been hailed as a nonracial democracy post-1994. While the history of South Africa did not begin with the arrival of the colonists, it remains true that the history of the South African church began with the Dutch (1652), followed by the French Huguenots (1668) and later the early German and British settlers.[3] It is also important to note that "the story of racial segregation and discrimination was part and parcel of the story of Christianity in South Africa" and that this understanding is central to any discussion on white supremacy in the church in South Africa today.[4] De Gruchy further outlines the manner in which not only was the growth of the Dutch Reformed Church (DRC) confined largely to white settlers, but that early mission work among the Indigenous population was curtailed due to the manner in which "the gospel of universal grace proclaimed to the Indigenous peoples collided with the Calvinist orthodoxy of the Dutch church."[5] De Gruchy continues that during the period of missionary zeal, white settlers were "largely unconvinced about the need for and desirability of such missionary endeavor," primarily due to the fact that not only did the missionaries evangelize Indigenous peoples, "they also took their side in the struggle for justice, rights and land."[6] While the missionary endeavor must also be read against the context of deep-seated beliefs in the supremacy of the white race and the complicity and nuanced relationships with colonial powers at the time, De Gruchy states that "it is true to say that the church's struggle against racism and injustice in South Africa only really begins with their witness in the nineteenth century."[7] Settler or mission churches, while in their initial establishment seldom formed separate denominations of synods, remained "in fact divided along racial lines."[8] It is perhaps equally important to note that while in 1829 the DRC Synod had insisted that the Lord's Supper should be administered to all baptized members, the reversal of this decision—resulting from the request of frontier congregations for "separate facilities and services for black converts"—would become the bedrock of racial segregation within the Dutch sister churches and would later form the religious roots of the ideology of separate development and the political policy of apartheid.[9] This double legacy of the church, both as complicit with colonial state power and control and as resistant to it, would continue well into the apartheid era and beyond.

While racial segregation and discrimination was practiced and codified into law during the colonial period, the advent of "formal" apartheid in 1948 saw the entrenching and expansion of a complete project to enforce total racial segregation and degradation in terms of segregated residential and business areas, public facilities, education, voting, and even social contact through over a hundred laws.[10] The efficacy of this project was firmly ungirded by what came to be known as a "theology of apartheid," which was promoted by the DRC and its sister churches. While the development of this theology certainly built on its white supremacist colonial roots and practices, it was undergirded by so-called scriptural proofs that maintained that the ideology and practice of apartheid (and therefore what we know as white supremacy today) were supported by scripture.[11]

The 1950s and 1960s saw religious organizations and churches begin to become more active in the anti-apartheid struggle, with the advent of organizations such as the Christian Institute and mobilization through ecumenical bodies such as the South African Council of Churches (SACC). Smit[12] notes that it was the leaders of the largely English-speaking mainline churches that were most outspoken in their opposition to apartheid, opposition which began during the first decade of apartheid rule. The 1970s heralded a new era in church resistance with the rise of Black Theology. Prominent anti-apartheid church leaders, such as Allan Boesak, incisively cut to the heart of racism and white supremacy in noting not only that "racism is an ideology which justifies white supremacy" but also that it is a sin, which "has defiled the body of Christ ... Christians and the Church have provided the moral and theological justification for racism and human degradation."[13] In Black Theology, many young Black Christians of that era found theological language for their opposition to the white supremacy embedded in church and society. In Black Theology, South African Black Theologians sought to dissect the "dehumanizing power of apartheid" as a structural sin and liberate Christianity from the whiteness of its racial bondage, calling on Black people to claim their freedom through Christ's liberating power.[14]

The 1980s saw the development of documents such as the Kairos Document (1985), which emerged at the height of the State of Emergency in South Africa as the anti-apartheid struggle continued and which challenged the church both in terms of its colonial inheritance and for churches to move from protest alone to action.[15] This document, furthermore, decried the silence of many white churches—liberal as they were—as being complicit in the sin of racism and the heresy of apartheid. In 1986 the DRC retracted its biblical justification for apartheid, and in 1990 the members of the DRC offered a full confession of guilt at the Rustenburg consultation, which is identified as the most representative gathering of South African churches until that time.[16]

The church's resistance and acquiescence to apartheid during this era, I would argue, should not always be read against the backdrop of the institutional response. It can be seen in the mass mobilization of Black youth, many of whom regarded themselves as committed Christians. It can also be seen in the military conscription and indoctrination of white youth as representatives of a violent and racist state, many of whom regarded themselves as committed Christians. The youth of the 1970s and 1980s are the parents and grandparents of today's youth, and this leads one to wonder how deep the roots of white supremacy go and how the outcomes we see now in terms of the growing resistance by the youth to the slow pace of transformation on the one hand and a rise in "color blindness" discourses and even neo-Nazi sentiments in white young adults, on the other hand, is rooted in the unexplored nature of white supremacy in South African society.[17]

With the advent of democracy, Archbishop Desmond Tutu declared the dawn of the "rainbow nation"—the breaking forth of a new era wherein all would be equal and free, and the churches and ecumenical bodies such as the SACC settled into a discourse of "reconstruction" and "reconciliation," which sought to promote social cohesion in step with a new political dispensation. It is also important to note that many theologians abandoned the notion of liberation and Black Theology in favor of these terms, believing that the need for resistance was over and that the church should move toward an era of assistance and support of the state.[18] The nightmare of apartheid and its white supremacist beliefs had been replaced by the dream of the rainbow nation, and church leaders and laity alike bought into this project with zeal. It has become increasingly clear, however, that the indirect effects of the previous dispensations coupled with widespread government corruption have left many South Africans of all races feeling as if the dream of a nonracial democracy has been deferred. It should also be noted, however, that the way in which corruption is framed within South Africa has racial undertones; and as racial polarization has increased worldwide, it has also seen an increase in South Africa. Lobby groups have emerged promoting the fake news of "white genocide" in South Africa, stirring right-wing sentiment, and the move by liberal centrist political parties to the right is worrying.[19] While churches certainly partook in anticorruption protests such as the #Zumamustfall protests against the previous president, work regarding the rising issue of racial polarization is taking place in pockets. Gatherings such as the Justice Conference held in 2017 and 2018[20] and organized largely by left-leaning evangelicals and the more recent "white work" attempts by the DRC[21] are two notable attempts to encourage dialogue around racial justice within the Christian faith community. It is also interesting to note that both these initiatives targeted young adults in their engagement.

Young Adults, Race, Class, and Its Effects in South Africa Today

Children born post-1994—the young adults of today—were termed "Born Free," having been born after the dawn of so-called democracy. Mandela's and Tutu's promotion of what has come to be called "rainbowism" by the youth, in particular, has left a bitter taste in the mouths of many—and more especially young Black South Africans—who feel that these leaders traded restitutive justice for cheap notions of reconciliation, which did not fully deal with the socioeconomic legacy of apartheid.[22] This legacy remains firmly aligned to the racist past and results in the Black youth of today facing many of the same realities faced by their parents and grandparents.[23]

While the laws enforcing segregation no longer exist, their effects remain inscribed on the substandard education of many Black children, the deplorable living conditions of many Black people, high unemployment rates that remain aligned to race, and the continued lack of upward mobility and social capital with regard to Black youth. Young people are currently the largest cohort of new job-seekers, and in a country where unemployment rates are high and remain aligned to racial inequalities of the past, this is a pressing concern.[24] A recent study on young adults in the town of Stellenbosch confirms this at grassroots and highlights the ways in which race-based inequality remains a lived reality for these young people. Ongoing spatial inequalities, still aligned to the old racial designations, mean that these young people noted that their access to basic services was aligned to where they resided, which in turn was still aligned to old apartheid racialized inequalities.[25] These factors, replicated throughout South Africa, have resulted in many youth contesting the notion of "Born Free" as the freedoms enshrined in the Bill of Rights do not appear to have materialized for many of the so-called Born-Frees.

In recent years, there has been a rise in youth activism, with youth in particular participating in various protests with regard to injustice—more often injustices deeply tied to our apartheid and colonial past. From a protest launched at a private girls' school still steeped in colonial traditions by one of its pupils in defense of her right to wear her natural hair in an afro, to the Shack Dwellers Movement, many of these protests have intersected with issues of lingering race-based inequality. Perhaps the most prominent protests by young adults have been the #FeesMustFall (#FMF) protests that spread across South African university campuses between 2015 and 2017. These protests called for an end to institutional racism and for a more decolonized and free education system that would grant access to all students seeking tertiary education. Du Toit et al.[26] note the following:

> Unfortunately, these protests also remind us that race still divides its citizens and that class consciousness has still not dominated race consciousness, making it problematic to forge solidarity between black and white youth.

The latter is both unsurprising and troubling, if one considers that in South Africa the notion of white supremacy has been linked to the socioeconomic and political oppression of the Black populace since colonialism. In the Stellenbosch study, race emerged as a major factor that was linked to lived experiences of inequality. While the study only asked one question that tied race to inequality, it emerged as a key feature. The empirical report found that "while outright racism was not on display, covert racism was on the rise and that this was best identified in the way young adults of color were treated as different or as less than white people or stereotyped and racially profiled."[27] Young adults of color listed being racially profiled as stealing while shopping in the central (and still largely white) part of town, or being treated with suspicion when jogging in areas that were formerly designated as "white" during the apartheid era. Durrheim et al. note that despite the enshrining of nonracism in our constitution and legislation prohibiting it, explicit and implicit racism—more especially in the form of racial stereotyping—remains.[28]

Other respondents talked about the fact that even within the university context, while "allowed to participate, you still feel excluded somehow, because there's been an (white) established group."[29] Embrick and Moore[30] draw on Yi-Fu Tan in noting that in "racialized social systems, both space and place are racialized such that the security and freedom emanating from social space and place flow disproportionately to Whites." White students were perceived as receiving more privileges from lecturers at the university, and these microaggressions were tied to what they viewed as an abuse of power, which was in turn tied to white privilege.

> White privilege for me is power, and abuse of power. There's no equality when you talk of white privilege, their whiteness scares us, us colored people, and as people

of color, and their whiteness really threatens us because they have the opportunity and we don't."

In what could be seen as positive and the basis for building solidarity and discourse in terms of racism and white supremacy between white and Black young adults, many of the white young adults of this study also, in part, recognized their privileges.

There has nevertheless been a rise in racial polarization and overt right-wing sentiment, especially at my own university, the University of Stellenbosch, a historically "whites-only" tertiary institution.[31] In its most extreme form, it is reflected in "Nazi-based posters" (direct copies of Hitler Youth posters), which invited students to a meeting of the "New Right" and to "Fight for Stellenbosch."[32] In its less overt form, the findings of the study revealed that some white young adults (albeit a minority) openly stated that they felt the current political and economic system rejects them and that they no longer possess privilege in terms of opportunities.[33] The latter, of course, while a strongly held perception, is rooted in the notion of white supremacy and the belief that white people should be at the apex of any privilege hierarchy. It is also patently untrue if one considers that only 1 percent of white adults are unemployed compared to over 60 percent of Black adults. Resane[34] notes that "racism expressed through supremacist attitudes, can be very deeply hidden, and that it can show up in our personal practices at unexpected times." Such perceptions and the emergence of these supremacist attitudes were also to be found in my classroom, moreover articulated by largely white male evangelical students who appeared to tout concepts such as "reverse racism" and claim color blindness and who constantly ignored the lived realities of poverty as expressed by their peers of color. Montano[35] argues that in theological education, such claims must be challenged and be seen for what it is—as rooted in white fragility and the ongoing systemic effects of white supremacy.

The "Hopeful *Sizwe*"? Young Adults, Agency, and a Challenge to the Church

Allan Boesak's book *Pharaohs on Both Sides of the Blood-Red Waters*[36] partly seeks to challenge the reader to recognize the role the youth have played in recent protests and revolutions for a more just world. Its subtitle contains the words "the power of the Hopeful *Sizwe*"—a reference to the role of hope in assisting people to challenge unjust systems and structures (*Sizwe* is Zulu for nation). This hope, Boesak notes, is a "hope against hope" rooted largely in young people's "faith and willingness to engage in sacrificial struggles for the cause of justice."[37] A recent Barna study on young adults, which included a South African country profile, indicates that faith plays an important role for these young adults in addressing issues such as poverty and injustice. In terms of the statistics, 68 percent of them believed that the Christian church was either definitely (24 percent) or probably (42 percent) making a difference with regard to these issues.[38]

Lee's study on young adult #FeesMustFall activists,[39] however, appeared to indicate that many of these young people felt that the theologies of their churches did not equip them to engage sufficiently and robustly enough with regard to their participation in this social movement. Weber[40] notes, furthermore, the strong calls by our own students during these #FeesMustFall protests to decolonize theology and theological training. The findings of the Stellenbosch study confirmed the need for churches and theological institutions alike to reexplore a hermeneutics around injustice. It was clear that across color lines, the majority of respondents believed that "the love of neighbor and the fact that 'God is love' should motivate one to both act and cross borders;" however, it was also stated that Jesus said the poor would always be with us or never condemned slavery.[41] In these findings it emerged that the anti-apartheid struggle's use of the Pentateuch and prophets was not familiar or taught in relationship to issues of race and class, which indicates a real need for churches to engage with young adults and provide them with the theological tools to engage injustice and equality.

Perhaps this seeming lack of engagement with these texts is part of the reason why some of the young adults in the study felt unsure as to how to articulate their role in social change and their own agency. From my own experience teaching a course on the church's role in poverty and inequality in South Africa—which includes looking at the ways in which race intersects with these notions—I have found that one of my classes, which engages students in corporate reading of the prophetic and justice texts found in the prophets and Pentateuch against the context of poverty, inequality, and race in South Africa, helps to shift students' understanding of the role of the scriptures in their own understandings of their positioning as agents of change.

What is clear from the findings of the study is that all of them—Black and white—believed that one of the key means to engaging inequalities that were racially aligned was to engage in dialogue and that the church needed to take the forefront in this.[42] It appears, at last in this study, that protest was not the main language with regard to engaging these issues—it was dialogue. During the research feedback session of the study itself, this notion was reaffirmed. Our research team invited clergy and young adults from the town to attend, with surprising results. Although we were initially fearful of bringing this group together, due to the racialized findings of the study, we were pleasantly surprised. We indicated from the outset why we needed to talk about race and also reflected on the ways in which those in the study had linked poverty, inequality, and race. Not only were these groups keen to dialogue across race and class lines with regard to the difficult issues in their own community, they were keen to see how they could become agents of change. As a team, we left feeling both hopeful and motivated to create more space for dialogue on these issues.

The Synthesis Report ends with the following quote, which reminds us both of the different ways that hope may be understood by young adults of different races and the fact that the notion of hope continues to shape the hopeful action of these young adults across the boundaries of race and class:

> It must be said that despite the complex and painful nature of the topic we investigated, the notion of hope was ultimately on the horizon. White respondents were specifically asked what they hoped for and revealed that housing and employment for everyone was at the top of their list as this would reduce poverty and crime, however, they saw corruption and the current state of education as a

hindrance. Most Black respondents were hopeful that the country would change for the better and rooted their hopes for this change in their faith: "when you come and you are rooted in faith or a great foundation, you are able to persevere and remain hopeful that eventually things will work out just well for you." This hope, however, was rooted in reality, as revealed by the fact that a number of the participants indicated that their ability to speak about inequality gave them the spiritual and emotional resources to continue to work for change. A Colored respondent noted in the words of Dr Martin Luther King Jr. that he held on to a dream of a different South Africa and that there was a need to work towards this dream—despite the harmful effects of the past (and arguably the present).[43]

Conclusion

To return to the words of Langston Hughes—has the dream deferred exploded? My short answer would be "not yet." There remains a "hopeful *Sizwe*" in the form of young adults who continue to challenge the church and academy to engage the lingering legacy of white supremacy, but it should be noted that this cohort of young people still experience not only the lingering socioeconomic effects of white supremacy but also its effects on their daily interactions and spaces in South African society, albeit now in more covert forms. It is also clear that there is rising racial polarization, in lockstep with the rest of the globe, and that the gains made at the dawn of our democracy in terms of racial reconciliation are threatened by the fact that we have not dealt sufficiently with the social, psychological, political, and economic wounds of the past. Nevertheless, it appears that young adults still believe that the church and academy have a central role to play in addressing racism and inequality as the fruits of white supremacy. The dream of the rainbow nation may have been deferred, but I am personally encouraged as I train the new generation of church leaders and theologians that they will continue to challenge us to root our hope not in the optimist dreams of a rainbow nation but in the costly discipleship it will require to fashion an antiracist church.

Notes

1. Kelebogile Resane, "White Fragility, White Supremacy and White Normativity Make Theological Dialogue on Race Difficult," *In Die Skriflig* 55, no. 1 (2021). https://doi.org/10.4102/ids.v55i1.2661.
2. This study sought to investigate the following question: "In what ways do the lived realities of the continued and intensified realities of inequality in post-Apartheid South Africa impact on lived theologizing and political agency of the 'born free' generation of South Africans (18–35 years) with regard to issues of social justice, inequality and reconciliation?" It was undertaken in the town of Stellenbosch (often popularly referred to as the most unequal town in South Africa) among young adults from three church congregations situated in communities within the town and which still today remain aligned to race. Approximately twelve young adults per congregation were interviewed as part of the study. The interviews were coded via

Atlas.ti using thematic analysis. The primary data utilized in this chapter is drawn from the research report that synthesized all the findings.
3. John De Gruchy, *The Church Struggle in South Africa* (Grand Rapids, MI: Eerdmans, 1979), 1.
4. Dirk J. Smit, *Essays in Public Theology: Collected Essays 1* (Stellenbosch: Sun Media, 2007), 17.
5. De Gruchy, *The Church Struggle in South Africa*, 4.
6. Ibid., 13.
7. Cf. Smit, *Essays in Public Theology*, 17. During the nineteenth century, that racial tension and conflict increased with British occupation, which resulted in laws that limited Black land ownership and raised Black taxes, and which in turn forced Blacks to sell their labor cheaply to white landowners. Further discriminatory laws followed in the twentieth century, which not only limited the movement of Black people but also dispossessed them of their land, denied them the control of social practices, and introduced job reservations. Such measures served imperial Britain who sought to secure cheap labor after the discovery of diamonds and gold. Cf. Smit, *Essays in Public Theology*, 16.
8. De Gruchy, *The Church Struggle in South Africa*, 18.
9. Smit, *Essays in Public Theology*, 17.
10. Ibid., 18.
11. Ibid., 19.
12. Ibid., 21. Cf. De Gruchy, *The Church Struggle in South Africa*, 59.
13. Allan Boesak, "He Made Us All, but …," in John De Gruchy, ed., *Apartheid Is a Heresy* (Claremont, CA: David Philip, 1983), 4–6.
14. De Gruchy, *The Church Struggle in South Africa*, 162, 163.
15. Other important documents included the Confession of Belhar (1986) and the EWISA (Evangelical Witness in South Africa) (1986).
16. Smit, *Essays in Public Theology*, 22.
17. These posters were based on Nazi youth posters.
18. Nadine Bowers Du Toit, "The Elephant in the Room: The Need to Re-discover the Intersection between Poverty, Powerlessness and Power in 'Theology and Development' Discourse," *HTS Teologiese Studies/Theological Studies* 72, no. 4 (2016). https://doi.org/10.4102/hts.v72i4.3459.
19. Digital Editors, "South African Election Results," *The South African*, June 1, 2019. www.thesouthafrican.com/news/2019-south-africa-election-results-natio nal-provincial-all-votes. Cf. Sheldon Morais, "What the Numbers Tell Us about the General Elections," *News24*, May 12, 2019. www.news24.com/elections/news/2019-vs-2014-what-the-numbers-tell-us-about-the-general-elections-20190512.
20. See www.thejusticeconference.co.za.
21. These are workshops largely led by Dr. Wilhelm Verwoerd, a reconciliation practitioner, which attempt to equip younger clergy with a consciousness of issues such as white privilege and to take account of their own histories in confronting racism.
22. Christoffel Thesnaar, "Decolonization and Renewed Racism: A Challenge and Opportunity for Reconciliation," *HTS Teologiese Studies/Theological Studies* 73, no. 3 (2017). https://doi.org/10.4102/hts.v73i3.3838.
23. Nadine Bowers Du Toit and Grace Nkomo, "The Ongoing Challenge of Restorative Justice in South Africa: How and Why Wealthy Suburban Congregations Are

Responding to Poverty and Inequality," *HTS Teologiese Studies/Theological Studies* 70, no. 2 (2014): 1–8.
24. Anita Cloete, "Youth Unemployment in South Africa. A Theological Reflection through the Lens of Human Dignity," *Missionalia* 43, no. 3 (2015): 513–25.
25. Bowers Du Toit, Dion Forster Nadine, Shantelle Weber, and Elisabet Le Roux, "Born Free? Born Free for What? Exploring the Lived Experiences of Christian Young Adults in South Africa with Regards to Inequality and Social Justice," *International Bulletin of Mission Research* 46, no. 2 (2022). https://doi.org/10.1177%2F23969393211010747.
26. Ibid., 8.
27. Nadine Bowers Du Toit, Dion Forster, Shantelle Weber, and Elisabet Le Roux, *Born Free? An Investigation into the Lived Theologies and Social Agency of Young Christians in Stellenbosch*, Empirical Research Case Study of "Colored" Young Adults Report, 2019.
28. Kevin Durrheim, Xoliswa Mtose, and Lyndsay Brown, *Race Trouble: Race, Identity and Inequality in Post-Apartheid South Africa* (Scottsville: Kwa-Zulu Natal Press, 2011), 32.
29. Du Toit et al., *Born Free*, 5.
30. David Embrick and Wendy Leo Moore, "White Space(s) and the Reproduction of White Supremacy," *American Behavioral Sciences* 64, no. 4 (2020): 1938.
31. The university trained some of the foremost Apartheid leaders, and although it has come a long way in terms of transformation, there remains a clear need for transformation.
32. Okuhle Hlati, "Former Stellenbosch Student Loses 'Nazi-Based Posters' Appeal," *Cape Times*, February 8, 2021. www. iol.co.za/capetimes/news/former-stellenbosch-student-loses-nazi-based-posters-appeal-03f878fb-e251-4797-8306-423b74f85db4. While these students were expelled and the university took a clear stand against them, it indicates that there is a rise in right-wing sentiment on campus—this was confirmed by other less overt incidents in the residential spaces.
33. Du Toit et al., *Born Free*.
34. Resane, "White Fragility, White Supremacy and White Normativity," 3.
35. Steffano Montano, "Addressing White Supremacy on Campus: Anti-Racist Pedagogy and Theological Education," *Religious Education* 114, no. 3 (2019): 274–86. https://doi.org/10.1080/00344087.2019.1603952.
36. Allan Boesak, *Pharaohs on Both Sides of the Blood-Red Waters: Prophetic Critique on Empire* (Eugene, OR: Cascade, 2017).
37. Boesak, *Pharaohs on Both Sides*, xviii.
38. Barna Report, *The Connected Generation: How Christian Leaders around the World Can Strengthen Faith and Well-Being among 18–35-Year-Olds* (Barna Group, 2019).
39. Jennifer Chi Lee, "Hope Has Two Daughters: The Intersections of Faith and Activism for Christian Fallists in South Africa," Masters Dissertation, Eastern Mennonite University, 2018.
40. Shantelle Weber, "Decolonising Youth Ministry Models? Challenges and Opportunities in Africa," *HTS Teologiese Studies/Theological Studies* 73, no. 4 (2017): a4796. https://doi.org/ 10.4102/hts.v73i4.4796.
41. Du Toit et al., *Born Free*.
42. Ibid.
43. Ibid.

Bibliography

Barna Report. *The Connected Generation: How Christian Leaders Around the World Can Strengthen Faith and Well-Being among 18–35-Year-Olds*. Ventura, CA: Barna Group, 2019.
Boesak, Allan. "He Made Us All, but …." In *Apartheid Is a Heresy*, edited by John De Gruchy. Claremont, CA: David Philip, 1983, pp. 1–9.
Boesak, Allan. *Pharaohs on Both Sides of the Blood-Red Waters: Prophetic Critique on Empire*. Eugene, OR: Cascade, 2017.
Bowers Du Toit, Nadine. "The Elephant in the Room: The Need to Re-discover the Intersection between Poverty, Powerlessness and Power in 'Theology and Development' Discourse." *HTS Teologiese Studies/Theological Studies* 72, no. 4 (2016): 1–9. https://doi.org/10.4102/hts.v72i4.3459.
Bowers Du Toit, Nadine, Dion Forster, Shantelle Weber, and Elisabet Le Roux. "Born Free? Born Free for What? Exploring the Lived Experiences of Christian Young Adults in South Africa with Regards to Inequality and Social Justice." *International Bulletin of Mission Research* 46, no 2. (2022). https://doi.org/10.1177%2F23969393211010747.
Bowers Du Toit, Nadine, Dion Forster, Shantelle Weber, and Elisabet Le Roux. *Born Free? An Investigation into the Lived Theologies and Social Agency of Young Christians in Stellenbosch*. Empirical Research Case Study of "Colored" Young Adults Report, 2019.
Bowers Du Toit, Nadine, and Grace Nkomo. "The Ongoing Challenge of Restorative Justice in South Africa: How and Why Wealthy Suburban Congregations Are Responding to Poverty and Inequality." *HTS Teologiese Studies/Theological Studies* 70, no. 2 (2014): 1–8.
Cloete, Anita. "Youth Unemployment in South Africa. A Theological Reflection through the Lens of Human Dignity." *Missionalia* 43, no. 3 (2015): 513–25.
De Gruchy, John. *The Church Struggle in South Africa*. Grand Rapids, MI: Eerdmans, 1979.
Digital Editors. "South African Election Results." *The South African*, June 1, 2019. www.thesouthafrican.com/news/2019-south-africa-election-results-national-provincial-all-votes.
Durrheim, Kevin, Xoliswa Mtose, and Lyndsay Brown. *Race Trouble: Race, Identity and Inequality in Post-Apartheid South Africa*. Scottsville: Kwa-Zulu Natal Press, 2011.
Embrick, David, and Wendy Leo Moore. "White Space(s) and the Reproduction of White Supremacy." *American Behavioral Sciences* 64, no. 4 (2020): 1935–45. https://doi.org/10.1177%2F0002764220975053.
Hlati, Okuhle. "Former Stellenbosch Student Loses 'Nazi-Based Posters' Appeal." *Cape Times*, February 8, 2021. www. iol.co.za/capetimes/news/former-stellenbosch-student-loses-nazi-based-posters-appeal-03f878fb-e251-4797-8306-423b74f85db4.
"The Justice Conference South Africa." www.thejusticeconference.co.za (accessed June 15, 2021).
Lee, Jennifer Chee. "Hope Has Two Daughters: The Intersections of Faith and Activism for Christian Fallists in South Africa." Masters Dissertation, Eastern Mennonite University, 2018.
Montano, Steffano. "Addressing White Supremacy on Campus: Anti-Racist Pedagogy and Theological Education." *Religious Education* 114, no. 3 (2019): 274–86. https://doi.org/10.1080/00344087.2019.1603952.
Morais, Sheldon. "What the Numbers Tell Us about the General Elections." *News24*, May 12, 2019. www.news24.com/elections/news/2019-vs-2014-what-the-numbers-tell-us-about-the-general-elections-20190512.

Resane, Kelebogile. "White Fragility, White Supremacy and White Normativity Make Theological Dialogue on Race Difficult." *In Die Skriflig* 55, no. 1 (2021). https://doi.org/10.4102/ids.v55i1.2661.

Smit, Dirk J. *Essays in Public Theology: Collected Essays 1*. Stellenbosch: Sun Media, 2007.

Thesnaar, Christoffel. "Decolonization and Renewed Racism: A Challenge and Opportunity for Reconciliation." *HTS Teologise Studies/Theological Studies* 73, no. 3 (2017). https://doi.org/10.4102/hts.v73i3.3838.

Weber, Shantelle. "Decolonising Youth Ministry Models? Challenges and Opportunities in Africa," *HTS Teologiese Studies/Theological Studies* 73, no. 4 (2017): a4796. https://doi.org/ 10.4102/hts.v73i4.4796.

12

African Traditional Pediatric Hospitals in Northern Nigeria: Shapeshifting Identities and the Future of World Christianity

Matthew Michael

Introduction

Modern pediatric studies have registered significant strides in the diagnosis and treatment of sick children around the world.[1] In the developed world, there are now advanced pediatric facilities, technologically driven pediatric spaces, and specialized centers for the study of children's health.[2] In spite of these global developments, however, children in sub-Saharan Africa live under the degenerating scourges of preventable illnesses, unmitigated poverty, and unbearable suffering without adequate pediatric facilities.[3]

On the African continent, children bear the formidable impact of the "24% of the global burden of disease" of the world, and sub-Saharan Africa, in particular, has only a minimal 3 percent of the standard healthcare delivery of the entire world.[4] Consequently, the mortality of children in modern Africa is one of the highest in the world, with the record of a child dying every minute from preventable diseases.[5] Of course, pediatric units in most government and private hospitals in Africa have little resources and manpower to cater to the overwhelming numbers of sick children who need health service.[6] The population of children has generally exploded with health facilities becoming unable to cope with the influx of sick children seeking medical attention. These challenges, exacerbated by poor governance, ill-thought health policies, and corruption, have rendered the pediatric units of most biomedical establishments inadequate to cater to the growing needs of children's health in sub-Saharan Africa. In recent times, the apparent needs of pediatric healthcare in modern Africa have led to the resurgence and patronage of traditional pediatric clinics in many parts of the continent.[7]

Historically, traditional pediatric clinics are built around shrines that are domiciled in families and administered by designated healers appointed through the consultation of ancestral oracles. While traditional pediatric hospitals have clearly existed in the past as important therapeutic sites, their emergence in contemporary times comes largely from the failure of the biomedical establishment and the growing recognition of the efficacies of traditional medicine in the pursuit of healing and wellness.[8] In Nigeria, the patronage of traditional pediatric hospitals has generally increased with culturally sensitive diagnoses and general treatments for sick children, thereby causing rivalry and competition between the pediatric units of biomedical establishments and traditional pediatric clinics in their herbal therapies.[9] Positioned in an extremely volatile terrain, traditional pediatric hospitals in northern Nigeria have navigated around the violent activities of Boko Haram, homegrown terrorist groups, and other intolerant Islamic groups to provide a therapeutic space in the quest for health and wellness of children in northern Nigeria. Apart from these conflicts, northern Nigeria is also saddled with enormous challenges of poverty—particularly seen in the recent description of this region as the poverty capital of the entire world.

Considering these preceding dynamics, the activities of traditional pediatric healers in the region provide therapeutic platforms against the constraining scourges of sickness, poverty, and death among children of this region.[10] Unfortunately, the significant presence of these specialized African healing spaces with traditional pediatric functions has generally remained unengaged in modern pediatric studies. While modern studies in biomedical research have investigated the challenges of global pediatric hospitals and the contextual challenges of pediatric units of biomedical hospitals in Africa, it has largely failed to study the importance of traditional African pediatric clinics and their significant role in the construction of wellness and well-being among African children. Considering this important trajectory, this chapter underscores the emerging operations of African traditional pediatric spaces and their attending importance for the future of World Christianity.

At the onset, I must underscore the connection of World Christianity to the immediate discourses on traditional African pediatric institutions on three important fronts.[11] First, the health and wellness of children are important concerns of World Christianity since the spiritual and physical growth of Christianity in the world are clearly conditioned on a healthy and vibrant child population.[12] Second, the network of cultural interaction and social negotiation at African pediatric sites has important bearings on World Christianity in its modern quest to understand the social and spiritual encounters between Christianity and pre-Christian religions as well as traditional institutions.[13] Lastly, the context of pediatric sites brings to the fore the intricate conversation between World Christianity and African spirituality, particularly at the crucial stage of children's health and care, which is critical to the social variegated mappings of Christianity within the template of its local environment.[14] On these different levels, African traditional pediatric hospitals have defining importance for World Christianity in forging new interests and conversations. Consequently, this chapter underscores the global significance of African pediatric hospitals in modern Africa in the construct of a fresh agenda for World Christianity.[15]

African Traditional Pediatric Clinics, Therapeutic Transversities, and Shapeshifting Identities

The transversities[16] of African traditional pediatric clinics placed them in direct conversation with African families whose sick babies threaten the lineage and social standing of parents because of the common perception of children as the embodiment of the hopes of parents and the entire community.[17] African traditional pediatric clinics present therapeutic sites that extend from the body of the sick child to the symbolic body of the entire family. In seeking healing and cure for the sick child, the African family seeks healing and cure for themselves because in the symbolic body of the child lies the communal embodiment of hope, physical existence, social relevance, and biological continuity of the entire family and the community.[18] This high premium placed on children comes from the important belief that the continuous existence of a family is closely tied to the birth, growth, and survival of children. African families without children are culturally outlawed and directly alienated from the entirety of the family and clan—because the future of the family is threatened by the absence of children. Consequently, barren women and impotent men in traditional African society are often stigmatized and totally alienated from the community because they are considered as terminal points in the competitive race of family survival. This high value placed on children has naturally placed additional value on the traditional pediatric sites since they provided rejuvenation and restoration of family lines and lineages through the treatment of bodily ailments of sick children.[19]

However, the importance of traditional pediatric hospitals in the transversities of social conversation in northern Nigeria transcends the mere discourses on healing and wellness and extends to the symbolic significance of the presence and dominance of these traditional institutions. Through traditional pediatric sites, African children are symbolically inducted back to the mothering care of traditional African religions. This mothering care of traditional African pediatric sites is clearly seen in the homecoming of sick children from both Christian and Muslim parents who seek the diagnosis and treatment of illness of their children at these traditional healing spaces.[20] The motherhood of traditional institutions suggests the strategic importance of women in the sustenance, care, and nursing of children in traditional African societies.[21] While there are men heading traditional pediatric clinics, the majority of the ones in northern Nigeria are led by mothers. They are popularly known as "mama yara," the Hausa phrase, meaning the "mother of children." From the study of twelve traditional pediatric hospitals, there are four evolving trends in the cultural operations and therapies of traditional pediatrics in northern Nigeria.[22]

First, most of these traditional pediatric sites in northern Nigeria have their origins in traditional religions. However, they have now carved a distinct identity for themselves that are no longer tied to the rituals and sacrifices associated with these traditional religions. For example, an herbal pediatric healer said, "I don't divine, I only give herbs."[23] Similarly, a popular *Mama Yaran* traditional pediatric healer in Kakuri in Kaduna also said, "I only use herbs for the treatments of these sick children. When mothers bring their sick children to me, I first diagnose the nature of the ailments, and then give appropriate herbs for cure."[24] The transitions of these traditional pediatric sites from shrines to traditional herbal clinics have defining importance in the modern expressions of African traditional religions within the bourgeoning presence of Christianity and Islam in northern Nigeria. Consequently, there is a gradual metamorphosis of the cultural identity of these traditional pediatric shrines from their intricate mystical backgrounds in traditional African religions to herbal pediatric centers.[25]

The evolution of pediatric sites suggests the cultural sensitivity of traditional African religions, particularly in its innate creativity to meet the existential needs for wellness within the changing religious dynamics and spiritual demographics of northern Nigeria.[26] While there are still shrines dedicated to the pediatric needs of children in northern Nigeria, the herbal ones exercise dominant influence and popularity.[27]

Secondly, traditional pediatric hospitals in northern Nigeria have become important sites for interreligious encounters. Both Christians and Muslims have continually patronized these traditional healing spaces in spite of the contentious relationship between Christians and Muslims in northern Nigeria.[28] Islamic terrorist groups had often waged wars against Christians and traditional institutions in the region. The deaths and massacres from these attacks have resulted in deepening the gulf among the already divided ethnic communities in northern Nigeria, placing a bulk of them into ethnic enclaves of Christian and Muslim communities. The exclusive geographies and border negotiations from these conflicts have created a rigged atmosphere of mutual suspicion, distrust, and animosity. However, in the traditional pediatric space, both Christians and Muslims engage themselves in subtle ecumenical discourse at the grassroots, which challenge the social stereotypes and conflicts among the adherents of Christians and Muslims in northern Nigeria. Interestingly, most traditional pediatric hospitals have in the "mothering spaces" of their healing spaces nurtured and cared for the children of both Christians and Muslims brought under their pediatric therapies.[29]

In addition, traditional pediatric hospitals in northern Nigeria employ Indigenous pharmacopeia. The traditional pharmacopeia uses local herbs, ingredients, resources, and therapies. This pharmacopeia has generally developed into traditional chemist and medicine stores that keep these herbal remedies in dry, fresh, or powder forms for the use of their sick clients. There are now assigned herbal spaces in most open markets in northern Nigeria where these traditional pediatric stands can showcase their pharmacopeia.

Lastly, traditional pediatric specialists in northern Nigeria have strategic internships and apprenticeships that intentionally train new generations of traditional healers in the arts of traditional healing and wellness. This important trend provides social longevity to the practices of pediatric medicine since new specialists are trained in herbs, traditional therapies, and cultural diagnoses that continually impose the cultural significance of these healing sites on the sacred demography of northern Nigeria. Seen from the preceding perspectives, traditional pediatric hospitals strategically empower African children with traditional and cultural resources at the critical period of childhood, thereby presenting them and their parents with an alternative worldview. Consequently, the appropriations of these pediatric healing spaces by Christians and Muslims underscore a therapeutic topography that welcomes, cares, and heals different sick persons across the exclusive borders and hostile rhetoric of faith traditions in northern Nigeria.[30]

Defining Significance of African Traditional Pediatric Clinics and the Future of World Christianity

There are four important deductions from these different developments in northern Nigeria for contemporary discourses on World Christianity, particularly in the creative encounter between Christianity and Indigenous pediatric institutions.[31] First, the strategic ecumenical space in the local operations of traditional pediatric clinics opens up new frontiers of interfaith discourses at the grassroots that have a potential to nurture and shape new relationships among Christians and Muslims.[32] In northern Nigeria, with its long history of religious violence, the interaction and joint appropriation of traditional healing spaces by both Christians and Muslims open up new opportunities for ecumenical engagements far from the problematic rhetoric of exclusivity as preserved in their mainstream orthodoxy. For example, Mama Sanei Afuwai said:

> Every ethnic group is welcomed, [we don't discriminate]. If sickness catches a child, every ethnic group that comes [to us]—will be given medicine. We don't discriminate whether a Muslim or a person from a different ethnic group ... the reason why we give medicine to everyone is that a child does not belong to a single person. If a disease is eating up a child, it is mandatory for us to give the child medicine for healing [without any consideration of the parents' tribe or religion].[33]

The offer of therapeutic services across the delicate religious borders has deep significance in the cultural and religious mapping of northern Nigeria. Mary Musa, a traditional pediatric healer in Goni Gora, whose father was killed in an earlier Christian and Muslim conflict in Rigassa, still dispensed herbal medicine to sick Muslim children. She said, "Muslim mothers bring their sick children to me from Rigassa, Tudun Wada, and Zaria ... I don't discriminate whether they are Hausas or Muslims, I just treat their sick children."[34]

The welcoming atmosphere of pediatric healing shrines promotes tolerance and respect in the collective quest for wellness among different faith traditions. This interesting conversation at African pediatric hospitals could enrich the discourses of World Christianity in its task of engaging the local religions and cultures that could add value to the contemporary discourses of Christianity.

Second, the evolving conversation among mothers and their sick children at pediatric hospitals has intergenerational benefits because it creates a narrative of interfaith dependence, collaboration, and appropriation of therapeutic resources across different faith traditions. While the children may not have a recollection of these appropriations of therapeutic resources from these traditional pediatric clinics, the stories of the impacts and influence of these traditional institutions will linger with them and their families. In my conversation with a *Mama Yara* from Kakuri, Kaduna, a number of mothers have testified how her pediatric therapies have benefited their children over the span of twenty years. One mother at this pediatric clinic said, "18 years ago, when my daughter was sick, I brought her to Mama here. She gave her medicine, and cured her. Our daughter is now in the University. This is the reason why I brought another of my children again today."[35] Several other mothers recalled the continuous pediatric help they have been receiving from Mama over the periods of five, ten, and fifteen years. These cherished stories of therapeutic assistance by traditional pediatric hospitals have an important place in the family stories. Significantly, the cultural reservoirs of therapeutic memories provided by these pediatric shrines continually impacted the social histories, spiritual encounters, and diverse negotiations of health and wellness in the lives of the families, particularly in the lives of children who have experienced healing. This childhood encounter has become part of their individual stories of therapeutic encounters with African traditional medicine.[36]

Situating this present discourse in the arena of memory-generating experience, African pediatric healers have moved beyond the mere creation of memories for these adherents of Christianity and Islam to the total construction of healing and wellness among the clients of African pediatric clinics, particularly in their subtle polemic against the exclusive rhetoric and spiritual borders imposed on the clients of these mainstream religions. Consequently, the exclusive rhetoric of their religious beliefs is often jettisoned and a new worldview is accepted that allows the creative appropriations of the therapeutic resources of African healing spaces. The induction of parents and children into the cultural universe of African pediatric spaces with evolving new memories for families are important cultural bridges for cross-religious encounters. For example, the mother of a sick child said:

> When I was a little girl, my mother told me that I was seriously ill and that they went everywhere looking for help for me, but mother was advised to see one mama—a healer and she gave my mother medicine, and I was healed. So when my own son became sick, I also decided to go for *Maman Yara* [pediatric healers] for help. This is the reason for my being here.[37]

There is an intergenerational significance of these stories that have stretched for decades among family members and been passed to children, thus placing the stories of these traditional pediatric sites in the collections of family stories. The critical importance of these pediatric encounters to family survival often underscores the importance of these shared stories among family members across generations. Describing the encounter of her family with a pediatric healer, Afuwai, a healer herself, said:

> We got this medicine from my grandmother, who before then was giving birth to children, but they were dying. She was told to go to Manchok to collect medicine. She now went to Manchok with her husband; and they gave them medicine ... they now said they should be given roots [of the healing plants] so that they also will help people at home with similar challenges [in Kagoro]. They took a goat there, and they joined their hands with the roots of the medicinal plant. From then onward they began also giving the medicine. It was from my grandmother,

and since she is no more, we her grandchildren began to give the same medicine ... Yes, we inherited her.[38]

The therapeutic impact of these stories and the webs of relationships here have significance for World Christianity, particularly since Christianity seeks to engage and converse with the intrigues, polemics, and agenda of pluralistic environments. The multilayer character of these different conversations with African Christian and Muslim families, and the repositioning of the contemporary African sacred geography in services of African healing shrines, offers creative negotiations between the exclusive orthodoxy of mainstream Christian and Muslim beliefs and their subversions by their adherents. To counteract this trend, Christians and Muslims have also developed traditional herbal platforms in imitations of these traditional hospitals in order to help their members seek healing and wellness within the exclusive borders of their Christian and Muslim orthodoxy. In spite of these Christian and Muslim herbal healers, patronage of traditional pediatric hospitals has continually soared because many clients, regarding pediatric needs, give priority to traditional hospitals rather than patronizing the exclusive operations and imitations of these traditional pediatric services by Christian and Muslim healers.

Lastly, the family memories and stories—discussed earlier—have fundamental significance in practical and pragmatic dimensions in northern Nigeria. In regard to the violent stage of northern Nigeria with entrenched radicalization of Islam and the growing fears of Christianity in the region, the healing memories and therapeutic encounters offered by African pediatric hospitals present a counterforce. It provides an oasis of tolerance in the desert of hate, mutual suspicion, and attacks in the contemporary war of dominance between Christianity and Islam. The sharing of traditional resources at African pediatric hospitals and the critical role of therapeutic memories, for both Muslims and Christians in the region, undermine the general rhetoric of killing, massacre, and kidnapping instigated by the radical expressions of Islam in the region.[39]

The future of Christianity in this region, as well as the violent context, will depend on its creative appropriation of Indigenous therapeutic and nontherapeutic traditions in waging a counterwar against the existing cultures of violence and hate.[40] Through these different appropriations of cultural resources of pre-Christian religions, World Christianity could stage a counterrevolution against structures of hate, radicalism, and insurgency via the instrumentality of conversations between Christianity and dominant cultures of violence in the therapeutic spaces of other faith traditions.

Conclusion

Traditional pediatric hospitals have continually provided strategic services for children across different religious borders, ethnic groups, and social classes of families in northern Nigeria.[41] Beyond their cultural and therapeutic importance, this chapter underscores the strategic challenge and importance of traditional pediatric hospitals for World Christianity, particularly in their quest for ecumenical and intergenerational operations that seek to create transversities (or a cross-border universe) where the children of both Muslims and Christians, rich and poor, and individuals of different ethnic groups and backgrounds have equal access to traditional therapeutic resources in their collective pursuits of healing and wellness.[42] The development underscores the shapeshifting identities of African traditional religions in their combative negotiations and creative engagement with a demographic space that is largely overtaken by Christian and Muslim presence. In this new environment, traditional pediatric healing spaces are freed from their original ritualistic observances to operate freely on a pure traditional herbal medication.

Consequently, this animated discourse in traditional pediatric medicine in northern Nigeria opens up a challenging frontier in the diverse mappings of World Christianity, especially in the active operations, changing identities, and resilience of Indigenous religions in their creative negotiations with modernity and local expressions of Christianity.[43]

Notes

1. See Tamara D. Simon, Sanjay Mahant, and Eyal Cohen, "Pediatric Hospital Medicine and Children with Medical Complexity: Past, Present, and Future," *Current Problems in Pediatric and Adolescent Health Care* 42, no. 5 (2012): 113–19.
2. See Bryan L. Burke and R. W. Ha, "Telemedicine: Pediatric Applications," *Pediatrics* 136, no. 1 (2015): 293–308.
3. See Larry G. P. Hadley, Bankole S. Rouma, and Yasser Saad-Eldin, "Challenge of Pediatric Oncology in Africa," *Seminars in Pediatric Surgery* 21, no. 1 (2012): 136–41.
4. See R. Albertyn, H. Rode, A. J. W. Millar, and J. Thomas, "Challenges Associated with Paediatric Pain Management in Sub-Saharan Africa," *International Journal of Surgery* 7 (2009): 91.
5. See World Health Organization, "A Child Dies Every Minute from Malaria in Africa." www.afro.who.int/news/child-dies-every-minute-malaria-africa (accessed April 9, 2021).
6. According to F. N. Bolu-Steve, A. A. Adegoke, and G. M. Kim-Ju, "Nearly half of all deaths prior to the age of five years globally occur in five nations: China, Democratic Republic of the Congo, India, Nigeria, and Pakistan, with almost a third of these deaths in India and Nigeria." See F. N. Bolu-Steve, A. A. Adegoke, and G. M. Kim-Ju, "Cultural Beliefs and Infant Mortality in Nigeria," *Hindawi: Educational Research International* (2020): 1–10.
7. For the patronage of traditional pediatric hospitals in sub-Saharan Africa, see Peter Bai James, Jon Wardle, Amie Steel, and Jon Adams, "Traditional, Complementary and Alternative Medicine in Sub-Saharan Africa: A Systematic View," *BMJ Global Health* 3, no. 5 (2018): 1–18. For the popularity of traditional pediatric hospitals in Nigeria, see T. E. Diamond, S. E. B. Ibeanusi, R. C. Echem, and C. C. Aniebo, "Extremity Amputations in Children from Complications of Traditional Bone Setters' Care Seen in a Tertiary Hospital in Port Harcourt, Nigeria," *Advances in Research* 14, no. 16 (2018): 1–7.
8. Concerning the history of pediatric hospitals in Nigeria, see Yakubu Alhassan, "Child Health Care in Nigeria: Historical Background," *Nigerian Journal of Paediatrics* 39, no. 1 (2012): 1–6.

9. See Lukman O. Abdur-Rahman, J. O. Taiwo, C. K. P. Ofoegbu, A. O. Adekanye, O. O. Ajide, C. Y. Ijagbemi, and B. A. Solagberu, "Community Survey of Childhood Injuries in North-Central Nigeria," *Annals of Pediatric Surgery* 11, no. 2 (2015): 136–9.
10. See Alhassan, "Child Health Care in Nigeria," 1–6.
11. Concerning the descriptions and perspectives in the studies of World Christianity, see Joel Cabrita and David Maxwell, "Introduction," in Joel Cabrita, David Maxwell, and Emma Wild-Wood, eds., *Relocating World Christianity* (Leiden: Brill, 2017), 1–44.
12. Women and children hold an important place in World Christianity. On the significance of women, see Dana L. Robert, "World Christianity as a Women's Movement," *International Bulletin of Mission Research* 30, no. 4 (2006): 160–88.
13. See Gavin D'Costa, *Christianity and World Religions: Disputed Questions in the Theology of Religions* (Malden, MA: Wiley-Blackwell, 2009), 1–54.
14. See J. Kwabena Asamoah-Gyadu, "Therapeutic Strategies in African Religions: Herbal Medicine, and Indigenous Christianity," *Studies in World Christianity* 20, no. 1 (2014): 70–90.
15. See Amuluche-Greg Nmamani, "The Flow of African Spirituality into World Christianity: A Case of Pneumatology and Migration," *Mission Studies* 32, no. 3 (2015): 331–52.
16. The word "transversities" has different connotations in many modern intellectual discourses. I use this term here, not in its strict scientific sense. By "transversities," I mean the social connections, religious interactions, and cultural movements of defining influences from pediatric sites to other spaces, thus collapsing erected religious borders and negotiating social boundaries. In short, transversities underscore the complex interactions between pediatric spaces and other spaces.
17. In spite of the defining presence of herbal healing spaces all across Africa, there is still a respectability accorded to biomedicine among African elites in the sphere of "biomedical absolutism," or what has been described as a kind of "biomedicocentrism." This belief often gives a "privileged role" or a near "infallible status" to formal medicine. See Robert Pool, "On the Creation and Dissolution of Ethnomedical Systems in the Medical Ethnography of Africa," *Africa: Journal of the International African Institute* 64, no. 1 (1994): 1–20.
18. See Anne Trine Kjørholt, "Childhood as Symbolic Space: Searching for Authentic Voices in Era of Globalisation," *Childhood's Geographies* 5 (2007): 29–42.
19. Silke J. Dyer, "The Value of Children in African Countries: Insights from Studies on Infertility," *Journal of Psychosomatic Obstetrics & Gynecology* 28, no. 2 (2007): 69–77.
20. See Erika Brady, "Introduction," in *Healing Logics: Culture and Medicine in Modern Health Belief Systems* (Logan: Utah State University Press, 2001), 5.
21. African mothers play an important role in the procurement of healing for their sick children. This factor likely contributed to the emergence of mothers in northern Nigeria in charge of the pediatric healing spaces. See Alexendra M. Towns, Sandra Mengue Egi, and Tinde van Andel, "Traditional Medicine and Childcare in Western Africa: Mother's Knowledge, Folk Illnesses, and Patterns of Healthcare Seeking Behavior," *Plos One* 9, no. 8 (2014). https://doi.org/10.1371/journal.pone.0105972.
22. The research adopts an ethnographic method and chiefly describes the deeper interaction between Indigenous pediatric hospitals and African Christianity. While collaborative data were taken from Nasarawa state, Plateau state, and Zamfara state of northern Nigeria, the research focused primarily on traditional pediatric hospitals in Kaduna state. We sampled six traditional pediatric hospitals in Kakuri, Goni Gora, Malali, Television, Sabon Tasha, and Maraban Rido within the metropolis of Kaduna

state and additional sites at Kasuwan Magani, Kafanchan, and Kagoro in the southern part of Kaduna state. The research began in April 2019 and extended through 2021. It was intermittently stopped in March 2020 due to the global outbreak of Covid-19 and concluded by the end of February 2021. The crisis nature of the terrain was a constant challenge to this study because the sampled areas in Kaduna are prone to incessant activities of terrorism, banditry, and kidnapping. During the period of the research, we had about twelve focus groups in the sampled population of traditional pediatric hospitals with each focus group comprising seven to twelve persons. We interviewed approximately 150 clients of traditional pediatric hospitals, including key informant interviews, which comprised the healers and their apprentices.

23. Mary Musa, a traditional pediatric healer in Goni Gora, Kaduna state, in an interview with her on November 30, 2020.
24. The quotation is from a popular pediatric healer, Mama Yara, in Kakuri, Kaduna state, in an interview with her in May 2019.
25. Ezekwesili-Ofili Josephine Ozima and Okaka Antoinette Nwamaka Chinwe, "Herbal Medicine in African Traditional Medicine," in *Herbal Medicine* (London: IntechOpen, 2019), 191–214.
26. See Matthew Michael, Nathan Chiroma, and Hauwa'u Evelyn Yusuf, "Health and Integrative Wellness: Mapping Wellness and Its Cultural Psychology in Contemporary Africa," *International Bulletin of Mission Research* 45, no. 2 (2020): 1–10.
27. Concerning the trends of traditional medicine in northern Nigeria, see A. A. Abdullahi, "Trends and Challenges of Traditional Medicine in Africa," *African Journal of Traditional, Complementary, and Alternative Medicines* 8, no. 5 (2011): 115–23.
28. See Matthew Michael, "Faith Borders, Healing Territories & Interconnective Frontier? Wellness & Its Ecumenical Construct in African Shrines, Christian Prayerhouses, & Hospitals." *Numen* 22 (2019): 240–60.
29. Women healers are a common sight in northern Nigeria. For the active presence of women involvement in Bori healing, see Umar Habila Didam Danfulani, "Factors Contributing to the Survival of the Bori Cult in Northern Nigeria," *Numen* 46, no. 4 (1999): 412–47.
30. See Ojo, "Pentecostal Movement, Islam and the Contest for Public Space," 175–88.
31. Concerning the different trajectories in the studies of World Christianity, see Irvin, "World Christianity: A Genealogy," 5–22; Cabrita and Maxwell, "Introduction," *Relocating*, 1–44.
32. See Michael, "Faith Borders, Healing Territories & Interconnective Frontier?" 240–60.
33. Mama Sanei Afuwai runs a traditional pediatric clinic at Kagoro in Kaduna state. This excerpt comes from the interview of Sanei Afuwai on April 1, 2021.
34. Mary Musa, a traditional pediatric healer in Goni Gora, Kaduna state, in an interview with her on November 30, 2020.
35. An interview with Maman Yara in May 2019.
36. See A. Bohn and D Berntsen, "The Future Is Bright and Predictable: The Development of Prospective Life Stories across Childhood and Adolescence," *Developmental Psychology* 49, no. 7 (2013): 1232–41.
37. An interview with a client of Maman Yara in May 2019.
38. From the interview with Sanei Afuwai, a traditional pediatric healer at Kagoro, on April 1, 2021.
39. See Michael O. Sodipo, "Mitigating Radicalism in Northern Nigeria," *African Security Brief* 26 (2013): 1–8.

40. See Abdul Rauf Mustapha, *Sects and Social Disorder: Muslim Identities & Conflicts in Northern Nigeria* (Suffolk: James Currey, 2014).
41. Concerning African healing shrines in general and the strategic importance for border-crossing, see Michael, "Faith Borders, Healing Territories & Interconnective Frontier?" 240–60. Also see Matthew Michael and Umar Habila Dadem Danfulani, eds., *African Healing Shrines & Cultural Psychologies* (Oxford: Regnum, 2021).
42. See Michael and Danfulani, "Introduction," *African Healing Shrines & Cultural Psychologies*, 1–4.
43. During the period of data collection, I recognize the three research assistants namely Mr. Zwandien Bobai of ECWA Theological Seminary, Kagoro, Kaduna state; Pastor Emma Tanta, ECWA English Service, Dominion Avenue Narayi-Highcost, Kaduna state; and Mr. James Danladi, a PhD student at Nasarawa State University, Keffi, for all their assistance. I also appreciate the initial grant and support of Nagel Institute at Calvin University (Grand Rapids, Michigan) and Templeton Religion Trust (Nassau, Bahamas). I also acknowledge the support of two of my colleagues during this project: Dr. Nathan Chiroma, Pan Africa Christian University, Kenya; and Prof. Hauwa'u E. Yusuf, Department of Sociology, Kaduna State University, Nigeria.

Bibliography

Abdullahi, A. A. "Trends and Challenges of Traditional Medicine in Africa." *African Journal of Traditional, Complementary, and Alternative Medicines* 8, no. 5 (2011): 115–23.

Abdur-Rahman, Lukman O., J. O. Taiwo, C. K. P. Ofoegbu, A. O. Adekanye, O. O. Ajide, C. Y. Ijagbemi, and B. A. Solagberu. "Community Survey of Childhood Injuries in North-Central Nigeria." *Annals of Pediatric Surgery* 11, no. 2 (2015): 136–9.

Alhassan, Yakubu. "Child Health Care in Nigeria: Historical Background." *Nigerian Journal of Paediatrics* 39, no. 1 (2012): 1–6.

Asamoah-Gyadu, J. Kwabena. "Therapeutic Strategies in African Religions: Herbal Medicine, and Indigenous Christianity." *Studies in World Christianity* 20, no. 1 (2014): 70–90.

Bohn, A., and D Berntsen. "The Future Is Bright and Predictable: The Development of Prospective Life Stories across Childhood and Adolescence." *Developmental Psychology* 49, no. 7 (2013): 1232–41.

Bolu-Steve, Foluke Nike, A. A. Adegoke, and G. M. Kim-Ju. "Cultural Beliefs and Infant Mortality in Nigeria." *Hindawi: Educational Research International* (2020): 1–10.

Brady, Erika. "Introduction." In *Healing Logics: Culture and Medicine in Modern Health Belief Systems*, edited by Erika Brady. Logan: Utah State University Press, 2001, pp. 3–12.

Burke, Bryan L., and R. W. Hal. "Telemedicine: Pediatric Applications." *Pediatrics* 136, no. 1 (2015): 293–308.

Cabrita, Joel, and David Maxwell. "Introduction." In *Relocating World Christianity*, edited by Joel Cabrita, David Maxwell, and Emma Wild-Wood. Leiden: Brill, 2017, pp. 1–44.

D'Costa, Gavin. *Christianity and World Religions: Disputed Questions in the Theology of Religions*. Malden, MA: Wiley-Blackwell, 2009.

Danfulani, Umar Habila Didam. "Factors Contributing to the Survival of the Bori Cult in Northern Nigeria." *Numen* 46, no. 4 (1999): 412–47.

Diamond, T. E., S. E. B. Ibeanusi, R. C. Echem, and C. C. Aniebo. "Extremity Amputations in Children from Complications of Traditional Bone Setters' Care Seen in a Tertiary Hospital in Port Harcourt, Nigeria." *Advances in Research* 14, no. 16 (2018): 1–7.

Dyer, Silke J. "The Value of Children in African Countries: Insights from Studies on Infertility." *Journal of Psychosomatic Obstetrics & Gynecology* 28, no. 2 (2007): 69–77.

Hadley, Larry G. P., Bankole S. Rouma, and Yasser Saad-Eldin. "Challenge of Pediatric Oncology in Africa." *Seminars in Pediatric Surgery* 21, no. 1 (2012): 136–41.

Irvin, Dale T. "World Christianity: A Genealogy." *Journal of World Christianity* 9, no. 1 (2019): 5–22.

James, Peter Bai, Jon Wardle, Amie Steel, and Jon Adams. "Traditional, Complementary and Alternative Medicine in Sub-Saharan Africa: A Systematic View." *BMJ Global Health* 3, no. 5 (2018): 1–18.

Kjørholt, Anne Trine. "Childhood as Symbolic Space: Searching for Authentic Voices in Era of Globalisation." *Childhood's Geographies* 5 (2007): 29–42.

Michael, Matthew, and Umar Habila Dadem Danfulani, eds. *African Healing Shrines & Cultural Psychologies*. Oxford: Regnum, 2021.

Michael, Matthew, and Umar Habila Dadem Danfulani. "Faith Borders, Healing Territories & Interconnective Frontier? Wellness & Its Ecumenical Construct in African Shrines, Christian Prayerhouses, & Hospitals." *Numen* 22 (2019): 240–60.

Michael, Matthew, Nathan Chiroma, and Hauwa'u Evelyn Yusuf. "Health and Integrative Wellness: Mapping Wellness and Its Cultural Psychology in Contemporary Africa." *International Bulletin of Mission Research* 45, no. 2 (2020): 1–10.

Mustapha, Abdul Rauf. *Sects and Social Disorder: Muslim Identities & Conflicts in Northern Nigeria*. Suffolk: James Currey, 2014.

Nmamani, Amuluche-Greg. "The Flow of African Spirituality into World Christianity: A Case of Pneumatology and Migration." *Mission Studies* 32, no. 3 (2015): 331–52.

Ojo, Matthews A. "Pentecostal Movement, Islam and the Contest for Public Space in Northern Nigeria." *Islam and Christian-Muslim Relations* 18 (2007): 175–88.

Ozima, Ezekwesili-Ofili Josephine, and Okaka Antoinette Nwamaka Chinwe. "Herbal Medicine in African Traditional Medicine." In *Herbal Medicine*. London: IntechOpen, 2019, pp. 191–214.

Pool, Robert. "On the Creation and Dissolution of Ethnomedical Systems in the Medical Ethnography of Africa." *Africa: Journal of the International African Institute* 64, no. 1 (1994): 1–20.

Robert, Dana L. "World Christianity as a Women's Movement." *International Bulletin of Mission Research* 30, no. 4 (2006): 160–88.

Simon, Tamara D., Sanjay Mahant, and Eyal Cohen. "Pediatric Hospital Medicine and Children with Medical Complexity: Past, Present, and Future." *Current Problems in Pediatric and Adolescent Health Care* 42, no. 5 (2012): 113–19.

Sodipo, Michael O. "Mitigating Radicalism in Northern Nigeria." *African Security Brief* 26 (2013): 1–8.

Towns, Alexendra M., Sandra Mengue Egi, and Tinde van Andel. "Traditional Medicine and Childcare in Western Africa: Mother's Knowledge, Folk Illnesses, and Patterns of Healthcare Seeking Behavior." *Plos One* 9, no. 8 (2014). https://doi.org/10.1371/journal.pone.0105972.

World Health Organization. "A Child Dies Every Minute from Malaria in Africa." www.afro.who.int/news/child-dies-every-minute-malaria-africa (accessed April 9, 2021).

13

Ante-Sacred-Space and the Interreligious Sphere in a Covid-19 ICU Room

Izak Y. M. Lattu

Introduction

The pandemic has brought both positive and negative impacts to interreligious communities in Indonesia. Panic and frustration in the early stage of the Covid-19 outbreak created social and religious prejudice toward religious others. Interreligious prejudice amid the Covid-19 era has highlighted hidden conflicts in society. However, Covid-19 has also produced forms of social solidarity[1] and mutual understanding among interreligious communities in Indonesia. This civic initiative comes from below in everyday life through open-heartedness and willingness to interact and learn from others.

The new sacred space and interreligious sphere emerge from social solidarity and prayers among medical workers and patients in Covid-19 intensive care unit (ICU) rooms. In Indonesia, during the Covid-19 pandemic, interreligious engagements have served as touchstones for social camaraderie.[2] Indonesia, the world's biggest Muslim-majority country, with a significant Christian presence and national ideology supportive of interfaith understanding, has become a place for interreligious solidarity amid a global pandemic.[3] Many scholars have studied interreligious prayer and mutual understanding from different perspectives.[4] These scholars believe that interreligious prayer with religious others brings a feeling of unity, solidarity, and understanding. However, prayers among religious followers in ICU rooms at hospitals in Indonesia take on an informal quality.

Finding interreligious engagements central to social solidarity, this essay investigates interreligious prayer as an expression of how religious people, in a pandemic context, cross religious formalities and boundaries. Prayers from medical workers to patients or among medical workers have shaped a sense of interreligious understanding. The chapter employs spatial concepts from Lefebvre, Soja,[5] Jeffrey Alexander's civil sphere,[6] and Michel D'Certeau's tactic[7] to unpack the change of spatial understanding in a hospital ICU room and a new understanding of hospital anteroom in the pandemic era. Based on an autoethnography approach[8] and my own experience as a patient in an ICU room because of a Covid-19 infection, this essay argues that amid the Covid-19 pandemic, interreligious solidarity and prayer have transformed the room from medical care to a sacred space and interreligious sphere.

The Autoethnographic Method of a Covid-19 Survivor

On March 16, 2020, I flew from New York to Jakarta. I must have been exposed to Covid on the flight. As it was during the early stages of the pandemic, the medical workers in Indonesia were unsure on how to deal with a Covid-19 patient. The Covid-19 death rate in Indonesia was terrifying between March and April of 2020. Out of the five hundred patients nationwide in Indonesia during that one-month span, only a hundred survived, including me. Covid-19 had indeed created a national panic as every neighborhood gate was closed because people were afraid; meat in local stores was absent as a result of mass panic buying; religious communities closed their sanctuaries and prevented congregation members from attending in-person rituals.

Observation and autoethnographic data from a Covid-19 ICU room could contribute solid data for any academic research on the pandemic. Yet any inquiry, except for a research-patient like me, within a Covid-19 ICU room is considered hazardous academic action. When this research was finalized on September 20, 2021, global Covid-19 patient data from the World Health Organization confirmed 226,844,344 cases and 4,666,334 deaths. Consequently, my personal experience of being hospitalized provides data for interreligious studies through prayer and the creation of a civil sphere in the ICU room.

My research employs an autoethnographic method that is based on direct involvement and experience with other subjects in the field.[9] Autoethnography[10] helps bring my experience along with medical workers' knowledge regarding interreligious understanding through prayer within the ICU room and social comradeship in the anteroom. Focus group discussion and online interview with medical workers contribute to developing dense data to comprehend interreligious ground in the medical terrain. This piece contributes to the interreligious study through the interfaith voices and symbolic actions from a hazardous space: a Covid-19 ICU room. Interreligious engagement among vulnerable people creates a sense of comradeship and *communitas* beyond religious affiliation.[11]

Covid-19, Enemy Image, and the Majoritarian Turn

Religious leaders' response to the early stages of the Covid-19 outbreak in Indonesia reflects religious division and hidden conflict. An outstanding Indonesian Muslim leader from a more exclusivist side announced publicly that Covid-19 is "the army of Allah" who attacked the *Kuffur*.[12] Another Muslim leader, also from a fundamentalist group, claimed that the Covid-19 virus appeared because of "the habit of pork consumption."[13] In the same manner, Christian fundamentalist leaders in Indonesia believed that God and angels would protect Christians from Covid-19. "Do not be afraid to come physically to the church. God will protect you from the virus in the church."[14] Another Christian evangelical pastor believed that the virus would not infect Christians and thus Christians did not need the Covid-19 vaccine because "the blood of Christ" is the best inoculation."[15]

The Covid-19 pandemic has sharpened religious division on many levels. For instance, when I was infected, the battle of religious claim took place on social media where Muslim fundamentalist flyers read, "*Kaffirun* or infidels got infected by Covid-19," while another flyer circulated among Christian groups said, "Pray for Izak, the first Covid-19 patient in Salatiga city, so his recovery witnesses the healing power of Jesus Christ." The pandemic has unpacked hidden religious conflict among fundamentalist attitudes and imaginations that suppresses security and harmonious approaches. Although most Indonesians believe in pluralism (Bhinneka Tunggal Ika), fundamentalist groups remain influential.[16] Fundamentalist groups reproduce religiously motivated conflict on social media platforms linking quotidian segregation with screen enemy image. This pandemic has changed social media into a battleground and claim of salvation among religious followers in Indonesia.

Open relationships among religious followers in Indonesia have experienced conflict. Prior to 1981, interreligious prayer rituals were common practices in Indonesia.[17] However, Indonesia's Ulama Council (MUI) in 1981 issued a fatwa on Christmas to prohibit Muslims from attending any interreligious prayer ritual. Following the Indonesian Reformation (Reformasi) in 1998, religious pluralism has dominated discussion in the private and public spheres. Inspired by the idea of religious pluralism in national policy and cultural practices, interreligious prayers became a common action in Indonesia. In 1999, during the first period of Reformasi, Abdurahman Wahid (Gus Dur), a progressive Muslim ulama from Nahdlatul Ulama (NU), served as the president of the Republic of Indonesia. Gus Dur endorsed the public practice of progressive interreligious understanding, including public interreligious prayer. When Gus Dur stepped down, Megawati Soekarnoputri from a nationalist group took the presidential office in 2000. Under her presidency from 2000 to 2004, interreligious understanding in the Gus Dur era continued to dominate the Indonesian perspective on religious others.

Interreligious relations changed radically in 2004 after General Soesilo Bambang Yoedoyono won the election with massive support from Islamic political parties. During this period, Indonesians experienced strong religious segregation. Fundamentalist sentiment increased in public areas, especially in schools and government offices. Although the current nationalist government under Joko Widodo's presidency introduces and campaigns for progressive religious attitudes toward other religions (Wasatia Islam), religious fundamentalism remains strong among urban communities. The politics and discriminative policies have reduced the social sphere for interreligious engagements, which includes interreligious prayers.

From Hospital Anteroom to Ante-Sacred-Space

The treatment of Covid-19 has created a lived or third space[18] in Indonesian hospitals. The concept of lived space in Henri Lefebvre' sociological production was developed by Edward Soja as a third space, which is a "space where issues of race, class, and gender can be addressed simultaneously without privileging one over other."[19] Third space is a sphere where people find extraordinary openness and experience living beyond material structures and imagination, or real-and-imagined places. The spirit of capitalism might change hospitals from a space to deliver care and medical services to a place of financial capital and class production. The conceptual changes in medical service may highlight, to borrow from Lefebvre, a "social location of a highly exploit[ed] and carefully monitored passivity."[20]

When a hospital functions as a place of money production, it shifts to an "abstract space," to borrow from Lefebvre, an area that is dominated by exploitation and the values of capitalism.[21] As a result, the abstract space that is controlled by capitalism fractures society into social classes. Indonesian hospitals' abstract space fragmentation exists in inpatient classes: Class III, II, I, Very Important People (VIP), and VVIP (Very Very Important People). The classification of medical service in Indonesia's hospitals goes back to colonial times when *Vereenigde Oost-Indische Compagnie* (VOC), or the United East India Company, developed hospitals to meet the health needs of its Western employees. Indigenous Indonesians could only access the colonial hospital when their health issues related to Dutch interests. Colonial hospitals provided better health service for colonial masters than locals.[22] Here the Dutch colonial government introduced hospital classes to the health system. The colonial idea remains the main trajectory for health service in the Indonesian hospital system.

The Covid-19 pandemic has changed the classes in the hospitals. Complete financial support from the central government in Jakarta to all the hospitals and health centers in Indonesia that provide medical services for Covid-19 patients create no class in hospital health amenity to the pandemic victims. Every Indonesian hospital provides one isolation room for patients with light symptoms and an ICU room for patients with respiratory problems. When I was hospitalized in Dr Kariadi Central Government Hospital in Semarang, in March and April of 2020, I witnessed the collapse of the class system. Dr Kariadi Central Public Hospital (RSUP Dr. Kariadi) served everybody regardless of social status and background. Medical workers served patients from different social classes in the ICU room. This resulted in the shift from a capitalist space into a humanist space.

Covid-19 transformed medical workers and patients in ICU rooms. In these rooms, medical workers expressed deep care and understanding toward patients. The hospital policymaker I interviewed said that only the best medical workers serve in the Covid-19 ICU room. The argument supports my observation in the ICU room where I witnessed medical workers demonstrating deep care, empathy, and encouragement toward patients. Medical workers in this room served beyond their basic duties. Nurses and medical doctors prayed for patients who suffered respiratory problems. When serving in an ICU room, medical workers' focus went beyond the social and spiritual backgrounds of their patients. Treatment in these rooms has transformed patient and worker relationships from subject–object relation to intersubjective awareness. Medical workers' and patients' relationships, at least in my observation, achieved intersubjective rapport.

The changing of space during Covid-19 in the hospital takes place in the ICU's anteroom. Research from Iran has underlined the centrality of anterooms in hospitals during the Covid-19 pandemic. This study has investigated the use of anterooms to isolate patients, thus controlling the spread of Covid-19.[23] Shon et al., writing about the Korean hospital experience, have explored the concept of the anteroom as a preparation room for medical workers to serve Covid-19 patients.[24] This recent study's basic argument is that the anteroom has changed during the pandemic era from the hospital architectural boundary between isolation rooms and hallways to a preparatory space. In Indonesia, anterooms function as both preparatory and prayer spaces before entering the isolation room. Using van Gennep's liminal concept developed by Victor Turner,[25] the anteroom plays an important role as a liminal gate for medical workers to prepare psychologically and spiritually before encountering patients with Covid-19.

Anterooms have shifted, albeit temporarily, from architectural places to sacred spaces where people encounter the presence of God. Interreligious prayer reconstructs anterooms to become an ante-sacred-space where religious people pray jointly before serving Covid-19 patients. My research includes two hospitals in Indonesia: one in Semarang, a predominantly Muslim city in the western part of Indonesia, and another in Ambon, a predominantly Christian urban area in eastern Indonesia. The prayer in the anteroom may be led by one person according to the religious litany. The leader prays in the common Bahasa Indonesia language or another language that concludes with the joint unison of "Amen!" This form of praying together in an ICU anteroom goes beyond a multireligious prayer. Focus group discussions with medical workers on October 11, 2020, showed that the unisonant in the ICU anteroom created a shared feeling and concern among those involved in the invocation. "Amen," a unisonant phrase in this sense, is the symbolic action of interreligious inclusion.

Interreligious Tactic in a Covid-19 ICU Room

Religious communities in Indonesia experience social and political pressure from fundamentalist groups and political leaders at local and national levels, but manage to create informal spaces for interreligious engagement. Radical religious groups hamper initiatives for interreligious collaboration and relationships. Fundamentalist wings of dominant religious groups have tried to judge any interreligious reflection and action based on any given religious view and value. At the same time, political interest functions as a barrier for formal dialogue and performative action among religious groups in Indonesia. Interreligious communities that are based on nongovernmental initiatives and interreligious engagements are led by progressive religious groups.

Drawing on Michel D'Certeau's idea of tactic and strategy,[26] this essay perceives this initiative of people from different religious backgrounds in a hospital's ICU room amid the pandemic as an interreligious tactic from ordinary actors in everyday life, as opposed to a strategy of fundamentalist-dominant groups. While interreligious actors employ informality and need no physical place for dialogue, the dominant structural group uses power relations and requires a formal place for interreligious conversation. Formal dialogue tends to legitimate majoritarianism; majority rules over others.

Elsewhere I have stated that majoritarianism hinders any social activism and national policy that could lead to interreligious collaboration and mutual understanding.[27] Interreligious understanding, including interreligious prayer, in ICU rooms is a genuine tactic to develop a bigger sphere for mutual trust and collaboration.

Interreligious prayer requires mutual respect, humility, and empathy from both medical workers and patients alike. D'Certeau perceives tactics as "a calculated action determined by the absence of a proper locus."[28] When medical workers pray for patients who have different religious backgrounds, the prayer functions as a calculated action to develop religious understanding beyond formal interreligious places. Politicians through ideological penetration, local government through religious-based law, and ulama via religious fatwa have cultivated religious segregation. However, the prayer represents tactics as the tools of marginal communities.[29] When a nurse asked me to say a Christian prayer while she prayed according to a Muslim *do'a*, the moment transformed into an equal relationship based on "the absence of power," according to D'Certeau's tactical spirit.[30] Covid-19 has carved ICU rooms into a space where people are freely able to practice interreligious tactics and thus reject the domination of political strategy in everyday interfaith engagements. There is no political power that drives interreligious action in the ICU room; rather the spirit of humanity and empathy is what powers interreligious prayer.

People's tactics that are based on social activism from below in the ICU room illustrate an interfaith need for a noncoercive room to express interreligious understanding and collaboration. Echoing Joel Carpenter, people prefer initiatives from below rather than impositions from the world's great powers.[31] Interreligious prayer in the ICU room is the weapon of the weak to strengthen spiritual foundation and social recognition. People with Covid-19 have experienced marginalization in communities, and thus, interreligious prayer functions as topos for understanding and social support for the weak. Using Joel Carpenter's and Kevin den Dulk's words, "collective action is a vital tool for achieving this shift from survival to self-expression."[32] Interreligious prayer is a genuine expression of mutual understanding. The standard operating procedure to fight Covid-19 does not exist in hospital policy. No religious leader can enter an ICU room to pray for spiritual support for a patient. Interreligious prayer is an initiative from below to reject social segregation in everyday life and elite interreligious dialogue. Elite-based interreligious dialogue needs a formal room for conversation. However, initiatives from below do not need a special place. Rather, they need a special heart to understand and reach beyond formality.

Praying with patients in hospitals is common in many places. Peter Collins has researched hospital prayer requests from patients in British hospitals.[33] Collins focuses more on Christian Chaplaincy in the UK's hospitals who utilize Christian prayer to strengthen patients' spirituality during turmoil. However, my autoethnographic observation and focus group discussions in Indonesian hospitals focuses on how medical workers in Covid-19 ICU rooms utilize prayer for patients who are in either conscious or unconscious conditions. The medical workers have no chaplaincy training but seek to serve as "religious agents" who conduct prayers for Covid-19 patients in isolated rooms. Abby Day stated, "They actively engaged with God in their rituals of healing, primarily through prayer and recitation of scripture, and also believe that

God works through other agents."³⁴ Covid-19 patients, including me, believe that the Supreme Being works healing through the work and prayer of medical workers.

Covid-19 patients are vulnerable and desire help by any means, including prayers from others. Collins discusses "people who are suffering, who are most likely worried, stressed, anxious and afraid,"³⁵ and this rings true as I experienced feelings of worry, stress, anxiety, and fear when hospitalized. In this ICU room, all patients were on a ventilator. Therefore, patients totally depend on medical workers. The day before I was transferred from a regular isolation room to an ICU room, I talked to my wife about the possibility of death. It echoed my fearfulness and also resembled other Covid-19 patients' feelings—the legitimate fear of dying. Being hospitalized in this room, patients depend on constant assistance, including prayer from medical workers.

During an interreligious prayer in a Covid-19 ICU room, medical workers and patients are fully aware of faith disparities. However, the patient gives consent for medical workers to pray as an agent to assist spiritual edification. Medical workers I interviewed confessed, "I had a Covid-19 patient who has a religion other than mine. She asked me to pray for her everyday. I am aware of religious differences, therefore I used universal language when I prayed with the patient. This is the way we support patients to fight the virus." When medical workers from different religious affiliations pray, patients are able to communicate to the Divine through agents that have different religious litany and dogma. Therefore, prayer speech uses a common language and universal tune without attaching the prayer to any religious litany.

When a medical worker asked for my consent to pray before my treatment, I was tremendously encouraged because an agent mediates the relationship with the Supreme Being. The medical worker had a different religious background than mine, but prayer testifies: "When you were in sedative condition, long sleep because of the medication, in Covid-19 room, although you are unconscious, my coworkers and I kept talking and supporting you. I prayed for you in my religious prayer and asked you also to pray—you were still unconscious—before I gave you medicine through the vein catheter." In relation to agents, patients, and interreligious prayers, the medical workers prayed through the combination of a particular religious phrase in Bahasa Indonesian. The prayer entered my consciousness, and I translated the agent's religious language into a universal language—a common religious language—and altered the prayer into my religious language.

Relations in the ICU room reflect everyday relationships where Indonesians from different religious backgrounds employ "tactics" to develop social-mutual engagements that are dissimilar to elite strategies that divide people based on religious backgrounds. Relationships in the ICU room at the micro civil sphere, as stated by Alexander,³⁶ are based on everyday initiatives for mutual engagements. This micro-level engagement is incompatible with macro-level political spheres that are based on ballot and elite interest. Using Jeffrey Alexander's perspective, the Covid-19 ICU room has shifted from a place of treatment to a civil sphere.³⁷ Medical workers and Covid-19 patients in the ICU room are actors of the civil sphere, who shared and connected through collective solidarity among people of different religions. Interreligious prayer in this sense is a reflection of respect and trust in the goodwill of religious others in the Covid-19 ICU room.

The respecting of the social trust formed in the ICU room is an action of inclusion and recognition toward various religious backgrounds. Alexander compared this process to one similar to incorporation.[38] The incorporation of people from different religious backgrounds into prayers in the Covid-19 ICU room brings a spirit of equality and respect. Interreligious solidarity emerges in the ICU room because medical workers recognize patients as "suffering others." Interreligious respect takes place in Covid-19 ICU rooms because of the honor and recognition of other humans.

Conclusion

Open-heartedness and willingness to engage with religious others in the Covid-19 ICU room have shifted the hospital from a capitalist space to a humanist sphere. While the class system in Indonesian hospitals was rooted in Dutch and Western supremacy during colonial times, the Covid-19 pandemic eliminated this system altogether. Everyone was treated equally in Covid-19 ICU rooms regardless of social status or religious background. The change of spatial concepts also occurred in the anteroom; it became a liminal sacred space where medical workers prayed in interreligious and strong spirit to serve Covid-19 patients.

Interreligious prayer and social solidarity in Covid-19 ICU rooms is an initiative and tactic from below where people from different religions developed social trust and collaboration. The interreligious prayer serves as a tactic for people who experience marginalization because of structural policies to segregate religious followers. Living with religious others is a habitus of peace and respect that will help to craft an interreligious sphere in a dangerous place like the Covid-19 ICU room. This habitus is a self-expression of Indonesian interreligious understanding in everyday life. Therefore, interreligious prayer in the Covid-19 ICU room is a weapon of the weak for interreligious engagements. Segregation in doctrinal teaching and political strategy cannot hamper Indonesian religious people from working collectively in understanding and trust during the pandemic.

Notes

1. Slavoj Zizek, *Pandemic: Covid-19 Shakes the World* (New York: OR Books, 2020); Marina Sitrin and Colectiva Sembrar, eds., *Pandemic Solidarity: Mutual Aid during the Covid-19 Crisis* (London: Pluto Press, 2020); Hal Brands and Francis J. Gavin, *Covid-19 and the World Order: The Future of Conflict, Competition and Cooperation* (Baltimore, MD: John Hopkins University Press, 2020); Christian Fuchs, *Communicating Covid-19: Everyday Life, Digital Capitalism and Conspiracy Theories in Pandemic Times* (Bingley: Emerald, 2021).
2. Murtini Hehanussa, Kristi, and Wiwin S. A. Rohmawati, *Daya Juang Perempuan Lintas Iman Menghadapi Pandemi* (Yogkarta: Srikandi Lintas Iman, 2020); Dicky Sofyan and Muhammad Wildan, *Virus, Manusia, Tuhan: Refleksi Lintas Iman Tentang Covid-19* (Jakarta: Gramedia, 2020); Mohammad Amin, *Covid-19 dari Perspektif Sains Biologi, Sosial dan Agama* (Jakarta: Intelegensi Media).

3. P. Jessy Ismoyo, Linda Susilowati, Wilson Therik, and Izak Lattu, eds., *Crossing the Boundaries: Covid-19 Pandemic, Social Solidarity and Interreligious Engagement in Indonesia* (Salatiga: Satya Wacana University Press, 2021); Hamdan Daulay, Khoiro Umatin, Zaen Musyirifin, Mikhriani, Hikmah Endraswati, and Theresia Octastefan, *Covid-19 dan Transformasi Keagamaan* (Yogyakarta: Lembaga Ladang Kata dan UIN Sunan Kalijaga, 2020); Fatma Lestari, Hasbullah Thabrany, Budi Haryanto, Sudarto Ronoatmodjo, and R. Hadianto, *Indonesia's Experience in Covid-19 Control* (Jakarta: Badan Nasional Penanggulangan Bencana, 2020).
4. Gavin D'Costa, "Interreligious Prayer between Christians and Muslims," *Journal of Islam and Christian-Muslim Relations* 24, no. 1 (January 2013): 1–14; Marriane Moyaert, "Inappropriate Behavior? On the Ritual Core of Religion and Its Challenges to Interreligious Hospitality," *Journal for the Academic Study of Religion* 27, no. 2 (2014): 222–42; Michael Amadoloss, "Inter-Religious Worship." In Cathrine Cornille, ed., *The Wiley-Blackwell Companion to Inter-Religious Dialogue* (Oxford: Wiley-Blackwell, 2013), 87–98; Abu-Nimer Muhammed, "The Miracle of Transformation through Interfaith Dialogue: Are You a Believer?" In David R. Smoch, ed., *Interfaith Dialogue and Peacebuilding* (Washington, DC: United States Institute of Peace Press, 2002).
5. Henri Lefebvre, *The Production of Space* (Oxford: Blackwell, [1974] 1991); Edward Soja, *Thirdspace: Journeys to Los Angeles and Other Real-and-Imagined Places* (Oxford: Blackwell Publishers, 1996).
6. Jeffrey C. Alexander, *The Civil Sphere* (Oxford: Oxford University Press, 2006).
7. Michel D'Certeau, *The Practice of Everyday Life* (Berkeley: University of California Press, 1984).
8. Stacy H. Jones, Tony E. Adams, and Carolyn Ellis, *Handbook of Autoethnography* (London: Routledge, 2013).
9. Robin M. Boylorn and Mark P. Orbe, *Critical Autoethnography: Intersecting Cultural Identities in Everyday Life* (Walnut Creek, CA: Left Coast Press, 2014); Amir Marvasti, *Qualitative Research in Sociology* (London: Sage Publications, 2004).
10. Jones et al., *Handbook of Autoethnography*.
11. Izak Y. M. Lattu, *Memoar Covid-19: Catatan Autoetnografi Penyintas* (Salatiga: Satya Wacana University Press, 2021).
12. GMG Crew, "Ustadz Abdul Somad Virus Corona Adalah Tentara Allah," February 17, 2020. www.youtube.com/watch?v=C6cixYXh4RM (accessed October 14, 2021).
13. GituDOANG, "MUI Sebut Konsumsi Babi Sebab Masuknya Corona Di DKI (BERITA TERKINI)," March 4, 2020. www.youtube.com/watch?v=ky6YpMzHm9E (accessed October 14, 2021).
14. GSJS Jakarta, "Pesan Daud Tony Mengenai Virus Corona COVID-19," March 24, 2020. www.youtube.com/watch?v=RTMHSFM7XHM (accessed October 14, 2021).
15. tvOneNews, "Tak Percaya Covid, Jemaat Gereja di Papua Ramai-ramai Bakar Masker | tvOne Minute," August 2, 2021. www.youtube.com/watch?v=t-zZvd65sP0 (accessed October 14, 2021).
16. Izak Y. M. Lattu, "Menggugat Majoritarianisme, Menegaskan Covenantal Pluralism in Indonesia," in *Festschrift Riwanto Tirtosudarmo, PhD* (Jakarta: Kompas Press, 2022). See also Robert W. Hefner, "Islam and Covenantal Pluralism in Indonesia: A Critical Juncture Analysis," *Review of Faith and International Affairs* 18, no. 2 (Summer 2020): 1–17.
17. Rumadi, *Fatwa Hubungan Antaragama di Indonesia* (Jakarta: Gramedia Pustaka, 2016).

18. Lefebvre, *The Production of Space*; Soja, *Thirdspace*.
19. Soja, *Thirdspace*, 5.
20. Lefebvre, *The Production of Space*, 384.
21. Ibid.
22. Laksono Trisnantoro, *Memahami Penggunaan Ilmu Ekonomi dalam Manajemen Rumah Sakit* (Yogyakarta: Gadjah Mada University Press, 2018), 4–22.
23. H. Ahmadi Choukolaei, S. Shafaee Tilaki, and A. Abraham, "Evaluation of Isolation Room and Anteroom of Hospitals in Corona Conditions (Case Study: Sari, Iran)," in C. Kahraman, S. Cebi, S. Cevik Onar, B. Oztaysi, A. C. Tolga, and I. U. Sari, eds., *Intelligent and Fuzzy Techniques for Emerging Conditions and Digital Transformation* (Cham: Springer, 2022). https://doi.org/10.1007/978-3-030-85626-7_90.
24. Soonyoung Shon, Hwasook Cho, Minseo Sung, Jinyoung Kang, Younsuk Choi, Sanghun Lee, and Kyoung Ja Moon, "Operationalization of an Expanded Anteroom in a Covid-19 Dedicated Hospital, South Korea." www.preprints.org/manuscript/202012.0485/v1.
25. Arnold van Gennep, *The Rites of Passage* (Chicago: University of Chicago Press, 1960); Victor Turner, *The Ritual Process: Structure and Anti-structure* (New York: Aldine de Gruyter, [1969] 1997).
26. D'Certeau, *The Practice of Everyday Life*.
27. Izak Lattu, "Beyond Interreligious Dialogue: Oral-Based Interreligious Engagements in Indonesia," *Annual Review of the Sociology of Religion* 10 (2019): 70–90; Hefner, "Islam and Covenantal Pluralism," 12.
28. D'Certeau, *The Practice of Everyday*, 37.
29. Ibid.
30. Ibid., 38.
31. Joel A. Carpenter, "Preface," in Lamin Saneh and Joel A. Carpenter, eds., *The Changing Face of Christianity: Africa, The West and The World* (Oxford: Oxford University Press, 2005).
32. Joel A. Carpenter and Kevin den Dulk, "Introduction," in *Christianity in Chinese Public Life: Religion, Society and the Rule of Law* (New York: Palgrave Macmillan, 2014), 6.
33. Peter Collins, "An Analysis of Hospital Chapel Prayer Request," in Giuseppe Giordan and Linda Woodhead, eds., *A Sociology of Prayer* (Farnham: Ashgate, 2015).
34. Abby Day, *Sociology of Religion: Overview and Analysis of Contemporary Religion* (London: Routledge, 2020).
35. Collins, "An Analysis of Hospital," 207.
36. Alexander, *The Civil Sphere*.
37. Ibid., 402.
38. Ibid., 504.

Bibliography

Abu-Nimer, Muhammed. "The Miracle of Transformation through Interfaith Dialogue: Are You a Believer?" In *Interfaith Dialogue and Peacebuilding*, edited by David R. Smoch. Washington, DC: United States Institute of Peace Press, 2002.

Alexander, Jeffrey C. *The Civil Sphere*. Oxford: Oxford University Press, 2006.

Amadoloss, Michael. "Inter-Religious Worship." In *The Wiley-Blackwell Companion to Inter-Religious Dialogue*, edited by Cathrine Cornille. Oxford: Wiley-Blackwell, 2013.
Amin, Mohammad. *Covid-19 dari Perspektif Sains Biologi, Sosial dan Agama*. Jakarta: Intelegensi Media, 2020.
Boylorn, Robin M., and Mark P. Orbe. *Critical Authoethnography: Intersecting Cultural Identities in Everyday Life*. Walnut Creek, CA: Left Coast Press, 2014.
Brands, Hal, and Francis J. Gavin. *Covid-19 and the World Order: The Future of Conflict, Competition and Cooperation*. Baltimore, MD: John Hopkins University Press, 2020.
Buber, Martin. *I and Thou* (trans. Ronald G. Smit). Edinburgh: T&T Clark, 1937.
Carpenter, Joel A. "Preface." In *The Changing Face of Christianity: Africa, the West and the World*, edited by Lamin Saneh and Joel A. Carpenter. Oxford: Oxford University Press, 2005, pp. vii–ix.
Carpenter, Joel A., and Kevin den Dulk. "Introduction." In *Christianity in Chinese Public Life: Religion, Society and the Rule of Law*. New York: Palgrave Macmillan, 2014, pp. 1–10.
Choukolaei, Ahmadi H., S. Shafaee Tilaki, and A. Abraham. "Evaluation of Isolation Room and Anteroom of Hospitals in Corona Conditions (Case Study: Sari, Iran)." In *Intelligent and Fuzzy Techniques for Emerging Conditions and Digital Transformation*, edited by C. Kahraman, S. Cebi, S.Cevik Onar, B. Oztaysi, A. C. Tolga, and I. U. Sari. Cham: Springer, 2021, pp. 775–86. https://doi.org/10.1007/978-3-030-85626-7_90.
Collins, Peter. "An Analysis of Hospital Chapel Prayer Request." In *A Sociology of Prayer*, edited by Giuseppe Giordan and Linda Woodhead. Farnham: Ashgate, 2015, 191–212.
D'Certeau, Michel. *The Practice of Everyday Life*. Berkeley: University of California Press, 1984.
D'Costa, Gavin. "Interreligious Prayer between Christians and Muslims." *Journal of Islam and Christian-Muslim Relations* 24 (2013): 1–14.
Daulay, Hamdan, Khoiro Umatin, Zaen Musyirifin, Mikhriani, Hikmah Endraswati, and Theresia Octastefani. *Covid-19 dan Transformasi Keagamaan*. Yogyakarta: Lembaga Ladang Kata dan UIN Sunan Kalijaga, 2020.
Day, Abby. *Sociology of Religion: Overview and Analysis of Contemporary Religion*. London: Routledge, 2020.
Fuchs, Christian. *Communicating Covid-19: Everyday Life, Digital Capitalism and Conspiracy Theories in Pandemic Times*. Bingley: Emerald, 2021.
GituDOANG. "MUI Sebut Konsumsi Babi Sebab Masuknya Corona Di DKI (BERITA TERKINI)." March, 4 2020. www.youtube.com/watch?v=ky6YpMzHm9E (accessed October 14, 2021).
GMG Crew. "Ustadz Abdul Somad Virus Corona Adalah Tentara Allah." February 17, 2020. www.youtube.com/watch?v=C6cixYXh4RM (accessed October 14, 2021).
GSJS Jakarta. "Pesan Daud Tony Mengenai Virus Corona COVID-19." March 24, 2020. www.youtube.com/watch?v=RTMHSFM7XHM (accessed October 14, 2021).
Hefner, Robert W. "Islam and Covenantal Pluralism in Indonesia: A Critical Juncture Analysis." *Review of Faith and International Affairs* 18 (2020): 1–17.
Hehanussa, Murtini Kristi, and Wiwin S. A. Rohmawati. *Daya Juang Perempuan Lintas Iman Menghadapi Pandemi*. Yogkarta: Srikandi Lintas Iman, 2020.
Ismoyo, P. Jessy, Linda Susilowati, Wilson Therik, and Izak Lattu. *Crossing the Boundaries: Covid-19 Pandemic, Social Solidarity and Interreligious Engagement in Indonesia*. Salatiga: Satya Wacana University Press, 2021.

Jones, Stacy H., Tony E. Adams, and Carolyn Ellis. *Handbook of Autoethnography.* London: Routledge, 2013.
Lattu, Izak Y. M. "Beyond Interreligious Dialogue: Oral-Based Interreligious Engagements in Indonesia." *Annual Review of the Sociology of Religion* 10 (2019): 70–90.
Lattu, Izak Y. M. *Memoar Covid-19: Catatan Autoetnografi Penyintas.* Salatiga: Satya Wacana University Press, 2021.
Lattu, Izak Y. M. "Menggugat Majoritarianisme, Menegaskan Covenantal Pluralism in Indonesia." In *Festschrift Riwanto Tirtosudarmo, PhD.* Jakarta: Kompas Press, 2022, pp. 110–21.
Lefebvre, Henri. *The Production of Space.* Oxford: Blackwell, [1974] 1991.
Lestari, Fatma, Hasbullah Thabrany, Budi Haryanto, Sudarto Ronoatmodjo, and R. Hadianto. *Indonesia's Experience in Covid-19 Control.* Jakarta: Badan Nasional Penanggulangan Bencana, 2020.
Marvasti, Amir. *Qualitative Research in Sociology.* London: Sage Publications, 2004.
Moyaert, Marriane. "Inappropriate Behavior? On the Ritual Core of Religion and Its Challenges to Interreligious Hospitality." *Journal for the Academic Study of Religion* 27 (2014): 222–42.
Rumadi. *Fatwa Hubungan Antaragama di Indonesia.* Jakarta: Gramedia Pustaka, 2016.
Shon, Soonyoung, Hwasook Cho, Minseo Sung, Jinyoung Kang, Younsuk Choi, Sanghun Lee, and Kyoung Ja Moon. "Operationalization of an Expanded Anteroom in a Covid-19 Dedicated Hospital, South Korea." www.preprints.org/manuscript/202012.0485/v1.
Sitrin, Marina, and Colectiva Sembrar. *Pandemic Solidarity: Mutual Aid during the Covid-19 Crisis.* London: Pluto Press, 2020.
Sofyan, Dicky, and Muhammad Wildan. *Virus, Manusia, Tuhan: Refleksi Lintas Iman Tentang Covid-19.* Jakarta: Gramedia, 2020.
Soja, Edward. *Thirdspace: Journeys to Los Angeles and Other Real-and-Imagined Places.* Oxford: Blackwell Publishers, 1996.
Trisnantoro, Laksono. *Memahami Penggunaan Ilmu Ekonomi dalam Manajemen Rumah Sakit.* Yogyakarta: Gadjah Mada University Press, 2018.
Turner, Victor. *The Ritual Process: Structure and Anti-Structure.* New York: Aldine de Gruyter, [1969] 1997.
tvOneNews. "Tak Percaya Covid, Jemaat Gereja di Papua Ramai-ramai Bakar Masker | tvOne Minute." August 2, 2021. www.youtube.com/watch?v=t-zZvd65sP0 (accessed October 14, 2021).
van Gennep, Arnold. *The Rites of Passage.* Chicago: University of Chicago Press, 1960.
Zizek, Slavoj. *Covid-19 Shakes the World.* New York: OR Books, 2020.

14

Ubuntuism and Africa: Actualized, Misappropriated, Endangered, and Reappraised

Francis B. Nyamnjoh

Ubuntu

In this chapter, I seek to give currency to concepts such as African communitarianism, Ubuntu, Africanness, Afrocentricity, Afrocentrism, Africanity, Afrikology, humanness, wholeness, and reciprocal altruism. Like pan-Africanism and the concept of African Renaissance, such apparently collectivist pretensions are suggestive of the potential in seeing and articulating identity-making and belonging as flexible, inclusive, dynamic, and complex aspirations and processes. Similar to the unity, solidarities, and relevance craved, the micro- and macro-level importance of these identities in the making are simultaneously abstract and grounded, local and global. They are far less about single identities than about offering mental and fantasy spaces for disparate identities to aspire to inspire coexistence in freedom and dignity.

Inclusivity is an established theme in popular culture in Africa, from song lyrics to home entertainment videos, television series, drama sketches on radio, and novel narratives. Collective success is emphasized, and individuals may not begin to consider themselves to have succeeded unless they can demonstrate the extent to which they have actively included intimate and even distant others: family members and friends, fellow villagers, and even fellow nationals depending on one's stature and networks. Elsewhere, millionaires and billionaires are men and women with tangible personal assets to substantiate their claims to riches. The logic of collective success in many African circles means that no one can truly be considered successful, if they have not involved themselves in ad infinitum redistribution of their accumulations, spreading them broadly and deeply.[1] The worldviews, cultural traditions, and practices that inform such investment in interconnections, interdependencies, and inclusivity draw from and promote philosophies of personhood, being, becoming, and belonging as a permanent work in progress in recognition of incompleteness as a normal order of things and beings.[2]

Ubuntu is a Nguni word widely used in South Africa by Zulu, Xhosa, Swati, and Ndebele peoples and increasingly adopted by other groups within the country and across Africa and the world. Among isiXhosa-speaking South Africans, the expression is usually *Ubuntu ungamuntu ngabanye abantu,* translated roughly as "people are people through other people." The singular is *umntu ngumntu ngabantu*: "a person is a person through other people" or "a human being is a human being because of other human beings."[3] More colloquially, "I am because you are" or "We are together." It should be added, however, that it is not enough to recognize and be conscious of togetherness to fulfill Ubuntu. There is a need for collective social action that ensures genuine participation and inclusivity for all. As a philosophy of life, Ubuntu "espouses a fundamental respect in the rights of others, as well as a deep allegiance to the collective identity," through compassion, interconnectedness, interdependence, and deep-rootedness in community.[4] Ubuntu encourages a definition and understanding of individuals "primarily through their relationships with others rather than by their status as discrete individuals."[5]

This philosophy of incompleteness and of self-activation through relationships of interdependence, shared throughout most of the African continent (not necessarily using the same terminology), "regulates the exercise of individual rights by emphasizing sharing and co-responsibility and the mutual enjoyment of rights by all."[6] It posits that humans are "related to and depending on each other" and "are responsible for ensuring that others have everything that they need."[7]

According to Desmond Tutu, whose articulations on Ubuntu as resilience and fortitude through forgiveness were at the heart of the South African Truth and Reconciliation Commission process,[8] one has Ubuntu ("Yu, u nobuntu") when one is "generous, hospitable, friendly, caring and compassionate." Ubuntu "has to do with what it means to be truly human, to know that you are bound up with others in the bundle of life."[9]

Ubuntuism in Practice and Perspective

Ubuntu can be considered as a social organizing principle at the heart of which is the humility of incompleteness and the quest for conviviality.[10] It can inspire stable relationships in the communities in which it is practiced by encouraging individuals to recognize the interconnections that make their sociality possible as well as to "learn how to create mutual interests, giving mutual satisfaction." Ubuntu seeks to socialize those who embrace it to recognize the virtues of giving, receiving, and giving in turn. It is about enabling life and living for all and sundry through the circulation of things, debt, and indebtedness. It is a deterrent to what Mauss terms "the brutish pursuit of individual ends," which is "harmful to the ends and the peace of all ... and rebounds on the individual himself."[11]

By encouraging the circulation of things, Ubuntu provides a framework for happiness through selfless giving, one in which poverty and wealth are constantly on the move, changing hands and changing places, ensuring that everyone shall have their fair share of opportunity and possibility—of sunshine, rainfall, windfall, pitfall, and downfall—in life.[12] The notion of Ubuntu and its ethic of caring, sharing, and considerateness are not uniquely African, even if African civilizations are widely understood to be governed by its philosophy.

What, in the everyday lives of those implicated, does it mean to live out the claim that a person is a person because of others? What does it mean to recognize, embrace, and act in tune with incompleteness not as a lack but as a disposition for living and letting live? In other words, what are the challenges, and how are these challenges negotiated, to ensure fulfillment of the maxim that "to be a human be-ing is to affirm one's humanity by recognizing the humanity of others and, on that basis, establish humane relations with them"?[13]

The Ubuntu suggestion that "humans depend completely on one another for their development" is similar to Mauss' notion of "the gift," which encourages a life of mutuality, obligation, and reciprocity and emphasizes a continuous act of sharing to maintain a balance of reciprocity between oneself and others.[14] The obligatory circulation of wealth entails an obligation to reciprocate and to make oneself available to others in ways that allow for the maintenance of the giving and receiving cycle.[15] As Mauss puts it, "To refuse to give, to fail to invite, just as to refuse to accept, is tantamount to declaring war; it is to reject the bond of alliance and commonality."[16]

A truly rich person, quite paradoxically, is someone engaged in an ongoing process of material impoverishment, someone constantly reaching out to involve others in their material possibilities and promise. A gift from them to others is a gift not just in material terms but an extension of themselves. Giving abundantly enriches them abundantly. Through sharing, they activate and maintain relationships. Marcel Mauss calls this "an intermingling." "Souls are mixed with things; things with souls." "Lives are mingled together."[17] To be a rich and selfless person relationally is to be a person consumed by others in deed, body, mind, and soul. Fortune can never really substitute the ultimate gift of all—the gift of oneself, one's soul, or one's essence—because things are only a substitute or proxy for the gift of self, which is what others really desire and appreciate.

This idea of gifts and giving is very prominent in many religions. In Christianity, for example, the Bible urges self-abnegation through selflessness in giving, promising salvation for walking in humility, and making a virtue of poverty: Matt. 5:42 says, "Give to the one who asks you and do not turn away from the one who wants to borrow from you." Prov. 19:17: "The one who is gracious to the poor lends to the Lord, and the Lord will repay him for his good deed." Prov. 28:27 states that "whoever gives to the poor will lack nothing," and Cor. 9:7 states that "God loves a cheerful giver."

In a sense, poverty and abnegation could be perceived as a technology of self-edification through self-abnegation to ensure that individuals are able to attain "a certain state of happiness, purity, wisdom, perfection, or immortality"[18] comparable to the beatitudes of heaven. Seen in this light, it is easy to understand the degree to which personal riches can be an embarrassment, a curse, an encumbrance, or a crown of thorns, especially when the rich person fails to ensure circulation by passing the riches onto others, needy or not.

Gifts postpone the ultimate sacrifice, enabling the giver to live, like Abraham in the Bible who sacrificed a ram so Isaac might live. The more personal the gift and the more history it has accumulated, the more likely it is to be accepted as a substitute, double, or lookalike of the gift-giver by the receiver. David Graeber argues that because money is too generic to accumulate history, it cannot add to the holder's identity in the same manner that other things can.[19] Because of its ephemeral, here-and-now character, money, paradoxical as it might seem, lacks the social-marker capacity to activate the receiver to the same degree of potency required for social visibility as would a more personal thing that has accumulated history or that is capable of such history.

Ultimately, within the framework of incompleteness, being human as a permanent work in progress is all about debt and indebtedness. It is about the need to recognize and provide for the fact that life is all about the circulation of debt—that it is important to recognize the reality of one's eternal indebtedness to others—be these fellow humans, the natural environment and its resources, or the suprasensory forces and one's ancestors and forebears.

Debt embodies the essence of morality and informs everything we do.[20] In contexts of sociality where a person invariably leans on others to achieve something, the sentiment of one good turn deserves another is common currency. Even if a person is not in debt financially or materially, they might owe debts of gratitude. This could well be the reason—over and above as a means of escaping taxation—why even in contexts of entrenched capitalism many a billionaire or millionaire tend to start a foundation and engage in philanthropy. A truly wealthy person is someone with little or nothing to show for their sweat and toil, not because he or she is lazy, has failed to make it in life, or has been the victim of dispossession or a devaluation of the local currency, but because they have, willingly or reluctantly, sacrificed their "wealth in things" for "wealth in people."[21]

Ubuntuism and the Seesaw of Opportunity and Opportunism

Ubuntuism is an invitation to accept and embrace that no humanity is complete if it entails wasting away the humanity of others, however justifiable that might seem in the short term. When are claims of Ubuntuism an opportunity for collective success and social inclusivity, and when are they a mere ploy for opportunism? An individual toiling away in a distant land might be a victim of various claims by family, friends, and acquaintances who are not themselves ready to reciprocate when the individual comes knocking with claims and demands of their own. How then does one differentiate opportunity from opportunism? When should relationship claims be taken seriously, and when should they be ignored?

To the Nigerian actor and comedian Nkem Owoh, one should be wary of those who come claiming relationships only when one's circumstances have improved. He addresses this in his song "Know Me When I'm Poor."[22] It is when a person is poor that he or she knows those who clearly care about him or her.

Here are some examples of opportunities and opportunism within Ubuntuism.

Tensions between African Migrants and Families and Friends Left Behind

The capitalist economy and increasing globalization have brought about even greater agility among Africans compelled to seek ever greener pastures away from their home villages, hometowns, home cities, and even countries and home continents. Family and friends left behind by Africans migrating from their villages, towns, cities, and countries look for ever more creative ways and means to extend themselves and their arms to keep track of kin and friends and ensure that the successes of kin and friends are constantly extended to include them.

It is with this background that I invite you to explore with me some of the tensions between African migrants and their families and friends left behind. To every story of disappointment and the opportunism in claims and denials of Ubuntu, there are counter-stories of solidarity, mutuality, and collective responsibility that have developed through migrants responding to the obligation to share their wealth, however hard earned, with the community of family and friends left behind.

There are cases in which remittances have sustained families in a myriad of ways. However, even when migrants bend over backward to redistribute their wealth with parents and other relations back in their home country and village, it is not always guaranteed that their efforts are appreciated.

Honorine Express (stage name) is a US-based Cameroonian migrant renowned for her YouTube videos castigating opportunistic relationships between diaspora Cameroonians and family and friends back in Cameroon. Her posting titled "Demanding and Ungrateful Family Members" captures the intricacies of relentless demands by family members.[23]

In December 2018, I participated in a panel discussion at the Royal Netherlands Academy of Science on the commodification of football and the exploitation of African footballers in Europe by their clubs and agents. Many African footballers in Europe would argue that such exploitation is also by families and friends back home in Africa.

A story that resonates with issues raised by Honorine Express in her video postings is the one of renowned Togolese international footballer Emmanuel Adebayor. He has played for several top European clubs, including Monaco, Arsenal, Manchester City, and Tottenham Hotspurs.

On May 6, 2015, I accessed a detailed Facebook posting in English and French[24] in which he complained about the catalog of ingratitudes his Togolese family had repeatedly shown him despite his generosity in their regard. He explains that finally coming out in the open with the story has less to do with "money" and more to do with the hope that "all families can learn from what happened in mine."

Adebayor recounts how at the age of seventeen he built a house for his family with his first wages as a footballer. This was to ensure that his family was safe. When he was awarded the trophy for African Player of the Year in 2008, he took his mother along with him to share the honor and "to thank her for everything." That same year, he "brought her to London for various medical checkups," but when his daughter was born and he called his mother to announce the birth, the mother did not want to hear about it. "She immediately hung up the phone."

Despite their differences, he continued to support his mother. He sponsored her travel to Lagos to meet with Nigerian Prophet T. B. Joshua. He also gave her "a great amount of money to start a business" and allowed her to put his name and picture on the items she sold for publicity. Faced with his mother's lack of appreciation, he asks: "What else can a son do in his power to support his family?"

Doing even more does not seem to bring recognition and gratitude in his case. He bought a fifteen-room house in East Legon, Ghana, for USD 1.2 million and found it normal to let his older sister Yabo and half-brother Daniel stay in the house. When he decided to go to the house on vacation a few months later, he was surprised to see many cars in the driveway and to discover that his sister had decided to rent out the house without informing him. She had also kicked Daniel out of the house. "When I called her and asked for an explanation, she took about 30 minutes to abuse and insult me over the phone," accusing him of being ungrateful. "I called my mother to explain the situation and she did the same as my sister."

Being accused of ingratitude by those he cared about was beyond his comprehension.

Adebayor does not seem to be lucky with his family. Even his brother Rotimi, whom he sponsored into a football academy in France, resorted to stealing the phones of other players—"Within a few months; out of 27 players, he stole 21 phones." He went on to steal jerseys of renowned players.

Rotimi repeatedly benefited from Emmanuel's recognition that "blood is thicker than water." But Rotimi would not give up stealing and abusing the privileges of "I am your brother." He would not apply himself as much as he was expected to with the chances he got.

When in 2005 Adebayor organized a meeting "to solve our family issues," his entire family was of the opinion that "I should build each family member a house and give each of them a monthly wage." It seems Adebayor is seen and related to by the rest of his family as a wallet on legs. They do not relent in asking him to redistribute his wealth to them and are vehemently hostile to any idea of him expanding the pool of those he helps. "Every time I try to help the people in need, they had to question me and all of them thought it was a bad idea." To conclude, "Today I am still alive and they have already shared all my goods, just in case I die."[25]

There is little in the attitude and behavior of his family to suggest that Adebayor owns himself, let alone his wealth. He is eaten, but not allowed to eat. It is normal in claims of Ubuntu to assume that one's fortunes or riches do not belong to one alone, that one has the duty to share one's success with others—both intimate and distant. In the case of Adebayor, his family does not even appear to expect him to claim any of his hard-earned riches. They treat him like a hen that lays golden eggs and that is strictly forbidden from claiming any egg for itself. In the eyes of his family, however much of his riches he shares with them, he is expected to share even more—to give away until there is nothing left to give. Only then would he be forgiven and forgotten by them. After usurping his wealth, they will have usurped him completely—mind, body, and soul—leaving him truly dead to them.

Despite not having been to school, Adebayor is proud of his achievements, and especially of what he did for his family, ungrateful though they are. Every now and again, he feels like committing suicide because of the family pressures. "For everyone who knows me, I'd do anything for my country and my people," he concludes his story.[26]

In three Facebook posts, Adebayor shares with us not only a story of how he went from humble beginnings to fame as a footballer, but more importantly the selfless generosity with which he greeted his good fortune. As Antoinette Muller puts it in a commentary, Adebayor has "gone from having no football boots to earning enough to provide, not only for himself, but for his family, and be in a position to support a number of charity projects across Africa," and "his actions mostly suggest that he is a good egg, who cares deeply for his fellow humans."[27]

Adebayor's story is more common than many reading his Facebook posts might imagine.

His story raises some perplexing questions. What could have provoked a renowned international footballer of his caliber to the point of washing his family linen on Facebook? Is his intention limited to what he claims—so that "all families could learn from what happened"? Could this also be a way of loosening his daughter from the entrapment imposed by his insatiable family members?

Adebayor portrays himself as an excellent example of an inclusive achiever through selfless contributions to others and their welfare. He would like to redistribute what he accumulates beyond the narrow confines of his immediate family, if only they disabuse themselves of insisting on the lion's share. Family members actively discouraged any attempt to spread the wealth to help other people. They would rather his Ubuntu start and end with them.

The fact that the story is told entirely from Adebayor's perspective—the perspective of the hunted and not the hunter—begs the questions: Why, given his stature and prominence, did Adebayor yield to this predatory dimension of his family? He could easily have argued, as some purportedly self-made others would, that it was within his right as an individual who had made it big to seek to protect his hard-earned wealth. Why did he not take this step? Is it enough to explain his position simply in terms of blood being thicker than water?

By seeking to take care of the family beyond mere reproduction of his father through birth, and by accommodating his family members even in their excesses, Adebayor makes a compelling case for inclusiveness, considerateness, generosity, and humaneness not dissimilar to the case made by Nelson Mandela for Ubuntu to which we alluded in the beginning.

Reflections on the Future of Ubuntuism

Ubuntuism is neither fixed nor claimed or practiced homogeneously across Africa. In some countries such as South Africa, it is an ideal to be recuperated, resurrected, or rediscovered through conscious acts of creative imagination and practice. The recuperation of Ubuntu is urgent, given surging economic downturns and ever-diminishing possibilities for the rights and entitlements promised all and sundry under the post-Apartheid constitution, which, paradoxically, does not give Ubuntu the centrality it deserves.

How do Africans who travel out of their communities in quest of greener pastures and those they leave behind forge a common future? How should they link up to demand that Europe and the West by extension assume their obligations toward a continent systematically dispossessed throughout histories of unequal encounters and unreciprocated generosity? Let us consider remittances.

The interconnections between gift and market economies materialize in the lives of African migrants and the relationships they seek to maintain with their home countries. Africans in the diaspora remit significant amounts of money to the continent yearly.

They are superexploited by the opportunism of families and friends back home and also by companies such as Western Union and MoneyGram, which thrive on weak competition, concentration of market power, and weak financial regulation to charge exorbitantly for remitting to Africa. Paul Collier asserts that the flow of remittances can be regarded as "an inadvertent aid program to host countries" from the countries of origin of the migrants in question.[28]

Many African migrants are very careful about how and to whom they remit and follow up on their investments judiciously, and many have fallen prey to the sort of opportunism described by Emmanuel Adebayor. Increasingly, however, Africans abroad and in general are wising up to the tricks of family and friends. Notwithstanding such alertness, it is hardly correct to blame the opportunism of relations and friends back home entirely on the waywardness and unethical behavior of the individuals involved. Structural factors informing growing global inequalities and the tendency to privilege the market over all other forms of economy play an important role in determining relationships of opportunity and opportunism—at global and local levels, by individuals, states, and corporations, among other actors.

Adebayor's negative experience explains in part why remittances by African migrants abroad have a "significant positive impact on income inequalities in African countries,"[29] even when the fact of remitting does not necessarily achieve the envisaged outcome for those doing the remitting.[30] Remittances, it has been noted, also contribute significantly to economic growth in Africa,[31] with Singh et al. suggesting that "countries with well-functioning domestic institutions" appear to "be better at unlocking the potential for remittances to contribute to faster economic growth."[32]

As the popular term "black tax" suggests, remittances are a form of taxation directly by family and friends who feel entitled to partake of the personal success of migrants.[33] Like with other forms of taxes—if social media commentary berating relatives and friends for constantly insisting on compliance willy-nilly are anything to go by—those who pay black tax are not always enthusiastic about doing so.

Stories like that of Adebayor provide a moral lens through which to understand the opportunism of Ubuntu. Individuals caught between cultures and continents navigate market and gift economies to express their connectedness and humanity. Surging opportunism and the corruption of Ubuntu that comes with it are a clarion call to rediscover, reinvent, and reinvest in the interconnections and interdependencies between market and gift economies, obligation and reciprocity, autonomy and sociality. Put differently, opportunism out of control is a clarion call to reunite the hunter and the hunted, each with the capacity to tell the story of the hunt, ever conscious as they both should be of the prospect that the hunter can be hunted, and the hunted be the hunter.

Humanity, human rights, and democracy cannot be considered apart from the economies and inequalities resulting from the global integration of markets that is leaving many behind. What practical prospects and possibilities are there for Ubuntuism in the twenty-first century? This is an age of crude paradoxes: incredulous wealth amidst implausible penury; phenomenal food wastage amidst mountains and valleys of hunger; concentration of resources in the hands and homes of a few while productive resources around the world are being devastated.

Theoretically, Ubuntuism would and should triumph in a context like our current world, where there is more than enough wealth to go around and more than enough resources for everyone to enjoy at least a minimal standard of living. The problem, in its simplest form, is one of equity and distribution. We do not use the world's resources wisely. We hoard and even destroy them. What about those excluded from their fair share of opportunity? The existential situation is absurd.

Africa might be "poor" according to economists, but is certainly not materially or otherwise poor. Africa is rich in social, cultural, conceptual, symbolic, and other forms of capital. Marketization, monetization, commodification, and rationalization are not the only, nor necessarily the most important, system of value for social life. What may be considered "poor" are systems and structures that do not recognize and provide for incompleteness and conviviality.

The tendency to focus overly on economic wealth and monetary and commodity value of sociality is delusory. It creates an illusion of the omnipotence of economics—and a particular form of economics: that of the market economy. Wealth in things and a fixation on economic capital and a logic of rational choice seem rather reductive when placed alongside philosophies and practices of inclusiveness, African or otherwise. Partaking in a cosmological epistemology of infinite possibilities of forms and transformations of being allows one to see things in people, and people in things.

I have broached the context of globalization and histories of unequal encounters that have shaped relations in Africa and beyond under global capitalism. I have argued that, in the spirit of Ubuntu, Africans, their identities, and mobilities are part and parcel of the experience of being human in a world on the move. And their contributions are needed in today's world more than ever.

Notes

This essay was first prepared and presented as the Africa Day Memorial Lecture, University of the Free State, Bloemfontein, May 22, 2019. It was subsequently published in *Alternation* Special Edition 36 (2020): 31–49. We are pleased to republish it here in honor of Joel Carpenter, for whom Ubuntuism and humility have been and remain dear.

1. F. B. Nyamnjoh and M. Rowlands, "Elite Associations and the Politics of Belonging in Cameroon," *Africa* 68, no. 3 (1998): 320–37; F. B. Nyamnjoh, "'A Child Is One Person's Only in the Womb': Domestication, Agency and Subjectivity in the Cameroonian Grassfields," in R. Werbner, ed., *Postcolonial Subjectivities in Africa* (London: Zed, 2002), 111–38; F. B. Nyamnjoh, "Cameroonian Bushfalling: Negotiation of Identity and Belonging in Fiction and Ethnography," *American Ethnologist* 38, no. 4 (2011): 701–13; F. B. Nyamnjoh, "Politics of Back-Scratching in Cameroon and Beyond," in Petr Drulák and Šárka Moravcová, eds., *Non-Western Reflection on Politics* (Frankfurt am Main: Peter Lang, 2013), 35–53; F. B. Nyamnjoh, *C'est l'homme qui fait l'homme: Cul-de-Sac Ubuntu-ism in Côte d'Ivoire* (Bamenda: Langaa, 2015).

2. F. B. Nyamnjoh, "Incompleteness: Frontier Africa and the Currency of Conviviality," *Journal of Asian and African Studies* 52, no. 3 (2017): 253–70; F. B. Nyamnjoh, *Drinking from the Cosmic Gourd: How Amos Tutuola Can Change Our Minds* (Bamenda: Langaa, 2018).
3. M. Letseka, "In Defense of Ubuntu," *Studies in Philosophy and Education* 31 (2012): 48. https://doi.org/10.1007/s11217-011-9267-2.
4. N. C. Mabovula, "The Erosion of African Communal Values: A Reappraisal of the African Ubuntu Philosophy," *Inkanyiso: Journal of Humanities and Social Sciences* 3, no. 1 (2011): 40.
5. A. Whitworth and K. Wilkinson, "Tackling Child Poverty in South Africa: Implications of Ubuntu for the System of Social Grants," *Development Southern Africa* 30, no. 1 (2013): 121. https://doi.org/10.1080/0376835X.2013.756219.
6. Mabovula, "The Erosion of African Communal Values," 40.
7. Whitworth and Wilkinson, "Tackling Child Poverty in South Africa," 125.
8. R. H. Bell, *Understanding African Philosophy: A Cross-Cultural Approach to Classical and Contemporary Issues* (New York: Routledge, 2002), 85–107.
9. D. Tutu, *God Has a Dream: A Vision of Hope for Our Times* (Cape Town: Double Day Publishers, 2004), 26.
10. Nyamnjoh, "Incompleteness," 2017; Nyamnjoh, *Drinking from the Cosmic Gourd*, 2018.
11. M. Mauss, *The Gift: The Form and Reason for Exchange in Archaic Societies* (New York: W. W. Norton, [1950] 1990), 82–7.
12. G. Agamben, *The Highest Poverty: Monastic Rules and Form-of-Life* (Stanford, CA: Stanford University Press, 2013).
13. M. B. Ramose, *African Philosophy through Ubuntu* (Harare: Mond Books, 1999), 52.
14. C. G. Christians, "Ubuntu and Communitarianism in Media Ethics," *Ecquid Novi* 25, no. 2 (2004): 244.
15. Mauss, *The Gift*, 8–18.
16. Ibid., 13.
17. Ibid., 20.
18. M. Foucault, "Technologies of the Self," in L. H. Martin, H. Gutman, and P. H. Hutton, eds., *Technologies of the Self: A Seminar with Michel Foucault* (Amherst: University of Massachusetts Press, 1988), 18.
19. D. Graeber, *Towards an Anthropological Theory of Value: The False Coin of Our Own Dreams* (New York: Palgrave, 2001).
20. D. Graeber, *Debt: The First 5,000 Years* (New York: Melville House, 2011), 89–126. See also David Graeber, "The Moral Power of Debt." www.bbc.co.uk/programmes/b05447pc (accessed May 27, 2015).
21. J. Guyer and S. M. E. Belinga, "Wealth in People as Wealth in Knowledge: Accumulation and Composition in Equatorial Africa," *Journal of African History* 26, no. 1 (1995): 91–120.
22. www.youtube.com/watch?v=z0JGB0PV0mE (accessed March 9, 2014).
23. Honorine Express, "Demanding and Ungrateful Family Members." www.youtube.com/watch?v=OJ3wZ97Ab0w (accessed August 7, 2015).
24. See www.facebook.com/permalink.php?story_fbid=1650071258554893&id=1377345199160835&substory_index=0 (accessed May 6, 2015).
25. The full Facebook post in French by Emmanuel Adebayor at these links: www.facebook.com/permalink.php?story_fbid=1650071258554893&id=1377345199160

835&substory_index=0; www.facebook.com/permalink.php?story_fbid=165170314 1725038&id=1377345199160835&substory_index=0
26. www.facebook.com/permalink.php?story_fbid=1656411337920885&id=137734519 9160835&substory_index=0 (accessed May 22, 2015).
27. Antoinette Muller, "Stranger in a Strange Land: Adebayor's Silent Struggles," May 22, 2015. www.dailymaverick.co.za/article/2015-05-22-stranger-in-a-strange-land-adebay ors-silent-struggles/#.VV7gxUYe4TY (accessed May 25, 2015).
28. P. Collier, *Exodus: Immigration and Multiculturalism in the 21st Century* (London: Penguin Books, 2013), 226.
29. J. C. Anyangwu, "International Remittances and Income Inequality in Africa," Working Paper No. 135 (African Development Bank Group, August 2011).
30. Collier, *Exodus*, 206–13.
31. E. K. K. Lartey, "Remittances, Investment and Growth in Sub-Saharan Africa," *Journal of International Trade and Economic Development: An International and Comparative Review* 22, no. 7 (2013): 1038–58.
32. R. J. Singh, M. Haacker, K. Lee, and M. Le Goff, "Determinants and Macroeconomic Impact of Remittances in Sub-Saharan Africa," *Journal of African Economies* 20, no. 2 (2010): 312.
33. A. Manqoyi, "Researching Cannibalising Obligations in Post-Apartheid South Africa," in Francis B. Nyamnjoh, ed., *Eating and Being Eaten: Cannibalism as Food for Thought* (Bamenda: Langaa, 2018), 197–222.

Bibliography

Agamben, G. *The Highest Poverty: Monastic Rules and Form-of-Life*. Stanford, CA: Stanford University Press, 2013.
Anyangwu, J. C. "International Remittances and Income Inequality in Africa." Working Paper No.135. African Development Bank Group, August 2011.
Bell, R. H. *Understanding African Philosophy: A Cross-Cultural Approach to Classical and Contemporary Issues*. New York: Routledge, 2002.
Christians, C. G. "Ubuntu and Communitarianism in Media Ethics." *Ecquid Novi*, 25, no. 2 (2004): 235–56.
Collier, P. *Exodus: Immigration and Multiculturalism in the 21st Century*. London: Penguin Books, 2013.
Foucault, M. "Technologies of the Self." In *Technologies of the Self: A Seminar with Michel Foucault*, edited by L. H. Martin, H. Gutman and P. H. Hutton. Amherst: University of Massachusetts Press, 1988, pp. 16–49.
Graeber, D. *Debt: The First 5,000 Years*. New York: Melville House, 2011.
Graeber, D. *Towards an Anthropological Theory of Value: The False Coin of Our Own Dreams*. New York: Palgrave, 2001.
Guyer, J., and S. M. E. Belinga. "Wealth in People as Wealth in Knowledge: Accumulation and Composition in Equatorial Africa." *Journal of African History* 26, no. 1 (1995): 91–120.
Lartey, E. K. K. "Remittances, Investment and Growth in Sub-Saharan Africa." *Journal of International Trade and Economic Development: An International and Comparative Review* 22, no. 7 (2013): 1038–58.

Letseka, M. "In Defense of Ubuntu." *Studies in Philosophy and Education* 31 (2012): 47–60. https://doi.org/10.1007/s11217-011-9267-2.

Mabovula, N. C. "The Erosion of African Communal Values: A Reappraisal of the African Ubuntu Philosophy." *Inkanyiso: Journal of Humanities and Social Sciences* 3, no. 1 (2011): 38–47.

Manqoyi, A. "Researching Cannibalising Obligations in Post-Apartheid South Africa." In *Eating and Being Eaten: Cannibalism as Food for Thought*, edited by Francis B. Nyamnjoh. Bamenda: Langaa, 2018, pp. 197–222.

Mauss, M. *The Gift: The Form and Reason for Exchange in Archaic Societies*. New York: W. W. Norton, [1950] 1990.

Nyamnjoh, F. B. "'A Child Is One Person's Only in the Womb': Domestication, Agency and Subjectivity in the Cameroonian Grassfields," In *Postcolonial Subjectivities in Africa*, edited by R. Werbner. London: Zed, 2002, pp. 111–38.

Nyamnjoh, F. B. "Cameroonian Bushfalling: Negotiation of Identity and Belonging in Fiction and Ethnography." *American Ethnologist* 38, no. 4 (2011): 701–13.

Nyamnjoh, F. B. "Politics of Back-Scratching in Cameroon and Beyond." In *Non-Western Reflection on Politics*, edited by Petr Drulák and Šárka Moravcová. Frankfurt am Main: Peter Lang, 2013, pp. 35–53.

Nyamnjoh, F. B. *C'est l'homme qui fait l'homme: Cul-de-Sac Ubuntu-ism in Côte d'Ivoire*. Bamenda: Langaa, 2015.

Nyamnjoh, F. B. "Incompleteness: Frontier Africa and the Currency of Conviviality." *Journal of Asian and African Studies* 52, no. 3 (2017): 253–70.

Nyamnjoh, F. B. *Drinking from the Cosmic Gourd: How Amos Tutuola Can Change Our Minds*. Bamenda: Langaa, 2018.

Nyamnjoh, F. B., and M. Rowlands. "Elite Associations and the Politics of Belonging in Cameroon." *Africa* 68, no. 3 (1998): 320–37.

Ramose, M. B. *African Philosophy through Ubuntu*. Harare: Mond Books, 1999.

Singh, R. J., M.Haacker, K. Lee, and M. Le Goff. "Determinants and Macroeconomic Impact of Remittances in Sub-Saharan Africa." *Journal of African Economies* 20, no. 2 (2010): 312–40.

Tutu, D. *God Has a Dream: A Vision of Hope for Our Times*. Cape Town: Double Day Publishers, 2004.

Whitworth, A., and K. Wilkinson. "Tackling Child Poverty in South Africa: Implications of Ubuntu for the System of Social Grants." *Development Southern Africa* 30, no. 1 (2013): 121–34. https://doi.org/10.1080/0376835X.2013.756219.

15

The Significance of Ancestors in Shaping and Understanding Christian Theology: A Samoan Perspective

Featunai Liuaana

Introduction: Genealogy and Ancestors

When Samoa celebrated its forty-seventh year of independence in 2009, the Head of State spoke on the theme "We Are What We Remember." He said, in part:

> Independence Day is a day of remembrance .... It is a day where we celebrate remembrance of history, traditions, and culture, of struggle and sacrifice, values, and vision. We celebrate Independence because knowing who we are is important. We remember that God is the source of life and frames our destinies. We remember our *spiritual mentors and our loved ones*.[1]

Efi reiterated three important features of Samoan life—Identity, God, and Ancestors. All three are interrelated and provide not only meaning but also substance of life. However, it is the influence of ancestors in the primal religion of Samoa that has shaped Samoan interpretation and understanding of Christian theology.

For Samoans, ancestors imply genealogy, which is primarily focused on the ascent and descent of rulers and nobles to legitimize claims to power, authority, and wealth. But, in recent times, genealogy has included the ancestral lineage of all people;[2] Samoans focus on both understandings of genealogy. Samoan ancestors are "spiritual mentors and loved ones" that connect the past to the present. In their ancestors, Samoans reflect on their origin and the sacred, find their identity, and define their relationship to their spiritual world.

Samoa genealogies rely on the memory of the living, which is the boundary between the secular and the sacred. And yet, Samoans expect their ancestors' genealogy to exist firmly in the sacred, because it legitimizes the lineage of the ancestors in the genealogy and the holders of *matai* (chief)[3] titles, *pule* (authority), *malosi* (power), and *mana* (sacredness).[4] In order to extend the existence of their ancestors and genealogy beyond the secular, Samoans advanced myths and oral traditions to fill the void. In doing so, the *matai* titles automatically extend beyond the memory of the living (secular) into the realm of the unknown (sacred). Subsequently, Samoan genealogies contain *matai* titles, which act as pointers to the original or first ancestors. Such genealogies authenticate family bloodlines and bind the first ancestor to future ancestors (descendants) who hold the same *matai* titles passed on in each family. Samoans who had no *matai* titles were represented by the ancestors who held the *matai* titles of their families. In the Samoan primal context, everyone was, is, and will be an ancestor.

The Samoan word *tuaā* is translated "ancestor" and refers to ancestors who are still in the memories of the living. The ancestors beyond the memory of the living are referred to as *tuaā ua mavae*,[5] but it still falls short of the sacred. Apart from *tuaā* and *tuaā ua mavae*, there are no other Samoan words to accurately express the importance of "ancestor" for Samoans. However, in perusing oral traditions and Samoan myths, I contend that the Samoan primal words for ancestor were *aitu* and *atua*. This goes against the popular consensus that *aitu* and *atua* mean "god."[6] Scholars of Pacific anthropology, history, sociology, theology, apostles of Samoan primal traditions, and keepers of Samoan customs would cry "rubbish," with a few turning in their graves vowing to send the spirits of their ancestors to deal with such sacrilege. Nevertheless, it is an assertion not lightly made without a reflective academic assessment, especially when many of the scholars of Samoan primal and antiquity have relied on biased missionary interpretations of the Samoan primal worldview.

Samoa had sporadic contacts with the outside world prior to the missionary era.[7] However, it was the missionaries of the London Missionary Society (LMS) who first fully dialogued and interacted with Samoans in their primal context, and I believe they were the perpetrators who reinterpreted Samoan primal worldview to articulate new Christian concepts. The culturally shocked LMS took apart the Samoan primal worldview and replaced it with their English Victorian Protestant worldview, which was further colored with a French Counter-Reformation Catholic worldview.[8] Samoan primal concepts were given new nuances of meaning to suit Christian beliefs and missionary ideology. And in the reshuffling of primal culture, customs, traditions, and religious beliefs, the missionaries dissected, redefined, exchanged, transformed, repackaged, substituted, and even eradicated much that gave meaning and definition to the existence of ancestors and the sacred in the Samoan primal worldview.

The LMS eschewed Samoan's veneration of ancestors as ancestor worship in their effort to redefine the meaning of *atua* and *aitu*. The missionaries knew that the practice of ancestor worship was a common phenomenon among other cultures encountered in their mission enterprises and found it a stumbling block in evangelization and conversion.[9] For Samoans, ancestor veneration honored the deeds and memories of their ancestors. In doing so, their ancestors would continue to provide for their future ancestors' (descendants) well-being—a common trait with other cultures.[10] The Protestant and Catholic missions in Samoa refused to acknowledge that Samoans venerated their ancestors, even though the notion of venerating the dead, and "Veneration of the Saints," would not have been lost to the missionaries or gone unnoticed by the Samoans. It was a common ritual in early nineteenth-century England to visit graves of ancestors, leaving flowers and praying for or asking favors from ancestors.[11] And no doubt, many of the early missionaries to Samoa would have participated as venerators, and not worshipers, of their ancestors. Samoans venerating *aitu* and *atua* (ancestors) did not constitute any belief that ancestors who passed on from the secular world became deities as the missionaries had concocted and condemned.

It was unfortunate that the early missionaries chose to reinterpret Samoan veneration of their *aitu* and *atua* as ancestor worship and transfer *aitu* and *atua* to accommodate the lack of a Samoan word for "god."[12] It was an act of sacrilege that pierced the heart of Samoan reverence for ancestors, especially the idea of sending *aitu* (ancestors) to the realm of *Sheol* (hell) as pagan gods, ghosts, and evil spirits. It transferred *aitu* (ancestors) outside the Samoan primal worldview and had an adverse effect on Samoans' understanding and acceptance of Christian theology on many levels.[13] However, in equating *atua* (ancestor) with God, various *matai* found legitimacy for their sacredness and divine nature. And the Samoan premise that God from the beginning of time ordained *matai* descendants of their *atua* (ancestor) to rule Samoa found new support and meaning at a sacred level and prompted many Samoan *matai* to presume they were gods on earth. The source of their sacredness is God, the new Christian *atua*.[14] Thus, the functions and actions of the ancestors in the primal, especially in relation to an ancestor's responsibility to the family, to the land, and to the spiritual need of those under their guidance, became more sacred in the roles and responsibilities of the *matai* as a descendant of God, or, at least, a descendant made in the image of God.

Samoan Primal Context of the Ancestors

The primal context of *aitu* and *atua* must be understood in relation to Samoa's history and location in the Pacific. Samoa, meaning sacred-center (Sa-moa) and honored by scholars as the "Cradle of the Pacific," was populated through successive, and yet distinct, migrations between 1000 BC and 300 AD, namely Lapita, Tagaloa, and Pulotu. Lapitans used Samoa sporadically as an outpost for trade, but it was the Tagaloan and Pulotuan migrations that gave the Samoans their identity as a people.[15]

There are many oral traditions describing the Tagaloa settlement of Samoa. Tagaloa—from *taga*, meaning a bag or enclosure, and *loa*, meaning eternal or extending forever—is revered as one who is timeless and eternal and encompasses all things. Tagaloa was the great ancestor of the first migration of Samoan people and is venerated accordingly. However, the veneration of Tagaloa as a great *atua* (ancestor) changed when myths and oral traditions were retold in line with the missionaries' reorganization of Samoa's primal worldview. Samoan oral traditions reinvented Tagaloa as Tagaloalagi (god of the sky) and highlighted his descendants Tagaloafa'atupunu'u (originator of lands), Tagaloatolonu'u (settler of lands), Tagaloanofonu'u (dweller of lands), Tagaloasu'enu'u (explorer of lands), and Tagaloava'aimamao (the seer). Together all the rituals, altars, and agents associated with the veneration of Tagaloa and his descendants in primal Samoa, which the missionaries saw as evidence of ancestral worship, were all condemned to *Sheol*.

The Pulotuans, on the other hand, were powerful, destructive, resilient, revengeful, and aggressive people. They kept close to the sea and preferred to reside near the coast. They were intimately in tune with nature and the supernatural. The Pulotuans originated from Pulotu, the home of all *aitu* (ancestors) and the abode of the afterlife.[16] They had a definite notion of soul (*loto*) and spirit (*agaga*), especially in relation to the spirits of the dead. The Pulotuan worldview left open communications between the world of the living and their ancestors in Pulotu. According to Samoan primal traditions, the location of two circular basins on the west coast of Savai'i Island in Samoa was the closest point of contact to the original homeland—Pulotu.[17]

Tagaloan and Pulotuan relationships were not always affable. And even though they interacted intimately through intermarriages, they failed to unite as one people as they kept to their own environment. However, at some point of time, the two groups could no longer coexist peacefully,[18] and, consequently, the Tagaloans left Samoa and migrated eastward. But a significant Tagaloan remnant remained in Samoa and were integrated into the Pulotuan primal context, and a compromised Samoan primal religious system took root.[19] The first missionaries discovered that the Samoans had developed a religious organization that influenced and controlled the lives of Samoans from birth to death. It controlled its social, economic, political, and religious life through constant interactions with, and veneration of, their *aitu* and *atua* (Pulotuan and Tagaloan ancestors). Such interactions and venerations were eradicated when the missionaries equated the *aitu* (ancestor) with demons and evil spirits, while the *atua* (ancestor) was highjacked to legitimize Christian theology. The missionaries enforced it vigorously, but the Samoans never entirely embraced it.

The "God with No Name" and Ancestors

In attributing the words *aitu* and *atua* to ancestors, it meant there was no word for "god" in the Samoan primal worldview. John Williams, an LMS missionary, asked a chief of Rarotonga about Samoan religion and was bluntly told, "those godless Samoans."[20] It was not that Samoans had no gods, but the fact that there was no word for god that made the Samoans "godless." Furthermore, after the Tagaloans left Samoa, all Tagaloan shrines, altars, and religious artifacts were abandoned and no longer visible when the LMS first met the "godless Samoans."[21] But in reality, the missionaries discovered that Samoa had gods galore, each with a name and a function.

According to the LMS missionary George Turner, Samoans were assigned personal gods at birth and would honor them for their entire life. In addition, Samoans had the protection and guidance of their family gods, village gods, district gods, and national gods. The many gods represented a higher consciousness that the Samoans could not make real, but real enough to be conceived in their minds and worshiped through inanimate and animate objects that surrounded their primal context.[22] The inanimate and animate objects were called *tupua* (idols), but the missionaries called them "gods" to fit their own mindset. It was this inability of the missionaries to grasp the Samoan primal worldview that led to a belief that Samoans had no understanding of a higher being that the missionaries called "God."

While Samoans may not have known "God" per se, they did know of a higher being whom they could not label or name. Samoans were not alone in being unable to conceive the sacred as "God." In Hinduism, many gods represent the existence of a higher being, but they can only refer to that higher being as "The One,"[23] and in Buddhism, that higher being is labeled "The Ultimate."[24] And even scholars of World Religions who struggle with this question refer to the existence of a higher being as "The Other."[25] The Taiwanese Indigenous people Seediq also have an idea of a higher being, but cannot give it a name as they have no idea of its being or form.[26] This being the case, it is noted that being unable to give a higher being a name is biblical. For instance, in the book of Exodus, God gives his name to Moses as "I am who I am."[27] In Athens, the Apostle Paul was inspired to preach the Christian God when he saw a pagan altar with a sign that said "To an unknown god."[28] Even the Epicureans and Stoics had a notion of a higher being beyond their many gods on display, but could only refer to it as the "unknown god." For Samoans, being unable to conceive a word for "God" in their primal worldview does not mean they were incapable of comprehending a higher being without a name.

Ancestors and Christian Theology

In pre-Christian Samoa, the *matai* held a sacred function in all matters pertaining to families, villages, and district, which included worship, war, fishing, canoe-making, house-building, and invoking *aitu* and *atua* (ancestors).[29] The *matai* represents the stored wisdom of past ancestors and is a legacy for future ancestors to interact in all matters that offer a pathway to forgiveness and reconciliation, salvation for the sinner, as well as entrusting faith and hope, wholeness, healing, and well-being, to the afflicted and guiding the dead to the afterlife. The *matai* also evoked their ancestors when the lives of family members were threatened or taken, and properties destroyed, as well as to guide and assist the family *matai* in achieving a positive outcome other than death.[30] These primal tasks continue as part of the roles and responsibilities of the *matai* in Christian Samoa today. It reiterates that there is still much to be offered by the ancestors of the past to the present and future ancestors in dealing with issues that affect every aspect of life. It is, therefore, important that Samoan primal concepts continue to be mined, reasserted, revisited, and viewed with fresh eyes and insights, so that the primal may be expressed again as the preface to any theological reflection. In the Samoan primal, several concepts underpinning the importance of ancestors and their contribution to theological thinking and practical application in the spiritual life of its people need to go through this process. But, due to space constraints, I will only highlight "sin and forgiveness" for clarification.[31]

The Primal Concept of Sin and Forgiveness

The ideas of forgiveness, retribution, and reconciliation were complex in the Samoan primal worldview. To understand its subtleness, one needs to understand Samoan primal worship and the roles and responsibilities of the ancestors and *matai* in it. An important characteristic of the Samoan primal worship was the nonexistence of a prayer of forgiveness. But it did not mean Samoans were immune from committing *agasala* (sin), on the contrary.[32] If a Samoan committed *agasala*, their ancestors would let them know through sickness, body deformity, and even death, thus the irrelevancy of a prayer for forgiveness when the ancestors had already punished them for their *agasala*.

However, the taking of a life, eloping with a *matai*'s wife, or the destruction of a *matai*'s property were *agasala* too great in magnitude for the ancestors of the offending family to punish, and only one punishment was warranted—death. Now the life of the offending family was in the hands of the ancestors of the offended family. However, the ancestors of the offending family can only guide in initiating reconciliation through the *ifoga*.[33]

The *ifoga* remains the highest act of reconciliation in Samoa today, and it is a shameful ordeal for any *matai* and their ancestors to endure. The *ifoga* takes place before dawn under the cover of darkness in front of the offended family's house to give the impression they have been prostrating all night. The highest ranked *matai* of the offending family, covered with an *ie toga* (fine mat),[34] prostrates on the ground, with his whole family prostrating uncovered alongside. The timeframe for the *ifoga* is determined by the *matai* of the offended family; it can take a few minutes, several days, or even longer. Rain or shine, the offending family will remain prostrated until the *matai* of the offended family decides the outcome.

There are only two outcomes possible. First, the *matai* of the offended family will end the life of the *matai* under the fine mat as compensation for the offense committed. In which case, the offending family would wrap the deceased with the fine mat, a symbolic act of covering their shame, and leave without further recourse. The penalty for the *agasala* has been fully paid, and both families would eventually reconcile and begin the process of healing. Second, the *matai* of the offended family would remove the fine mat and accept an apology offered by the offending family. In doing so, the process of reconciliation begins immediately. Dialogue takes place with a verbal confession, a request for forgiveness, and an offer of compensation, which all contribute to healing taking place in relationships, health, and well-being.[35]

The primal action of *ifoga* shows that prayers of confession mean little if they are not expressed in actions. For Samoans, actions are important when it comes to forgiveness and reconciliation, before any exchange of words, especially when a life is at stake. Samoans believe that if one is truly repentant, then they may be willing to offer their life to secure forgiveness and reconciliation, as Jesus did on the cross. For many Samoan churches today, the primal concept of *ifoga* has substituted the prayer of confession to the "God without a name" and the unseen power in the sacred realm of the ancestors. Christ forgave sinners during his earthly ministry. But eventually words were not enough. Christ offered himself as the ultimate word for the forgiveness of sin, as well as put into action, once and for all, our final reconciliation with God.

Ancestors in Limbo as the Church Searches for Understanding

Since the arrival of missionaries in Samoa, the churches' teachings have condemned the existence and invocation of *atua* and *aitu* (ancestors) and any references to ancestor spirits that contradict Christian theology. It created a Samoan theology black market to coexist with the missionaries' infallible theology. The misuse of the *atua* and *aitu* concept is a pivotal aspect of this dilemma. Samoan churches continue to teach that ancestors no longer have *mana* (power) because they have been defeated by the *mana* of the *Atua* (God) through Jesus Christ. However, when confronted with *ma'i aitu*,[36] many church members have been forced to respect their ancestors because *ma'i aitu* is seen as a positive confrontation for families with the sacred. Samoans still believe *atua* and *aitu* are vehicles for healing and blessings today. Church members have been willing to face humiliation and accept excommunication rather than suffer in the hands of their *atua* and *aitu*. The clergy continue to witness the growing participation of members evoking *atua* and *aitu* as part of their Christian faith. And many clergy, despite their Christian theological training, are caught between a rock and a hard place. They are, after all, by-products of the Samoan primal tradition.

Samoan Christians, like those in Africa, South America, and Asia, are increasingly conscious of their primal experiences. Many are at a crossroads in preserving the "Enlightenment" theological understanding of their missionary mentors against a strong shift toward primal religious underpinnings such as *atua* and *aitu*.[37] Samoan churches want to maintain, and be identified with, their missionary roots, but Samoan Christians want to openly take up their primal inheritance. It is hypocritical to support the primal and yet, as an institution, reject it. Otele Perelini, a Samoan scholar of primal religion, wrote:

> Jesus did not come to defeat the [*atua* and] *aitu* nor annul family ancestral spirits, but to deliver men and women from the forces of evil and malicious beings. The parallel drawn between [*atua* and] *aitu* possession and demon possession has undoubtedly led to the negation of [*atua* and] *aitu* within Samoan Christianity.[38]

The Samoan Church can no longer ignore the changing face of Christianity in its relationship with primal concepts as a vehicle to understanding its Christian faith. Primal concepts and experiences have already found their way into Christian experiences in various cultures to make Christianity more meaningful. Even in Samoa, every time people gather for *tapua'iga* (worship/prayer) they gather as the body of Christ—together with their *atua* and *aitu* who have gone before them—to worship the sacred beyond the secular—God.

Today, Sunday worship liturgies of many Samoan churches, and *tapua'iga* for many community undertakings, reflect the silent mood of the primal worship of the *aitu* and *atua*. Furthermore, the primal remnant of the family *tapua'iga afiafi* (evening prayers) is still the heart and soul of Samoan Christianity today. Samoan villages still ring bells, blow conch shells, and beat drums to signal the start of curfews and the beginning of *lotu afiafi*. The family gather to offer prayers, with the father still playing the role of the *taulāitu*.[39] The contributions of Christianity to the evening *lotu afiafi* today include hymns and the Bible. There is also in Samoa today an increase in the importance and role of the *taulāsea*,[40] which has further heightened the awareness of the existence of primal substructures within the Samoan Christian framework. And the popularity of *taulāsea* has not only increased the competition with Christian clergy as spiritual healers within the community but has also given confidence to those who have absorbed primal traditions into their Christian experiences. It also gives comfort to those still trapped within the Enlightenment mindset of the Victorian English Protestants, and the Catholic French Counter-Reformation, to explore their primal roots.

Samoan clergy are encouraged to be anchors of the *Atua* (*taulāitu*), as well as anchors of the *atua* and *aitu* (ancestors). Only then will Samoans make sense of Jesus being their "greatest ancestor,"[41] because Samoans have Jesus' DNA as the Gospel of Matthew's genealogy of Jesus attests. For Samoan Christians, Jesus being their greatest ancestor legitimizes their connection to the sacred—to God the creator of ancestors.[42] For Samoan *matai*, who have Jesus as their greatest ancestor, God had decreed Samoa to be ruled by their descendants—the *matai*. And through each *matai* every Samoan is connected to their ancestors who, like Jesus, have helped pave the way for a blessed afterlife.

In everyday affairs, Samoans still do everything under the guidance and protection of the *Atua* (God) and *atua* and *aitu* (ancestors), albeit in a passive and subversive manner. Sometimes, it is difficult to determine whether the *Atua* (God) or *atua* and *aitu* (ancestors) receive more attention. Every day in Samoan family and village undertakings, education, occupation, life's crisis, feasting, sports, and community gatherings, there is a continuous presence of the *atua* and *aitu* (ancestors) alongside the *Atua* (God). Everything Samoans do begins and ends with prayers, and every small portion of food, every little drops of water and *ava*[43] are still offered to acknowledge the *Atua* (God) and, indirectly, to pay respect to the *atua* and *aitu* (ancestors). No one can deny the revelations and evidence of God's presence in Samoan primal traditions. To do so is to deny God Himself and the existence of ancestors. Samoans want to regain the personal relationship they once enjoyed with their *atua* and *aitu* (ancestors), which the openness of their unique primal worldview provided. Samoa, after all, is Sa-moa (sacred-center), and for a primal religion to be a substructure of Samoan Christianity, Samoans must engage the present, to enable them to return to the future and move forward to their past,[44] so that Christ may be experienced holistically within the framework of Christianity. The best way forward is to heed the words of another great ancestor in the Christian faith, Augustine of Hippo, who testified, "Crede ut intellegas."[45]

Notes

1. Tuiatua T. Efi, "We Are What We Remember: Speech at 47th Independence of Samoa," *Samoa Observer*, June 3, 2009, emphasis added.
2. Teo Tuvale, T. E. Faletoese, and F. L. Kirisome, *O le Tusi Faalupega* (Apia: Malua Printing Press, 1900); Augustin Kramer, *Samoa Islands*, vol. 1 (trans. Theodore Verhaaren) (Auckland: Polynesia Press, 1995).
3. *Matai* status in Samoa is determined by their genealogies. See Featunai Liuaana, "Resurrecting Aitu as a Contemporary Theological Concept," BD Thesis, Pacific Theological College, 1991, 7–17.
4. The three attributes of a *matai* with *mana* being the supernatural power emanating from the sacred. See Otele S. Perelini, "A Comparison of Jesus' Healing with Healing

in Traditional and Christian Samoa," PhD Dissertation, Edinburgh University, 1992, 25-8. Professor Asamoah-Gyadu shared that African traditional chiefs were representatives of their ancestors. J. Kwabena Asamoah-Gyadu, "Drinking from Our Own Wells: The Primal Imagination and Christian Religious Innovation in Contemporary Africa," Primal Religion as the Substructure of Christianity Seminar, ACI, Akropong-Akuapem, Ghana, October 13-25, 2008.
5. *Tuaā* means "back of" or "behind of," and *tuaā ua mavae* means "ancestors who passed on long ago."
6. For example, Turner, *Samoa: A Hundred Years Ago and Long Before* (Suva: University of the South Pacific, 1984); Richard Goodman, "Some Aitu Beliefs of Modern Samoans," *Journal of Polynesian Society* 80 (1971): 463-79.
7. Between 1722 and 1824, six explorers visited Samoa, including Louis-Antoine de Bougainville who named Samoa *L'Archipel des Navigteus*. See Andrew Sharp, *The Discovery of the Pacific Islands* (Oxford: Clarendon, 1960); John Dunmore, *French Explorers in the Pacific*, vol. 1 (Oxford: Clarendon, 1965); Louis-Antoine de Bougainville, *A Voyage Round the World* (New York: Da Capo, 1772).
8. The LMS arrived in 1830. In 1835 the Wesleyan-Methodist reaffirmed the English Victorian worldview. The Catholics arrived in 1845. See Neil Gunson, *Messengers of Grace* (Oxford: Oxford University, 1978).
9. The animistic tribes of northern Philippines practiced ancestor worship before 1900. It was observed among Hindus and practiced by Indigenous Africans despite adopting Christianity. See Neal Ocampo, "Ancestor Veneration," November 12, 2018. https://fili pinoconjurerootwork.blogspot.com/2018/11/ancestral-veneration; Leme, "Ancestor Worship Philippines," November 9, 2020. https://lemeforense.com.br/site/article. php?e262ad=ancestor-worship-philippines.
10. Ghana's annual *Odwira* festival emphasized the cleansing of the town and the remembrance of ancestors. The ancestors were invited to participate in the *Odwira*. The Ghanaian believe that the dead, the living, and those not yet born are part and parcel of the community. Food was offered to the ancestors, and the people and the chiefs were blessed in the presence of the ancestor. I participated in the *Odwira* in relation to the Primal Religion as the Substructure of Christianity Seminar at Akrofi-Christaller Institute of Theology, Mission, Culture in Akropong-Akuapem, Ghana, October 13-24, 2008.
11. James Hastings, ed., *Encyclopedia of Religion and Ethics*, vol. 4 (Edinburg: T&T Clarke, 1911), 415-653.
12. There were similar practices by missionaries in Africa. See Lamin Sanneh, *Whose Religion Is Christianity: The Gospel beyond the West* (Grand Rapids, MI: William B. Eerdmans, 2003), 55-9.
13. For a discussion on the Samoan primal worldview and understanding of hell, see Liuaana, "Resurrecting Aitu," 51-66; see also E. S. Graighill Handy, "Polynesian Religion," in *Bernice P. Bishop Museum Bulletin No. 34* (New York: Kraus Reprint, 1971), 321-30.
14. Using the word *atua* for God in the Samoan Bible has helped to promote such ideologies, as in Luke 3:23-38, which traces the genealogy of Jesus back to God.
15. Joseph Finney, "The Meaning of the Name Samoa," *Journal of the Polynesian Society* 82, no. 3 (1873): 301-3; Roger C. Green, *Lapita: The Prehistory of Polynesia* (Cambridge, MA: Harvard University, 1979), 27-59.
16. Paul Geraghty, "Pulotu, Polynesia Homeland," *Journal of the Polynesian Society* 102, no. 4 (1993): 343-84.

17. John B. Stairs, *Old Samoa or Flotsam and Jetsam from the Pacific Ocean* (London: The Religious Tract Society, 1897), 210–40; Liuaana, "Resurrecting Aitu," 10–29.
18. Oral traditions relay constant conflicts between the two groups. For instance, the Pulotuan Lufasiāitu attacked the Tagaloans for stealing his properties. The conflict ended when Tagaloa gave his daughter as a peace offering.
19. In the Rotuman bible *aitu* is used for "God," and *atua* for "demon." The Marquesas ceremonial drink (betel-pepper) is *kavakava-atua*, but *avaava-aitu* in Tahiti. The interchangeable use of *aitu* and *atua* reflects earlier interactions of the two groups. Rotuman were Pulotuans, and Tahitian and Marquesians were Tagaloans. See Walter Ivens, "The Polynesian Word Atua: Its Derivation and Use," *Man* 24 (September 1924): 133–6.
20. John Williams, *A Narrative of Missionary Enterprises in the South Sea Islands* (London: John Snow, 1840), 142. This dilemma is also found in the primal religion of some Taiwanese tribes. See Wallis Ukan, "Grafting onto the Primal Religion: Re-thinking the Relation between TYCM Primal Religion and Christianity in Taiwan," Primal Religion as the Substructure of Christianity Seminar, Nagel Institute for the Study of World Religion, Michigan, July 1–17, 2007, 3–10.
21. Recent archaeological discovery in Samoa of *Pulemelei* has revealed Tagaloan shrines and altars.
22. Turner, *Samoa: A Hundred Years*, 27–67.
23. John B. Noss, *Man's Religion*, rev. ed. (New York: Macmillan, 1956), 113–40, 224–74.
24. Noss, *Man's Religion*, 155–80. For a broader understanding of the concept of "Ultimate Reality," see also Bahai World Centre, *Tablets of Bahaullah* (trans. Habib Taherzadel) (Haifa: Bahai World Centre, 1978).
25. For a good perspective on the subject, see Ilai Alon, Ithamar Gruenwald, and Itamar Singer, "Concepts of the Other in Near Eastern Religions," in *Israel Oriental Studies No. 14* (New York: E. J. Brill, 1994).
26. Ukan, "Grafting onto the Primal," 4–6.
27. *The Renouré Spiritual Formation Bible*, New Revised Standard Version (San Francisco: Harper, 1989), Exod. 3:14f.
28. Ibid., Acts 17:23.
29. See Augustin Kramer, *Samoa Islands*, vol. 2 (trans. Theodore Verhaaren) (Auckland: Polynesia Press, 1995); Turner, *Samoa: A Hundred Years*.
30. The ancestors were evoked through worship called *tapua'iga*—"sacred of the family."
31. Other Samoa primal concepts for discussion include salvation and eternal life, sickness and healing, blessings and cursing, and births and deaths. For further insights, see Harold Turner, *Australian Essays in World Religions* (Bedford Park: Australian Association for the Study of Religions, 1977), 27–37.
32. *Agasala* means "wrong action" or "punishable act."
33. *Ifoga* means "bow down" or "to prostrate."
34. The *ie toga* is a symbol of wealth, celebration, redemption, honor, and forgiveness.
35. For an excellent discussion on Samoa primal and Christian healing, see Perelini, "A Comparison of Jesus."
36. It is sickness caused by an *aitu* (ancestor). Such sickness in primal Samoa were either punishment for *agasal* or a message from an ancestor that needed to be communicated to the family. See Perelini, "A Comparison of Jesus," 243.
37. Similar trends occur among Christian Aimara of Bolivia. See Marcelo Vargas, "The Identity of Aimara Neopentecostals from 'Power of God' Church in La Paz, Bolivia,"

Primal Religion as the Substructure of Christianity Seminar, ACI, Akropong-Akuapem, Ghana, October 13-25, 2008.
38. The [*atua* and] is the writer's insertion. See Perelini, "A Comparison of Jesus," 244.
39. *Taula'itu* means anchor of the *aitu* (ancestors) or priest.
40. *Taulāsea* is the Samoan word for "Healer," who relies on Jesus' power and *mana* (power) of the *aitu* and *atua* (ancestors) for healing.
41. Professor Benhardt Y. Quarshie wrote, "Jesus is the maker of ancestors." See "Paul and the Primal Substructure of Christianity: Missiological Reflections on the Epistle to the Galatians," *Journal of African Christian Thought* 12, no.1 (June 2009): 8–14.
42. *The Renouré Spiritual Formation Bible*, Matt. 1: 1–16.
43. *Piper Methysticum* is a ceremonial drink served to chiefs. Before drinking it, a small portion is tipped out as an offering to the *atua* and *aitu* (ancestors) and to God.
44. This is the uniqueness of the Samoa primal worldview, which is not discussed in this essay. Samoans see the world as three tiers on one plane and understand God, Life, and Death in a circular context of coming from the sacred and returning to the sacred. Thus, the Samoans believe they come from their ancestral homeland Pulotu at birth and return to Pulotu at death. So, whether you go back or forward, you still return to the source.
45. "Believe so that you may understand."

Bibliography

Alon, Ilai Ithamar Gruenwald, and Itamar Singer, eds. "Concepts of the Other in Near Eastern Religions." *Israel Oriental Studies No. 14*. New York: E. J. Brill, 1994.

Asamoah-Gyadu, J. Kwabena. "Drinking from Our Own Wells: The Primal Imagination and Christian Religious Innovation in Contemporary Africa." Primal Religion as the Substructure of Christianity Seminar, ACI, Akropong-Akuapem, Ghana, October 13-25, 2008.

Bahai World Centre. *Tablets of Bahaullah* (trans. Habib Taherzadel). Haifa: Bahai World Centre, 1978.

Charlot, John. "The War between the Gods of Upolu and Savaii." *Journal of Pacific History* 23 (April 1988): 80–5.

de Bougainville, Louis-Antoine. *A Voyage Round the World*. New York: Da Capo, 1772.

Dunmore, John. *French Explorers in the Pacific*, vol. 1. Oxford: Clarendon, 1965.

Efi, Tuiatua T. "We Are What We Remember: Speech at 47th Independence Celebration of Samoa." *Samoa Observer*, June 3, 2009.

Finney, Joseph. "The Meaning of the Name Samoa." *Journal of the Polynesian Society* 82, no. 3 (1873): 301–3.

Geraghty, Paul. "Pulotu, Polynesia Homeland." *Journal of the Polynesian Society* 102, no. 4 (1993): 343–84.

Goodman, Richard. "Some Aitu Beliefs of Modern Samoans." *Journal of Polynesian Society* 80 (1971): 463–79.

Green, Roger C. *Lapita: The Prehistory of Polynesia*. Cambridge, MA: Harvard University, 1979.

Gunson, Neil. *Messengers of Grace*. Oxford: Oxford University, 1978.

Handy, E. S. Graighill. "Polynesian Religion." In *Bernice P. Bishop Museum Bulletin No. 34*. New York: Kraus Reprint, 1971.

Hastings, James, ed. *Encyclopedia of Religion and Ethics*, vol. 4. Edinburg: T&T Clarke, 1911.
Ivens, Walter. "The Polynesian Word Atua: Its Derivation and Use." *Man* 24 (September 1924): 133-6.
Kramer, Augustin. *Samoa Islands*, vol. 1 (trans. Theodore Verhaaren). Auckland: Polynesia Press, 1994.
Kramer, Augustin. *Samoa Islands*, vol. 2 (trans. Theodore Verhaaren). Auckland: Polynesia Press, 1995.
Leme. "Ancestor Worship Philippines." November 9, 2020. https://lemeforense.com.br/site/article.php?e262ad=ancestor-worship-philippines.
Liuaana, Featunai. "Resurrecting Aitu as a Contemporary Theological Concept." BD Thesis, Pacific Theological College, 1991.
Noss, John B. *Man's Religion*, rev. ed. New York: Macmillan, 1956.
Ocampo, Neal. "Ancestor Veneration." November 12, 2018. https:/filipinoconjurerootwork.blogspot.com/2018/11/ancestral-veneration.html.
Perelini, Otele S. "A Comparison of Jesus' Healing with Healing in Traditional and Christian Samoa." PhD Dissertation, Edinburg University, 1992.
Quarshie, Benhardt Y. "Paul and the Primal Substructure of Christianity: Missiological Reflections on the Epistle to the Galatians." *Journal of African Christian Thought* 12, no. 1 (June 2009): 8-14.
The Renouré Spiritual Formation Bible, New Revised Standard Version. San Francisco, CA: Harper, 1989.
Sanneh, Lamin. *Whose Religion Is Christianity: The Gospel beyond the West*. Grand Rapids, MI: William B. Eerdmans, 2003.
Sharp, Andrew. *The Discovery of the Pacific Islands*. Oxford: Clarendon, 1960.
Stairs, John B. *Old Samoa or Flotsam and Jetsam from the Pacific Ocean*. London: The Religious Tract Society, 1897.
Turner, George. *Samoa: A Hundred Years Ago and Long Before*. Suva: University of the South Pacific, 1984.
Turner, Harold. *Australian Essays in World Religions*. Bedford Park: Australian Association for the Study of Religions, 1977.
Tuvale, Teo, T. E. Faletoese, and F. L. Kirisome. *O le Tusi Faalupega*. Apia: Malua Printing Press, 1900.
Ukan, Wallis. "Grafting onto the Primal Religion: Re-thinking the Relation between TYCM Primal Religion and Christianity in Taiwan." Primal Religion as the Substructure of Christianity Seminar, Nagel Institute for the Study of World Religion, Michigan, July 7-17, 2007.
Vargas, Marcelo. "The Identity of Aimara Neopentecostals from 'Power of God' Church in La Paz, Bolivia." Primal Religion as the Substructure of Christianity Seminar, ACI, Akropong-Akuapem, Ghana, October 13-25, 2008.

16

Primal Religious Spirituality and Charismatic Revivalism: The Mizo Christian Experience

Lalsangkima Pachuau

Revivalism and the Primal Spirit

Not that our revered friend and colleague Joel Carpenter has anything to do with charismatic revivalism or primal religions, but my first connection with him happened to be a project that connects the two. I was privileged to be on a team working under the leadership of the late Kwame Bediako on a project called "Primal Religions as the Substructure of Christianity." The project was a collaborative work of the Nagel Institute for the Study of World Christianity, directed at the time by Joel Carpenter, and the Akrofi-Christaller Institute of Theology, Mission, and Culture, directed by Kwame and Mary Bediako in Ghana. In fact, this chapter is a revision of the work done for the project.[1] As the term revival or revivalism has been associated with Mizo Christianity, it centers on the spiritual experience reviving the religious fervor surrounding the belief in the vitality of the Holy Spirit of God. The Mizo Christian experience, the subject of this chapter, has two sources—the Christian revival movement inherited from the Welsh revival (1904) through the missionaries, and Indigenous primal spirituality. The former sparked the latter. With that thesis in mind, we trace the story of spiritual beliefs in the Mizo religious story.

The rise of Christianity in the majority world diversifies the face of Christianity and brings new features in the world of Christians. Indian Christianity sees a genuinely diverse form of religion from various people groups and the different Christian traditions. Even among the so-called tribal[2] Christians of India, great variations exist as a result of diverse regional, denominational, and cultural backgrounds. To exemplify the connection between pre-Christian spiritual beliefs and a Christian experience, I will do an explorative reading on Mizo Christianity back to its primal religious worldview. An advantage in doing this is that the entire Mizo community in Mizoram and those living nearby in India, Myanmar, and Bangladesh have become Christian. Mizo Christianity has a strong Indigenous character that is held in tension with features of Christianity it inherited from missionaries and borrowed from other missions and churches. In addition to the three historically mission-established churches—the Presbyterians, the

Baptist, and the Independent Church of Maraland—various Christian denominations have come and continue to coexist today. Many of the churches have been influenced deeply by the revivals that first came through the missionaries of the Welsh Calvinistic Mission to the Presbyterians.

All these revival-influenced churches share the tension between charismatic revivalism and the rationally driven church traditions they inherited. A number of newer churches, including different Pentecostal and independent charismatic congregations, branched out, more or less, from these main "mission churches." A visitor to a typical Mizo Christian worship service will notice that a pair of drums (in some churches only one drum) is the only set of musical instruments in most churches. Any hymn-singing, either translated hymns in Western tunes or Indigenous hymns either in tunes borrowed from Western music or Indigenous tunes, is done at the beat of the drum. A single larger drum is used to rhythmically beat Western tunes, and an additional smaller drum is added to sing in the Indigenous tunes. Yes, singing is so important for Mizo Christian worship as it serves to distinguish Mizo Christianity.

Mizos embraced Christianity within half a century of Christian missions in their region. The swiftness of the conversion to Christianity has been associated with the waves of revival movement that swept Mizo communities since the second decade of the twentieth century. Part of my thesis is that traditional Mizo beliefs in supernaturalism and active spirits in human lives and society find their continuity in the spirit-driven experience-centered charismatic revivals. The inherent connection between the two, I would contend, resulted in the speedy evangelization of the Mizo people and in giving birth to an indigenized Christianity. Perhaps, we may say that the resulting indigenized Christianity was unplanned as such, but a fortunate consequence. Because the word revival is closely connected to the history of Welsh Calvinistic Methodism and that any historical study on revivalism in the modern period of Christianity is incomplete without the mention of the "Wales revival," it is natural to think of revival as an important aspect of the Mizoram Presbyterian Church, a church planted by the Welsh Calvinistic Methodists (also called the Presbyterian Church of Wales). Almost all historical writings affirm the significant role revivals played in the evangelization of Mizo people. But the role of revivals in the establishment of Indigenous Mizo Christian identity, changes in the nature and characteristics of revivals in Mizoram that had taken place since the beginning, and its shifting place in the different periods of history have not been well studied until recently.[3]

Christian revival in Mizoram came in waves. The first revival in the series, sparked by the Wales revival of 1904, came through the revival in the Khasi hills. It was the most foreign to Mizo culture and relatively insignificant in its impact in comparison to succeeding revivals.[4] Because the nature and expressions changed so much between the first (Welsh-influenced) revival and the succeeding ones, it is worth observing the characteristic change as a distinct way of indigenization. The Welsh revival first sparked a revival in the Khasi hills, which was the main seat of the Welsh Calvinistic Mission in India from where it reached Mizoram, the next field of the mission. Through a group of early Christians who visited the Khasi hills, a revival was ignited in 1906. Many Mizo people accepted Christianity, but the revival's most significant impact was the confidence it gave to the small Christian community in their newfound faith. A few years after the first one died down, the second wave began in 1913, followed by the third and the most significant one in 1919. The fourth wave came about almost as a continuation of the third in the late 1920s and early 1930s. Since then, the waves of revivals come and go. If the movement has slowed down in one region, another region might see it heightening. New upsurges have often fueled new and contagious waves. A new wave from the early 1980s, for instance, helped the number of missionaries to multiply significantly. From one wave to another, the revival changes its course and character. While such other movements as the "born-again-movement" came as independent movements, they eventually weaved into charismatic revivals.

In an earlier study,[5] I concluded that waves of revival movements not only helped to evangelize Mizos but also indigenized Christianity to fit the worldview and ethos of the Mizo people. Here in the present chapter, I identify a factor I consider to be significant in defining Mizo Christianity, that is, the primal spiritual factor. This very factor also served as the seedbed of revival movements themselves. Without going into details, let me outline briefly how the revivals underwent gradual indigenization as succeeding waves saw manifestations through different Indigenous symbols and addressed contextual issues. First came the gradual indigenization of revival dance changing from the foreign foot-stomping dance (as was done in the Khasi hills) to Indigenous waving hands and the circle dance, which seemed to have been drawn from the *Puma Zai* movement around the same time. As I have argued earlier, the revival dance and the revival songs are connected to this Indigenous *Puma Zai* movement. *Puma Zai* (literally, the songs or song-type of Puma) was an emotionally charged non-Christian movement of singing-dancing in the first decade of the twentieth century. Although replaced eventually by Christianity and its revival songs, *Puma Zai* and its accompanying *Tlang Lam* (communal dance) have come to occupy important places in Mizo tradition. If the Mizo revival dance traced its origin to this traditional Mizo dance, so did the new revival songs.

Amidst the revivals' frenzy, a group of new Christian hymn-writers arose whose songs adopted Indigenous tunes meant for community singing. This is the second Indigenous feature that came from the revivals. Though the song-type appeared to be new and was called "the new hymns," it has strong resemblances and close links to the *Puma Zai* song-type. Some of *Puma Zai*'s songs composed at the time derided Christianity, which made some Christians consider it "anti-Christian." But the central features of the emerging revival dance and tunes were greatly influenced by the *Puma Zai* and its accompanying *Tlang Lam* movement. Thirdly, the new revival songs and dances were soon accompanied by Indigenous drums. The use of the drum was extended even for the translated hymns in Western tunes for which a single drum is used. For the singing of the new Indigenous hymns, two drums of varying sizes are used. These three elements—a new Indigenous family of hymns, which are sung at the beat of the traditional drum, accompanied by a distinctly Mizo revival dance—thus became the "symbols" of indigenization and marked off Mizo Christianity from other forms of Christianity.[6] As mentioned above, all hymn-singing is done with the help of drums today. Tunes are switched between Western and Indigenous ones even in one worship service, but all are sung to the beat of the drum or drums.

The belief in the domination of the world by spirits—benevolent and malevolent—lies behind the making of Mizo charismatic Christianity. Coupled with the communitarian nature of the society, the belief in the existence of a multitude of spirits inhabiting the earth fed Mizo Christianity and distinguished it clearly even from the mother churches. Undeniably, the ancient world of the New Testament shares a very similar worldview in which Jesus cast out demons who possessed individuals. The biblical worldview seemed closer for the Mizos than the views represented by the missionaries.

Mizo Primal Religion

Terms like animistic, primitive, and tribal acquire their pejorative connotations in modern times in part due to the new evolution-based categorization of societies. Because of their depreciatory connotations, there are objections to the use of these terms. In India, because the term "tribe" is a constitutional term to identify a large portion of the non-Indic (and "noncaste") group of people, it has been used widely without the accompanying pejorative baggage.[7] The terms "primitive" and "animistic" have, however, been contested for their pejorative connotations. The term primal has not really been depreciated.[8] Harold Turner has argued quite persuasively that primal religions reveal many of the basic or primary features of religion.

In writing this chapter, I cannot but continue an earlier work in which I have briefly argued that various features of the primal religion continued in Mizo Christianity.[9] Since I am going to focus my attention on the role and contributions of the belief in spirits in the transition from tribal or primal religion to Christianity, I will first look at the place of spirits in primal religion. E. B. Tylor has theorized animism as the most primitive form of religion, which is characterized by the belief in the inhabitation of most objects by souls or spirits. Some scholars in northeast India have understandably opposed the calling of primal religions "animistic" because it places the religion "at the bottom of the supposed line of religious evolution."[10] If animism is understood as inhabitation of the world by a multitude of spirits without Tylor's accompanying insistence that it is the most primitive, and thus backward, then what Tylor called animism is a suitable name for tribal or primal religions like the Mizos.

What does the Mizo primal religion consist of? Essentially, the belief in the Supreme Being (or Spirit), the belief in the existence of a multitude of benevolent and malevolent spirits and the accompanying propitiatory sacrifices to them, the practice of a clan-based *sakhua* (annual sacrifice for the protection and blessings of the clan), and the belief in life after death and the "religious" striving to reach *pialral* (heaven) constitute the Mizo religion.[11] The Mizos believe in the existence of *Pathian* (literally "the Holy Father"), the supreme being, as much as they believe in the presence of actively engaging malevolent spirits. They do not seek to reconcile the two, nor do they seek to reconcile the practice of sacrifices to the God of the ancestors in their clan-based sacrifices with the sacrifices to malevolent spirits for healing. *Pathian* is a distant being on whom the final fate of every human being rests. However, he is distant and does not involve himself in the day-to-day life of the people. The belief in *Pathian* (who would himself seem to be treated as Spirit) and the world populated by malevolent spirits again has little to do with how one goes to *pialral* (or heaven) after death. *Pialral* is reserved mainly for the rich who could offer prescribed public sacrifices and feasts, and for great hunters who have hunted down a strict list of wild animals.[12] Therefore, only a few people can go to *pialral*, and the rest go to *mithi khua* (village of the dead), which is described as dreary and lackluster. The image of *pialral* is inviting where one enjoys life with all the services one needs; *mithi khua* is dim and hazy.

Central to the everyday life of the people are the spirits, both malevolent and benevolent. Fortunes and misfortunes are believed to be caused by benevolent spirits and malevolent spirits, respectively. *Khuavang*, the chief benevolent spirit, though not always understood as identical to *Pathian* (the supreme being), is close to being equivalent to *Pathian* in the way she or he is addressed and described. Whereas the word *Pathian* is masculine, *Khuavang*, the god of blessing, is also referred to in the feminine as *Khuanu* in a poetical expression. It is to this spirit of blessing, *Khuavang* or *Khuanu*, that prayers for blessings are made and most blessings are attributed.[13] Are the two (*Pathian* and *Khuavang/Khuanu*) different names of the same being? Two well-known native Christian theologians and church leaders have expressed their opinion that the two refer to the same being.[14] The other best-known group of benevolent spirits are *Lasis* who own wild animals. They are known to be beautiful women with whom men, especially hunters, can have mysterious special relations. Successful hunters are often considered to have such a mysterious relationship with or being possessed by *Lasis*.

Added to *Pathian*, *Khuanu/Khuavang*, and *Lasi* are other good spirits such as guardian spirits of the village community to whom sacrifices are made, and the unnamed particular spirit or spirits each clan worshiped (*sakhua*). The object/s of these *sakhua* (or religious) sacrifices was/were not named and never clearly explained. Did different clans who sacrificed separately worship different spiritual objects or the same? Is *Pathian*, the supreme being, addressed differently in these different occasions? No explanation is given. The people addressed it simply on some occasions as "one worshiped by the ancestors." These spirits were to protect communities and clans from harmful incidents and accidents.

Whereas sacrifices were made to benevolent spirits less frequently and only on certain appointed and special occasions, sacrifices were offered to the malevolent or evil spirits much more frequently as needed. All sicknesses and diseases were believed to have been caused by these spirits. When one unknowingly displeases an evil spirit, the spirit brings sickness and even death unless he or she is content with sacrifice. Every sickness demands a sacrifice, and the priest would prescribe the right sacrifice by looking at the symptoms of sicknesses. In each case, the soul of the victim was believed to be captured and possessed by the spirit, resulting in the sickness. The evil spirit was to be appeased with food (often the best of food a family can afford) sacrificed in a ritual performed by a priest (or witch doctor). It was not so much morality or immorality that caused these spirits to act, but the spirits were believed to have likes and dislikes. Life was lived between the fear of angering malevolent spirits and the wish to be blessed by benevolent spirits.

The Historical Course of the Emergent Mizo Christianity

We have briefly highlighted how revivals came about and helped to indigenize Christianity. The process was not easy and was at times painful. As most historians of the Mizo church have shown, the first three revivals were congenial to the church and occurred in the mainline mission churches with no problem; the fourth revival was known for its excessiveness leading to disruptions and the church's eventual effort to control the movement. Disagreeing with the church's effort to suppress excessive forms, some left the mainline (mission) churches to form separate churches. Some of those who left the mainline churches came to form the United Pentecostal Church by joining the denomination in the early 1940s. Although we relate revivals and the indigenization of Christianity closely, the relationship was not obvious at the time. So, while objections to the excessive forms of the revivals have been raised since the fourth wave of the revivals in the 1930s, the churches came to deliberate the issue of Christianity's relation with culture after the 1960s. The attempt to control excessive revivals led to a general suspicion against traditional culture. Missionaries and some early Indigenous leaders of the church developed a propensity against Indigenous forms.

How, then, did Mizo Christianity become indigenized and acquire its charismatic nature? Despite objections by the official leaders (missionaries and some early native leaders), indigenization happened through the revivals as a people's movement. Waves of revival made evangelization a people's movement. Especially since the third wave when bands of evangelistic "visitors" from villages that experienced revival visited other villages, Christianity expanded like wildfire. Thus, through revivals, Mizos embraced Christianity en masse. While Christianity was embraced en masse, the people's Indigenous worldview and ethos could not be curbed. Instead, they became the driving force of the new religion. It was only natural for both the new religion and elements of the old tradition to merge and produce a blended Christianity. Because of opposition from the Indigenous leadership and missionaries, the blending also took a longer period. The objections, often strong at times, took different forms. When forced by a spontaneous people's movement through the indigenizing revivals, the church leadership gradually withdrew objections to some of these elements. The political situation in the 1960s led to the expulsion of all the missionaries by the government of India in 1968. Soon after, the two churches that served as the missionary seats also installed Indigenous drums in the church without any opposition.

At the heart of Mizo Christianity is singing as an expression of a spiritual longing for the life to come. It is not an exaggeration to say that Mizos are a singing people with rich poetry. It is said that every prosaic word has its poetic equivalent.[15] In the earliest period of Christianity, missionaries and early leaders objected to any use of Indigenous songs in poetic forms, and they did not permit the use of traditional drums. Only translated songs in prosaic forms of Western tunes were considered Christian. As the successive revivals turned more and more toward Indigenous expressions of spirituality, it was only natural for Indigenous individuals to create new songs out of prosaic languages. Between traditional pre-Christian songs and the newly introduced translated Western hymns, there emerged a new revival song-type popularly named

Lengkhawm Zai "community-gathering songs." This song-type was new at the time of its emergence in the 1920s in that it was not directly drawn from any particular pre-Christian song-type. As said earlier, however, there is no doubt of its traditional and Indigenous traits. It is totally different from Western tunes, and many translated Western hymns were revised into this new Indigenous tune-type. The new tune-type was influenced by a non-Christian singing movement called *Puma Zai*, which also greatly influenced the new revival dance. With the introduction of the traditional drum to beat this new song-type, the three (the drum, the tune-type, and the dance) formed the symbol of Mizo Christianity.

Tension mounted between missionary-controlled mainline church leadership and the revival-enthusiasts. The course of development finally took the middle of the road between the wishes of extreme revivalists and the official mission/church's suspicion against anything native. By extremists, we refer to some who held all forms of emotional expressions as the work of the Holy Spirit. Some had chosen a morally libertine position including immoral sexual behaviors as spiritual expressions. Against the direction taken by the church, that is, to officially discourage (in some cases to do away with) most or all Indigenous elements in the church, revivals gradually established Indigenous symbols in the church and wed Christianity with the native culture. Against the steps taken by the so-called extremists—many of whom later left the mission church and established Pentecostal denominations—to embrace only the native tunes of hymns and emotional expressions, Mizo Christianity came to interlace the Indigenous and traditional Christian symbols and practices. But the tension was not easy. It led to painful dissensions and disunity within the small Mizo community.

Primal Religious Tradition as the Substructure of Mizo Christianity

If Christmas were to be observed in place of all the traditional festivals of the people, Christmas would have to be celebrated in the way most familiar to the people, namely in the fashion of Mizo traditional festivals. At the center of the Christmas celebration is a community feast surrounded by community carols in native tunes. Till today, Christmas is associated with a community feast prepared and enjoyed by members of the community. Similarly, the observation of Good Friday has also gradually taken the form of an Indigenous community rite of condolence. Along came occasional "Pathian Chawimawi" (literally "glorification of God"), especially during revival moments in the church funded by individual family or groups or even a church. Except for the absence of the "holiday spirit" of Christmas and New Year, the occasion of *Pathian Chawimawi* is like a Christmas celebration marked by public feasting and singing. All these celebrations take the form of traditional annual festivals or *Kut* and the individual family-funded community celebrations of "sechhun" and "khuangchawi." As mentioned before, only the rich who can afford to feast the public as prescribed can go to *pialral* or heaven. The prescribed feastings are *sechhun* and *khuangchawi*. The communitarian nature of traditional festivities provides a firm ground for the community of faith, the church, to grow in the community.[16] Not only were the worldviews of the people picked up in Christianity, a large portion of the traditional ethos, including the traditional moral code called "tlawmngaihna" (a competition for selflessness that promotes sacrificing the self for the sake of the community), came to be Christianized.[17]

The clearest trace of primal worldview is to be seen in the very success of charismatic or revivalist Christianity among the Mizos. The success of charismatic Christianity is to be credited to its connectivity to the spirit-filled worldview of the people. Because spirits were part of the daily life of the people, in a sense they were felt to be very "real." Jesus' power over evil spirits and his exorcizing of such spirits from humans to heal them resonates very well with the people. Furthermore, a religion believed to be carried and overseen by a good or "holy spirit" not only made sense but also was appealing and most acceptable. It was not that revivals intentionally promoted the Indigenous elements we have described, such as the native drums, Indigenous hymns, and the revival dance; these elements emerged from the people when the people took over the new religion into their hands from foreign missionaries. Such overtaking happened when Christianity came to be introduced in the most acceptable channel, namely, spirit-driven charismatic revivals. One of the three great pioneering Indigenous hymn-writers, I interviewed C. Z. Huala in the early 1990s. In response to my question as to how he and other early native hymn-writers came up with the Indigenous tunes, he said, "We did not; it was the people who transformed the tune into their present tunes."[18] The community songs, then, were made by the community by singing them in the gatherings. It was a spontaneous outflow from the community's heart in the singing to express their newfound spiritual joy. It was only natural for the new Christians to indigenize hymns with tunes most congenial to their taste. Their natural expression of spiritual joy turned out to be a distinctive revival dance.

As indicated above, the supernatural worldview of the New Testament and Jesus' power over demons and other evil spirits resonate with the worldview of the people. There is no doubt that the common worldview is the most important factor for the early success of Christian evangelization in Mizoram. The very name *Pathian* for God provided a ready concept that was yet transformed and reformulated. Christianity transformed the view on *Pathian* by insisting that he is a loving God who cares and is willing to engage the people in their daily lives. In other words, it brought the distant *Pathian* closer by affirming him as a loving and caring father. The longing for *pialral* (or heaven in a poetical form) after death and the fear of living in a hollow and dull life of *mithi khua* found their counterparts in Christian teaching of life after death.

The idea that *Pathian* is good is not new, but his loving and caring nature to the extent of sacrificing his son for the sake of the world is a new teaching. Such a loving *Pathian* and his extraordinarily *tlawmngai* son, Jesus Christ, became extremely appealing to the Mizos. For a society that valorizes self-sacrifice for the sake of others above everything else, the teaching that Jesus Christ sacrificed his life for our sake was not only meaningful but also powerful. As I have described in an earlier work,[19] the most powerful theological piece in the conversion of the Mizos was the message of Jesus' victory over the demons. The *Christus Victor* was the healer of the sick and the liberator from the oppression of the *ramhuais* (literally jungle spirits used to translate demons in the New Testament). The healing and liberation by Jesus were introduced along with modern medicine and scientific education, and the two (Christianity and modern science) are often confused among Mizo Christians.

The Mizo word for "prophet" is *zawlnei*, which may be translated as "possessing someone or something beyond." Prophecy is believed to be possible only through Spirit possession. Being possessed and controlled by the Holy Spirit is valued highly, especially among revivalists, and it is in such a condition that most authoritative interpretations of the scripture are also made. As in the primal religious belief of being possessed by the good spirit, the act of possession is mutual, that is, possessing and being possessed. This is where the church has often faced difficult situations of dealing with spirit possessions. The mystery of the pronouncement of "God's word" is often exploited by giving undue importance to the unseen spirit. An overemphasis on the mysterious and spontaneous "revelation" with claims of being possessed by the spirit and being given prophecy outweigh the biblical message. When the emphasis falls on the mysterious possession by an unseen spirit over against the revealed Word of God, Christological boundaries can easily be overstepped. Such is not uncommon among revival enthusiasts.

Mizo Christianity by no means is indigenized Christianity par excellence. The indigenization happened not by intentional effort but almost as an accident. Any indigenized Christianity runs the risk of domesticating the religion, limiting its universal character and transforming power. While primal supernatural spirituality has contributed immensely to the "meaningful" communication and understanding of the Gospel, it also led to disunity. The emotionally driven charismatic Christianity tends to disunite the community and goes overboard against theological decorum. But such is Christianity that connects people with a strong belief system in the reality of the spirits in everyday life.

Notes

1. An earlier version of this essay was published as "Primal Spirituality as the Substructure of Christian Spirituality: The Case of Mizo Christianity in India," *Journal of African Christian Thought* 11, no. 2 (December 2008): 9–14.
2. The various people groups outside the caste system are categorized by the Indian Constitution as "scheduled tribes."
3. Although some of the viewpoints are disagreeable, the most comprehensive study with the detailed chronicling of the revivals is Vanlalchhuanawma, *Christianity and Subaltern Culture: Revival Movement as a Cultural Response to Westernisation in Mizoram* (Delhi: ISPCK, 2006).
4. Saiaithanga, *Mizo Kohhran Chanchin*. Lushai Theological Book Series, No. 8 (Aizawl: The Mizo Theological Literature Committee, 1969), 26.
5. Lalsangkima Pachuau, *Ethnic Identity and Christianity: A Socio-Historical and Missiological Study of Christianity in Northeast India with Special Reference to Mizoram* (Frankfurt am Main: Peter Lang, 2002).
6. For a detailed discussion, see ibid., 131–41.
7. Ibid., 34–43.

8. See, for instance, J. H. Thumra, "The Primal Religious Tradition," in P. S. Daniel, David C. Scott, and G. R. Singh, eds., *Religious Traditions of India* (Serampore: The Senate of Serampore College and ISPCK, 1988), 45–74. One tribal scholar, Renthy Keitzer, did raise objection to the use of "primal" as it is closely associated with "primitive." See Renthy Keitzer, "Tribal Theology in the Making," in S. Shimray, ed., *Tribal Theology: A Reader* (Jorhat: Tribal Study Center, 2003), 213–14.
9. Lalsangkima Pachuau, "Mizo '*Sakhua*' in Transition: Change and Continuity from Primal Religion to Christianity," *Missiology: An International Review* 34 (January 2006), 41–57.
10. A. Wati Longchar, *The Tribal Religious Traditions in North East India: An Introduction* (Jorhat: Eastern Theological College, 2000), 6.
11. This is a slightly revised version of an earlier description I made in Pachuau, "Mizo Sakhua in Transition," 42.
12. For a more detailed discussion, please see "Mizo '*Sakhua*' in Transition."
13. K. Zawla, *Mizo Pipute leh an Thlahte Chanchin*, 2nd ed. (Aizawl: The Author, 1976), 44.
14. These leader-theologians are Rev. Liangkhaia and Rev. Zairema. See Liangkhaia, "Mizo Sakhua," in *Mizo Zia-rang* (Aizawl: Mizo Academy of Letters, 1975), and Zairema, "The Mizos and Their Religions," in K. Thanzauva, ed., *Toward a Tribal Theology: The Mizo Perspective* (Jorhat: Mizo Theological Conference), 39.
15. Z. T. Sangkhuma, *Missionary-te Hnuhma* (Aizawl: M. C. Lalrinthanga, 1995), 42.
16. For further study on this issue, see K. Thanzauva, *Theology of Community: Tribal Theology in the Making* (Bangalore: Asian Trading Corporation, 2004).
17. See further M. Kipgen, "Tlawmngaihna and Christianity," *Tribal Theology: A Reader*, 79–104.
18. Interview, September 18, 1991, in the residence of Aizawl, Mizoram, India.
19. See Pachuau, "Mizo '*Sakhua*' in Transition."

Bibliography

Hiebert, Paul G. "The Flaw of the Excluded Middle." In *Perspectives on the Christian World Mission: A Reader*, 3rd ed., edited by Ralph Winter and Steven C. Hawthorne. Pasadena, CA: William Carey Library, 1999, pp. 416–18.

Keitzer, Renthy. "Tribal Theology in the Making." In *Tribal Theology: A Reader*, edited by S. Shimray. Jorhat: Tribal Study Center, Eastern Theological College, 2003, pp. 213–14.

Kipgen, M. "Tlawmngaihna and Christianity." In *Tribal Theology: A Reader*, edited by S. Shimray. Jorhat: Tribal Study Center, Eastern Theological College, 2003, pp. 79–104.

Liangkhaia. "Mizo Sakhua." In *Mizo Zia-rang*. Aizawl: Mizo Academy of Letters, 1975.

Longchar, A. Wati. *The Tribal Religious Traditions in North East India: An Introduction*. Jorhat: Eastern Theological College, 2000.

Pachuau, Lalsangkima. "Mizo '*Sakhua*' in Transition: Change and Continuity from Primal Religion to Christianity." *Missiology: An International Review* 34 (January 2006): 41–57.

Pachuau, Lalsangkima. "Primal Spirituality as the Substructure of Christian Spirituality: The Case of Mizo Christianity in India." *Journal of African Christian Thought* 11, no. 2 (December 2008): 9–14.

Pachuau, Lalsangkima. *Ethnic Identity and Christianity: A Socio-Historical and Missiological Study of Christianity in Northeast India with Special Reference to Mizoram*. Frankfurt am Main: Peter Lang, 2002.

Saiaithanga. *Mizo Kohhran Chanchin*. Lushai Theological Book Series, No. 8. Aizawl: The Mizo Theological Literature Committee, 1969.
Sangkhuma, Z. T. *Missionary-te Hnuhma*. Aizawl: M. C. Lalrinthanga, 1995.
Thanzauva, K. *Theology of Community: Tribal Theology in the Making*. Bangalore: Asian Trading Corporation, 2004.
Thumra, J. H. "The Primal Religious Tradition." In *Religious Traditions of India*, edited by P. S. Daniel, David C. Scott, and G. R. Singh. Serampore: The Senate of Serampore College and ISPCK, 1988, pp. 45–74.
Vanlalchhuanawma. *Christianity and Subaltern Culture: Revival Movement as a Cultural Response to Westernisation in Mizoram*. Delhi: ISPCK, 2006.
Yung, Hwa. "Pentecostalism and the Asian Church." In *Asian and Pentecostal: The Charismatic Face of Christianity in Asia*, edited by Allan Anderson and Edmond Tang. Oxford: Regnum Books International, 2005, pp. 37–57.
Zairema. "The Mizos and Their Religions." In *Toward a Tribal Theology: The Mizo Perspective*, edited by K. Thanzauva. Jorhat: Mizo Theological Conference.
Zawla, K. *Mizo Pipute leh an Thlahte Chanchin*, 2nd ed. Aizawl: The Author, 1976.

List of Contributors

Afe Adogame is the Maxwell M. Upson Professor of Religion and Society at Princeton Theological Seminary, New Jersey, USA. His research interests focus on interrogating new dynamics of religious experiences and expressions in Africa and the African diaspora; the interconnectedness between religion and migration, globalization, politics, economy, media, and the civil society. His most recent book is *Indigeneity in African Religions: Oza Worldviews, Cosmologies and Religious Cultures* (2021).

Rose Mary Amenga-Etego is Associate Professor in Religious Studies and Head of Department for the Study of Religions, University of Ghana, Legon. She is also a RITR Research Fellow at UNISA. Her research interest focuses on African indigenous religions with particular interest in indigenous development, gender issues in religion and culture, personhood, and health. Her publications include *Mending the Broken Pieces: Indigenous Religion and Sustainable Rural Development in Northern Ghana* (2011).

Aminta Arrington is Associate Professor of Intercultural Studies at John Brown University, Arkansas, USA. Her research interests focus on World Christianity, particularly Christianity in China, especially among its ethnic minorities. She is the World Christianity editor for the *Encyclopedia of the Bible and Its Reception*. Her most recent book is *Songs of the Lisu Hills: Practicing Christianity in Southwest China* (2020).

Mariano Ávila Arteaga is Emeritus Professor of New Testament at Calvin Theological Seminary, Grand Rapids, Michigan, USA. His research interests are in the field of justice and peace and how hermeneutics, biblical studies, and social and political sciences interconnect to address them. His most recent publications are a two-volume commentary on *Ephesians, Comentario Bíblico Iberoamericano: Efesios* (2018) and a chapter on Ephesians for the *Latinx Perspectives on the New Testament* (2022).

Raimundo C. Barreto is Associate Professor of World Christianity at Princeton Theological Seminary, New Jersey, USA. His research interests focus on World Christianity, particularly Latin American and Latinx Christianities, and their theological innovations, including liberation, indigenous, mujerista, and decolonial theologies. He is the editor of the Fortress Press series "World Christianity and Public Religion." His most recent book is *Protesting Poverty: Protestants, Social Ethics, and the Poor in Brazil* (2023).

Alexandre Brasil Fonseca is Dean of Personnel Management and Associate Professor at Universidade Federal do Rio de Janeiro, Brazil. He was special advisor to the president of Brazil on religious affairs, within the National Secretariat for Social Articulation

(2012–16). His research interests focus on religion and politics, inequalities, human rights, disinformation, the media, and health education. His most recent works are *Religious Intolerance in Brazil: An Analysis of the Social Reality* (2020) and *Evangelicals in Brazil: Analysis, Assessment, Challenge* (2019).

Nadine Bowers Du Toit is Associate Professor of Practical Theology (Community Development) at the University of Stellenbosch, South Africa. Her research interests focus on the intersections between religion, poverty, and inequality with a special focus on the role of faith communities in the South African context. She currently serves as the vice president of the International Academy of Practical Theology. Her most recent book is *Faith, Race and Inequality among Young Adults in South Africa: Contested and Contesting Discourses for a Better Future* (2022).

Won W. Lee is Professor of Old Testament and the Director of the Asian Studies Program at Calvin University, Grand Rapids, Michigan, USA. His research interests focus on exegesis and theology of the Hebrew Bible, especially the book of Numbers and Amos, and Korean diasporic biblical hermeneutics. His most recent works include *The Oxford Handbook of the Bible in Korea* (2022) and "The Structure of Amos 5:1–17: Reconsidered," *Journal of Biblical Interpretation in Context* (2019).

Izak Y. M. Lattu is Associate Professor of Interreligious Engagements at the Theology and Sociology of Religion Department, Satya Wacana Christian University, Salatiga, Indonesia and a regular visiting professor at the Center for Religious & Cross-Cultural Studies, Gadjah Mada University, and the American Study Area, the University of Indonesia. His research interests focus on interreligious engagements, indigenous knowledge, local theology, and the sociology of religion. His most recent book is *Memoar Covid-19: Autoetnografi Lintas Benua* (Covid-19 Memoir: A Cross-Continent Auto-Ethnography) (2022).

Featunai Liuaana is the Church Minister at the Congregational Christian Church of Samoa (CCCS) Sandringham, Auckland, New Zealand. A graduate of the Australian National University, Canberra, Australia, in church history, his research interest over the last decade has focused on World Christianity and Primal Religion. His recent contribution was to *Atlas of Global Christianity* (2009). He is currently working on the *Sulu* project, a CCCS church magazine in the Samoan language, first published in 1839 and still in publication today, which highlights the changes and development in Samoan primal context, literature content, thinking, and theology.

Li Ma is a social historian and Senior Research Fellow at Sage Creative Foundation, an interdisciplinary and intercultural think tank for scholars of Chinese descent. Her research interests include Christianity in China, women's history, and social history. She is the author of *Christian Women and Modern China: Recovering a Women's History of Chinese Protestantism* (2021).

List of Contributors

Melba Padilla Maggay is a literary writer, a social anthropologist, and President of the Institute for Studies in Asian Church and Culture and of the Micah Global, a network of about eight hundred faith-based development organizations worldwide. Her research interests are on the interface of religion, culture, and development. Her more recent books—*Global Kingdom, Global People* (2017), *The Gospel in Culture: Contextualization Issues through Asian Eyes* (2016), and *Rise Up and Walk: Religion and Culture in Empowering the Poor* (2016)—are examples of her interest in gospel and culture issues, and the impact of globalization and development metanarratives that have defined the trajectories of the economies of the Majority World.

Matthew Michael is Head of the Department of Philosophy and Religious Studies, Nasarawa State University, Keffi, Nigeria. His research interests are primarily centered on African Christianity in its diverse creative expressions at the grassroots. He recently led the research project "Triangulated Health & Integrative Wellness: The Mapping of Wellness and Its Cultural Psychology in Modern Africa," jointly sponsored by the Nagel Institute at Calvin University, Grand Rapids, Michigan, USA, and the Templeton Religion Trust. His book *African Healing Shrines & Cultural Psychologies* (2021) launches pioneering interests into the studies of African healing shrines in its ethnopsychological significance to African Christianity.

Retief Müller is Associate Professor of Theology at VID Specialized University in Stavanger, Norway. Until recently he served as Director of the Nagel Institute for the Study of World Christianity at Calvin University, Grand Rapids, Michigan, USA. His research focus is on southern African religious history and theology. His most recent book is *The Scots Afrikaners: Identity Politics and Intertwined Religious Cultures in Southern and Central Africa* (2022).

Mwenda Ntarangwi is a cultural anthropologist based in Kenya. Ntarangwi's scholarship and research hinge on the intersection between culture and performance, especially popular culture, as analyzed through the lens of symbolic interpretivism. His most recent book is *The Street Is My Pulpit: Hip Hop and Christianity in Kenya* (2016).

Francis B. Nyamnjoh is Professor of Social Anthropology at the University of Cape Town, South Africa. His current research interests include incompleteness, mobility, encounters, belonging, citizenship, and conviviality. His most recent book is *Incompleteness: Donald Trump, Populism and Citizenship* (2022).

Sung Deuk Oak is Dongsoon Im and Mija Im Endowed Chair Associate Professor of Korean Christianity at UCLA, Westwood, California, USA. His research focuses on the development of indigenous Korean Christianity. His most recent books are *The Making of Korean Christianity: Encounters of Korean Religions with Protestantism, 1876–1910* (2020, in Korean) and *The History of the Korean Bible Society. Vol. III. 1945–2002* (2020, in Korean).

Lalsangkima Pachuau is the John Wesley Beeson Professor of Christian Mission and Dean of Advanced Research Programs at Asbury Theological Seminary, Kentucky, USA. His research interests are in the areas of World Christianity, contextual theology, theology of mission, and how Christian faith witness intersects with other religions. Two of his most recent books are *God at Work in the World: Theology and Mission in the Global Church* (2022) and *World Christianity: A Historical and Theological Introduction* (2018).

Tite Tiénou is Research Professor and Director of the Paul G. Hiebert Center for World Christianity and Global Theology at Trinity Evangelical Divinity School, Deerfield, Illinois, USA. His research interests focus on race, ethnicity and theology, Christian theology in Africa, global theologies, and World Christianity.

Index

Africa vii–ix, 1, 3, 7, 9, 11–13, 31–2, 34–9, 44, 72, 91, 97–100, 105, 150–6, 173–4, 176–81, 191
   African Christianity 2, 31–2, 34, 37–8
   African Theological Initiative ix, 12–13
   South Africa 137–44, 173–4
   sub-Saharan Africa 149
ancestors 4, 176, 185–92, 200–1
anthropology 32–4, 36–7, 39, 59, 186
Apartheid viii, 72, 137–41, 179
Asia vii–ix, 7, 14, 31, 59, 59, 62, 123, 191
   Asian American 28, 43, 45
   East Asia 117, 119

Baptist 71, 103, 198
Bediako, Kwame vii, x, 12, 32, 38, 197
Bible 2, 20, 26, 35, 44–5, 47, 56, 64, 85, 88, 100–1, 103, 113–14, 116, 123, 128–9, 175, 191
   Biblical interpretation 3, 44–5, 103, 205
   the Bible belt 26–7
   the Moody Bible Institute 9, 26–7
Brazil 2, 21–3, 85, 88
Buddhism 189

Calvin ix, 3, 70–2, 77
   Calvinist 20, 138, 198
   Calvinist Reformation 69, 71, 74
   Calvin University (Calvin College) viii–ix, 1, 13, 31–2
capitalism 23, 118, 164, 176, 181
Carpenter, Joel vii–x, 1–2, 4, 7–14, 20–8, 31–5, 39, 166, 197
charismatic 35–6, 90, 105, 123, 197–205
China 3, 7, 11, 115, 123–32
Cold War 26
colonialism 3, 73–5, 98, 118, 137–8, 141
   colonization 43, 74, 82, 112
   cultural colonialism 73–4

community 12, 45, 62–3, 77, 83, 87, 98–9, 101–4, 125, 130–1, 140, 143, 151, 174, 177, 191–2, 197–9, 201–5
communist/ism 24, 109, 115–16, 119, 123, 126–31
Confucianism 125
contextualization 3, 55, 58–59, 66, 84–5
Covid-19 3, 158–68
customs 100, 113, 186

ecumenical 27, 83–8, 128, 139, 152–3, 155
ethnography 32–5, 37–9
   autoethnography 3, 161–2
Europe viii, 1, 34, 70, 82, 177, 179
   European 34, 76, 99–100
   European Enlightenment 3
   European Protestants 83
Evangelical ix, 9–10, 20–8, 35–6, 62, 70, 73–4, 82–4, 86–9, 98, 124, 129–30, 140, 142, 163
   Evangelicalism 2, 7–8, 25, 86, 132
   National Association of Evangelicals 24, 27
   neo-Evangelical 24, 27

fundamentalism viii, 1–2, 4, 8–10, 20–8, 73, 116, 137, 163
   American fundamentalism 20, 28
   Black fundamentalism 10
   Evangelical fundamentalism 21
   post-fundamentalism 24
   neo-fundamentalist 25

gender 88, 124, 126, 131, 164
Ghana ix, x, 3, 97–9, 101, 103–5, 178, 197
Global Christianity 7
Global North viii, 4
Global South vii, 1, 4
globalization viii, 2, 131–2, 176, 181
   globalization from below 8
Graham, Billy 25, 87, 129

healing 1–4, 114, 150–6, 163, 167, 189–91, 205
hermeneutics 63, 143
hybrid/hybridity 2, 43, 45
hymns 129–30, 191, 198–9, 202–4

identity 2, 10–11, 33, 37–8, 43, 45–52, 60, 64, 73, 83–4, 88–9, 102–4, 124, 131, 151–2, 173–5, 185–7, 198
imperialism 110, 118, 128
India 4, 38, 164, 197–8, 200, 202
   Indian Christianity 197
Indigenous viii, 58, 76–7, 88–9, 91, 97–105, 123, 125–7, 138, 152–3, 155–6, 164, 189, 197–9, 202–4
   Indigenous religions 98, 104, 156
Indonesia 3, 161–8
interconnectivity 1–4
interreligious 3, 45, 98, 102–4, 152, 161–8
Islam 44, 63–4, 98–9, 103–4, 150, 152, 154–5
   Islamization 44
   Islamists 63
   Muslim 55, 63–4, 104, 151–3, 155–6, 161–3, 165–6

Japan 45, 110, 112–14, 116–18, 126
   Japanese American 43
   Sino-Japanese 109, 111
Jerusalem 3, 109, 112, 114–16, 118–19
justice 65, 85, 87, 91, 138, 140, 142–3
   injustice 38–9, 82, 86–7, 91, 138, 141–3
   social justice 87, 90

Kairos document 139
Kenya 32, 35, 38
Korea 3, 46, 109, 109–19, 165
   Korean diaspora/diasporic 2, 43, 45, 47, 51
   Korean American 2, 43, 45
   Korean Christians 109–11, 114, 119
   Korean Protestantism 113, 115–16, 118–19
   US-Korean War 127–8

Latin America vii, viii, ix, 2, 3, 21, 28, 3, 56, 69–70, 72–5
   Latin American Protestant/Protestantism 82

liberation theology 81, 86–7, 89–90, 140
libertarianism 23

materialism 23, 45
megachurch 113
methodist 75, 100, 109, 111–16, 198
Mexican revolution 69, 76
migration 2, 187
mission ix, 3, 9–11, 21, 23, 25, 27, 43–4, 64, 82, 87–9, 97–103, 105, 109–11, 114, 118, 123–5, 128–9, 138, 197–8, 202–3
missionary 3, 4, 25, 27, 38 , 45, 63, 73, 81, 82–4, 97–105, 109–13, 115–17, 123–6, 131, 138, 186–8, 190–1, 197, 199–200, 202–4
Mizo Christianity 4, 197–205
modern/modernity 9–11, 21–2, 27, 36, 55, 69–70, 72–3, 75–7, 101, 104, 110, 124–5, 128, 130–1, 149–50, 152, 156, 198, 200, 205
morality/immorality 25, 39, 110, 112, 176, 201

Nagel Institute viii–x, 1, 13, 32, 197
nationalist/sm 84, 113–16, 118, 123–4, 127–8, 130–1, 163

Overseas Ministries Study Center (OMSC) ix, 11

pandemic 43, 161–5, 168
Pentecostal 35, 37, 86, 88, 90–1, 105, 198, 202–3
   neo-Pentecostalism 35
   Pentecostalism 27, 89, 91
   Pentecostalization 82, 89
Pew Charitable Trust ix, 10–13
Philippines 43, 55, 62–3, 131
postmodern 37, 55
prayer 3, 38, 47–48, 88, 102–3, 161–8, 189–92, 201
Presbyterian 109, 112–17, 197
   Presbyterian Church 110, 113–14, 118, 198
Protestant 3, 69–70, 72–6, 81–7, 89–91, 97–8, 118–19, 123–6, 186, 192
   Protestantism 70, 73–5, 81–4, 86, 89, 92, 109–10, 112–16, 123–4, 129, 131

Protestant schools 70, 75
Protestant reformation 69–70, 81–2
Pyongyang 3, 109–19

racism 137–9, 141–2, 144
reconciliation 38–9, 49, 139–40, 144, 174, 189, 190
reductionism 112, 116, 118
religion ix, 1–2, 4, 10, 13, 15, 19–28, 33–4, 37, 43–4, 51–2, 59, 61, 63, 70, 77, 98, 100–2, 104, 111, 116, 127, 129, 150–6, 163, 168–9, 175, 185, 188–9, 191–2, 197, 200, 202, 204–5
revival/ism 4, 8, 24–5, 27, 109, 112, 114–17, 119, 197–9, 202–5
ritual 59, 102, 131, 151, 156, 162–3, 186
Roman Catholic/Catholic 33, 59, 70–1, 73, 75, 85–6, 88–9, 97–9, 102, 112–15, 186, 192

Sacred 63, 102, 152, 155, 161–2, 165, 168, 185–92
sacrifice 61, 65, 151, 175–6, 185, 200–1, 204
Saint 38, 58, 70, 71, 99, 102, 129
Samoan 4, 185–92
Sanneh, Lamin vii, 11, 43–5, 51, 101
science 19–20, 33, 37, 55–6, 61, 70, 75, 81, 128–9, 177, 205
sectarianism 83
secular 54, 70–2, 85, 127, 185–7, 191
  secularism 26
  secularization 20, 45
Shaull, Richard 3, 81–2, 85
Shinto Shrine 117–18
social ethics 3, 82–3, 90
sovereignty 71, 74, 76

spirit ix, 24, 26, 31, 38, 45, 51, 56–7, 60, 62, 64, 66, 74, 88–90, 102–3, 164, 166, 168, 181, 186–9, 191, 197–8, 200–1, 203–5
spirituality 3, 4, 90–1, 103, 113, 130, 150, 166, 197, 202, 205
subversion 1–4, 155
syncretism 58
  syncretistic 63, 65, 103

Tabula rasa 3, 97–101, 103–5
theology viii–ix, 3–4, 9–10, 24, 31, 33, 35, 37–8, 58, 71–2, 75, 81, 85–91, 118, 129–30, 137–40, 143, 185–91, 197
tradition/al viii, ix, 2–3, 9, 20, 32, 37–8, 44–7, 55–63, 69–73, 76–7, 81–2, 91, 100, 104, 114, 124–5, 149–56, 173, 185–92, 197–9, 202–4
traditional pediatrics 151, 156
translatability 43–5, 50–1

Ubuntu 4, 32, 173–81
United States 2, 7–10, 19–23, 26, 28, 36, 45–6, 73–4, 82, 110, 125–9

veneration 4, 186–8

Walls, Andrew F. vii, 3, 81
white supremacy 3, 127–9, 141–2, 144
women 3, 58, 72, 77, 88, 90, 113, 123–31, 151, 173, 191, 201
World Christianity vii–x, 1–4, 7–11, 13–14, 31–2, 137, 149–50, 153, 155–6
worldview 19, 27, 44, 57, 59, 62, 70, 82, 90–1, 97, 100–1, 152, 154, 173, 186–9, 192, 197, 199–200, 202, 204

www.ingramcontent.com/pod-product-compliance
Lightning Source LLC
Chambersburg PA
CBHW052109300426
44116CB00010B/1598